TRIALS FROM CLASSICAL ATHENS

TRIALS FROM CLASSICAL ATHENS

Christopher Carey

London and New York

First published 1997
by Routledge
11 New Fetter Lane, London EC4P 4EE

Simultaneously published in the USA and Canada
by Routledge
29 West 35th Street, New York, NY 10001

Typeset in Garamond by
BC Typesetting, Bristol
Printed and bound in Great Britain by
Hartnolls Ltd, Bodmin, Cornwall

British Library Cataloguing in Publication Data
A catalogue record for this book is available from the British Library

Library of Congress Cataloging in Publication Data
A catalogue record for this book has been requested

ISBN 0–415–107–601
0–415–107–61X (pbk)

CONTENTS

	Preface	vii
	Introduction	1
1	HOMICIDE CASES	26
	General	26
	Case I: Lysias 1 – On the killing of Eratosthenes	27
	Case II: Antiphon 1 – Accusation of poisoning against the stepmother	36
	Case III: Antiphon 5 – On the killing of Herodes	42
	Case IV: Antiphon 6 – On the chorister	63
2	ASSAULT AND WOUNDING	75
	Case V: Lysias 3 – Reply to Simon, a defence	75
	Case VI: Demosthenes 54 – Against Konon for battery	84
	Case VII: Isokrates 20 – Against Lochites	97
3	SUITS CONCERNING PROPERTY	102
	Case VIII: Lysias 32 – Against Diogeiton	102
	Case IX: Isaios 3 – On the estate of Pyrrhos	109
	Case X: Isaios 4 – On the estate of Nikostratos	127
	Case XI: Demosthenes 55 – Reply to Kallikles on damage to a farm	133
4	CASES CONCERNING COMMERCE	142
	Case XII: Hypereides 3 – Against Athenogenes	142
	Case XIII: Demosthenes 35 – Reply to Lakritos' special plea	150
	Case XIV: Demosthenes 37 – Against Pantainetos	163

5 CASES CONCERNING CITIZENSHIP 180
Case XV: [Demosthenes] 59 – Against Neaira 180
Case XVI: Demosthenes 57 – Reply to Euboulides 212

6 SLANDER 233
Case XVII: Lysias 10 – Against Theomnestos 233

Appendix I: Athenian currency 240
Appendix II: The Athenian calendar 241
Selected further reading 242
Index 244

PREFACE

For most of this century, with the exception of a small and distinguished group of scholars (in particular Douglas MacDowell and Stephen Usher) British classicists have paid scant attention to Greek oratory and rhetoric, unlike their counterparts on mainland Europe. However, the recent past has seen a welcome resurgence of interest in Athenian oratory. This sea-change is partly to be explained in terms of the growth in interest in Athenian law, for which the oratorical texts are the most important surviving documents, partly by the current interest in the social and economic history of the ancient world, partly by an increased interest in the interaction between Athenian drama and the social and political values of the city. However, although the last few years have seen an increase in the number of commentaries on individual speeches, the Greekless reader still has to cast about among separate volumes in the Loeb collection for the relevant texts. This is especially problematic for anyone trying to introduce undergraduate and postgraduate students to Athenian law and legal procedure. The present volume, which began its life as a set of workaday translations for a course on Athenian law, seeks to bring together a number of the most interesting and informative texts in a single volume. It strives to fulfil a similar role to Kathleen Freeman's *The Murder of Herodes*, now half a century old, in providing a translation (less elegant than hers) with brief comments on legal issues and rhetorical strategy for the student interested in understanding the speeches as legal documents and exercises in the art of persuasion. A full new translation of the whole corpus of Athenian oratory is sorely needed, and will soon be provided thanks to an international project managed by Professor Michael Gagarin at Austin, Texas. In contrast, the present volume is highly selective (in particular, the major political speeches have been ignored for reasons of space) and reflects my own tastes, prejudices and whims. But I take comfort from the thought that the selection process is less dangerous in a collection of full texts than in an anthology of excerpts, the obvious alternative format considered and rejected for the book. In translating the texts I have tried to provide a readable English version which remains close to the original Greek. My success in this I leave for the reader to judge.

In any academic endeavour one accumulates debts. I wish to express my thanks to my colleagues at Royal Holloway for supporting the introduction of a course whose appeal seemed limited but whose popularity was a welcome surprise, and to the scholars whose research, in many languages, forms the invisible foundation on which the book rests. I owe particular thanks to Lene Rubinstein, who read and commented with her usual gentle astuteness on the introduction, and to Stephen Usher and Mike Edwards who commented in detail on most of the translations and improved the text in too many places to signal. For the errors which remain I should dearly like, but feel unable, to blame them; those, I am afraid, are all my own work.

Christopher Carey
Royal Holloway
14 September 1996

INTRODUCTION

GENERAL

The purpose of this section of the book is to provide a broad introduction to the Athenian legal system as a background for the specific cases which follow. It is neither full nor systematic. A full treatment of this theme would be beyond the scope of the book. For the reader who wishes to explore Athenian law and legal practice in greater depth there are three excellent books available. Even after a quarter of a century A.R.W. Harrison's *The Law of Athens* remains invaluable for its presentation of detail as well as the acuity with which issues are addressed, though for the Greekless reader it is somewhat opaque. Equally valuable, but very different, is D.M. MacDowell's *The Law in Classical Athens*, which combines thoroughness and attention to detail with a ready accessibility to the non-specialist and requires no knowledge of Greek. S.C. Todd's *The Shape of Athenian Law* provides both a broad overview of the Athenian system as a whole and a perceptive account of the methodological and informational problems of the study of Athenian law.

HISTORICAL SKETCH

There was never in the archaic or classical period a 'Greek' legal system. We find similarities in legal procedure and provision between different states and different periods. But it would be a mistake to envisage a single origin or a uniform development for the administration of justice in different parts of Greece. The Greek world (by which is meant the Greek peninsula and the regions colonized by the Greeks) was divided into independent states, largely along lines determined by geography. These states differed in their political structure, in aspects of cult practice, and in the content and application of their laws. Even where one state fell under the political control of another, it is uncertain in most cases how far the legal system of the dependent state would be affected beyond such changes as were necessary to secure political dependence. Accordingly we find substantial differences between the legal provisions of different states. To take a single example, in Athens a man might legally marry his half-sister if they shared a father but not if they shared a mother, while in Sparta the reverse was the case.[1] This diversity is acknowledged by Athenian litigants, who occasionally (as in Lys. 1.2) emphasize the importance of a legal provision by claiming (rightly or wrongly) that it is applied throughout Greece.

Of most of the legal systems of Greece we catch only occasional and partial glimpses. The state for which we have most information is Athens in the classical period – that is, the fifth and fourth centuries BC. Even for Athens our information is very limited.[2] For the period before the late fifth century we have very little contemporary evidence; our sources are nearly all looking backward, and not infrequently indulging in conjecture. Even for the classical period, our evidence is uneven. We often have to rely for information on litigants, who have good reason to present the law in a partisan way, and not infrequently we are faced with a single source which we have no means of checking against other texts. Any historical sketch must therefore be tentative.

Prior to the seventh century, Athens, in common with other Greek states, had no written laws. In the seventh century we find written laws emerging in a number of areas in Greece. The art of writing had been lost with the fall of the Mycenaean palace kingdoms and was not reintroduced into Greece until late in the eighth century BC. One of the first public uses of the new art was for the inscription of laws.[3] There can be no question of democratic intent at this period, but we may reasonably see a desire to place limits on the exercise of power by those in authority. The purpose was presumably to remove the content of the laws from the control of a narrow body of officials and place them in the open. The symbolic force of this move was enormous, since the open display of the laws is a formal statement both of the access of all citizens to the laws and of limitation on the authority of public officials, and the fixing of the text in stone contains a message of stability. In Athens the writing down of the laws is attributed to Drakon; the date we are given is 621/20.[4] As to the details of Drakon's code, we are in the dark. His laws were believed by later generations to have been extremely harsh, with the death penalty prescribed for a large number of offences. The tradition of severity is plausible, given the number of offences for which the death penalty was available even in the classical period; but since Drakon was inevitably defined by contrast with his successor Solon, who was characterized by tradition as the man who set Athens on the road to democracy, it is likely that some at least of the reputation for harshness is due to Solon's reputation for moderation. We may reasonably doubt how much later authorities actually knew of Drakon's laws. It is unclear whether Drakon actually enacted laws rather than merely codifying existing practice.

Certainly in the sphere of the administration of justice Drakon appears to have made no revolutionary changes. It seems from Aristotle[5] that the administration of justice in Athens at the end of the seventh century BC was in the hands of magistrates who had the authority to decide cases and impose penalties. These differ from the kings who dispense justice in Homer[6] and the local rulers who try cases in Hesiod's Boiotia[7] in that they are elective officials. But their aristocratic origin and small number mean that the administration of justice remains in the hands of the wealthy. The pivotal figure in the evolution towards the system in place in the classical period was Solon, who at the beginning of the sixth century was chosen to mediate between the conflicting interest groups of rich and poor. Among the structural changes attributed to him were two which were to have fundamental and lasting significance[8] – the introduction of the right of prosecution by any volunteer into a system which had previously been based on action by the individual victim (or in the case of homicide the relatives), and the introduction of the right of appeal (*ephesis*) to a court against the verdict of a magistrate. The former meant that in theory anyone could intervene to protect the weak, and the latter meant that final judgment (even if, as has been suggested[9] resort to the appeal mechanism spread only gradually) lay with a larger body which was not necessarily composed of the wealthy, since the judicial panels were open to all citizens.

The last decade of the sixth century and the first half of the fifth century saw a profound change in the Athenian political system. Athens after Solon was still essentially an aristocracy, but after the fall of the dictatorship of Peisistratos and his sons at the end of the sixth century a series of leaps took the city toward a direct democracy in which sovereign power lay with the Assembly of all adult citizen males. Although the democratic reforms of Kleisthenes at the end of the sixth century, as well as having implications for the legislative process, will certainly have had an impact on principle, practice and perception in the administration of justice,[10] it is difficult to ascribe changes in the legal system with confidence to Kleisthenes. The next major leap in the development of the legal system on which we can pronounce with confidence came in the fifth century. In the late 460s the aristocratic council of the Areopagos was stripped of its political powers and left with (the still important function of) jurisdiction in a number of cases, largely religious, in which Athenian conservatism on matters of religion precluded radical change. The rest of its areas of jurisdiction were transferred to the ordinary lawcourts, together with the Assembly and the Council of Five Hundred (the Boule). Since its political powers included supervision of the magistrates, one effect was to give the lawcourts a more prominent role in political cases. At about the same time Perikles introduced pay for the members of the panels of judges. This meant that poorer citizens were not precluded from serving on the juries by the need to earn money. The pay was set at two obols per day of service, but was later raised by Kleon in the 420s to three obols (half a drachma).

THE COURTS AND POLITICS

It will be seen that the evolution of the legal system was closely intertwined with the evolution of the constitution. The political importance of the courts was accepted by Aristotle, who in commenting on Solon's reforms observes that 'when the people have control of the vote they gain control of the political system';[11] the vote in question is that cast in court, not the vote in the Assembly. The courts were from the very first part and parcel of the political system, and if anything the courts became more rather than less political with time. The notion, common nowadays, that the courts should be separate from politics would no doubt have surprised the ordinary Athenian, as it would have surprised Aristotle. Under the democracy, the courts were used in part as a complement to the political activity of the Assembly. From the fifth century, in addition to hearing trials for political offences (such as receipt of bribes or treason), the courts functioned as part of the normal political process. From 415 BC at the latest (and possibly from as early as the reforms of Ephialtes in the 460s) new legislation could be challenged by a procedure called *graphe paranomon* (indictment for illegality) on the grounds that the means used was procedurally flawed or that the proposal contravened existing legislation.[12] If the measure had not yet been passed, further consideration was suspended while the case was heard by a court. In the event of conviction the measure fell and the proposer was liable to a punishment assessed by the court. Even after the measure had been passed, the proposer remained open to prosecution by *graphe paranomon* for a year. Three convictions brought loss of citizen rights. The vetting of public officials also involved the courts. All public officials were subject to a preliminary scrutiny (*dokimasia*) to ensure their suitability; this scrutiny either took place in a lawcourt or (in the case of officials subject to scrutiny by the Council) was subject to appeal to a lawcourt.[13] There were ten opportunities per year for the Assembly to vote officials out of office, and expulsion would normally lead to a trial. The courts also heard appeals from youths rejected by their deme (the smallest political unit of the Athenian state, membership of which allowed a man to exercise full citizen rights) when they applied for admission on reaching the age of eighteen. During the fourth century the use of the panels of judges (*dikastai*) who served in the courts was extended to include the vetting of new legislation and amendments to existing legislation. Above and beyond the overtly and unambiguously political use of the courts, we find politicians using non-political cases to harry their rivals and those associated with them, by bringing actions themselves, by using agents to prosecute, or by appearing as witness or supporting speaker in court.

Thus the courts were from the start, and remained, firmly embedded in the political system. While it would be a mistake to argue that all cases were political, or even that all cases involving wealthy men were political, we should remain alert to the possibility of hidden undercurrents beneath the seemingly lucid malice of litigation.

THE JUDGES

The essence of the Athenian system was that competing claims or versions of events should be presented for adjudication by a panel of ordinary citizens. In contrast to the administration of justice in archaic Athens as envisaged by Aristotle, judgment in the classical period was given not by a state official but by non-professionals. The name given to the individual member of the panels was *dikastes*, which I translate throughout as 'judge' for reasons which will become clear below. The qualifications for service on the court panels were more stringent than those for citizen status (before 451/0 an Athenian father and a free mother, after 451/0 two Athenian parents); to be a judge it was necessary in addition that a man should be over the age of thirty, evidently because experience and maturity were considered necessary. Much effort has been devoted to the task of identifying the socio-economic status of the judges. Statements made to the judges by litigants in surviving oratory, where they imply anything about the status of the addressees, suggest that they are not poor men. The problem of course is that such statements may be intended to flatter by assimilating individuals to a higher economic status than they actually possess. Probably the most useful starting point is the stipend paid to the judges. By the end of the fifth century the judge's pay was three obols (half a drachma) per day. At this period a labourer could earn a drachma a day; the judge's pay remained static throughout the fourth century, while inflation pushed the unskilled labourer's pay up to one and a half drachmas. So the judge's stipend will not have competed effectively with skilled or unskilled labour for the able bodied. Probably we should imagine the panels as consisting of men with sufficient private income (owners of shops or workshops, larger landowners living near the city) to allow free time, together with manual workers whose employment was seasonal, the elderly[14] and the infirm, temporarily or chronically. All who were empanelled as judges took an oath, which included a promise to judge according to the laws and decrees of the Assembly and the decrees of the Council (and failing legal provision to use their opinion of what was most just, *gnomei tei dikaiotatei*) and to listen to both sides of the case.[15]

The translation of *dikastes* as 'judge' is prompted by the difficulty caused by the more common translation, 'juror'. The latter term immediately suggests itself for the member of a group which collectively determines guilt or innocence, as the Athenian *dikastes* certainly did. But as a translation it obscures both the powers of the panel members and the scale of the panels. There was a presiding magistrate at each trial to control procedure. But he did not have the role of the modern judge as arbiter of law. There was no such legal authority in the court. The individual *dikastes* was left to interpret the law for himself. Nor did the presiding magistrate pass sentence as in our own courts. In some cases the penalty was fixed by law;[16] where there was no fixed penalty it was for litigants to propose alternative punishments[17] in case of conviction and for the judges to select the proposal which seemed more appropriate. The task of proposing a penalty which would both best suit the litigant's needs and at the same time avoid provoking the judges into accepting the rival proposal must have required subtle judgment.[18]

In size too the panels did not resemble modern juries. The smallest figure we are given for a panel of Athenian judges is 201 for private suits for sums below a thousand drachmas, with 401 empanelled for sums over a thousand drachmas.[19] In public suits we find panels ranging from 500 upwards in multiples of 500.[20] The judges also differed in their behaviour. In contrast with the calm and restrained demeanour expected of modern juries, we know that Athenian judges were very demonstrative in their response to what they heard in court. Plato (*Republic* 492b) lists the lawcourts alongside the Assembly, the theatre and the army camp as a place where people are noisy in approval or disapproval, shouting and banging. Plato of course was no friend of Athenian democracy; but it is revealing that speakers facing the courts will commonly ask the judges not to make a noise when they are about to say something controversial.[21] There are no special rules of behaviour. The response of the judge to what he hears in court is identical with that of the decent Athenian in everyday life. As a result, a large panel of Athenian judges must have been a very intimidating audience.

LITIGANTS AND LITIGATION

Access to the courts

Unrestricted access to the legal system, as to other areas of political life, was the prerogative of the Athenian citizen. For citizenship it was necessary before 451/0 to have an Athenian father and a free mother; after this date the qualification was stricter, Athenian parentage on both sides being necessary. At all times the rights of citizenship were open only to males. The world of the female was the household. Only males could hold office, attend meetings of the Assembly, serve on a judicial panel, or appear in court as prosecutor, defendant or witness. It has been maintained that women could appear as witnesses in homicide trials, but there is no solid evidence to support this belief. For all legal activity a woman was represented by an adult male, her *kyrios* (roughly 'guardian'), who would usually be her father (or his heir) before marriage and her husband once she was married. If action needed to be taken on her behalf, her *kyrios* would act for her.[22] If a woman was prosecuted, the action would be lodged against 'X and her *kyrios*', and her *kyrios* would conduct the case in court.[23] If evidence was needed from a woman, it would be given in court by her *kyrios*.[24]

However, not all males who satisfied the birth qualifications had full acccess to legal and political activity. It was possible in Athens to lose one's citizen rights, either wholly or in part. The term for loss of rights was *atimia*, and an individual subject to loss of rights was described as *atimos*, literally 'lacking honour', 'lacking privilege'. Partial loss of rights was imposed on individuals who collaborated with the oligarchic regimes which supplanted the democracy at the end of the fifth century. Partial *atimia* was also in some circumstances at least imposed on individuals who either dropped a public prosecution or failed to obtain 20 per cent of the votes cast.[25] Full *atimia* was imposed as a punishment for a number of serious offences, especially for military derelictions[26] and for abuse of one's parents, and for conduct unbecoming in a citizen, such as homosexual prostitution. Debtors to the state were automatically deprived of citizen rights (as was the heir, if the original debtor died without paying the debt) until the debt was repaid. Anyone subject to complete loss of rights was barred from the public temples, the agora (which was both the main marketplace and also the administrative and civic centre of the city), the Assembly and the courts. The *atimos* did not lose the protection of his person and property afforded by the laws, but would find it very difficult to protect his rights in view of his legal disabilities. He also retained the right to marry an Athenian female, though his marriage prospects would understandably be poor.

Athens also had a thriving immigrant community from the late archaic period onwards. The term for a non-Athenian residing in Athens was *metoikos*, usually anglicized as 'metic' and commonly translated 'resident alien'. The male resident alien, though denied all other political rights (including the right to marry an Athenian female after 451/0 and the right to own land in Attica), had almost unlimited access to the legal system (though some legal actions could only be brought by citizens). The female resident alien was in a similar position to the female of Athenian stock, in that she was usually subject to a *kyrios*. However, since a resident alien would not necessarily have an extended family within Attica (especially freed slaves, who if they continued to reside in Athens enjoyed metic status), a female metic might well have no living male relative to act as *kyrios*. The law acknowledged this by imposing the special tax to which resident aliens were liable (*metoikion*) on unattached metic females as well as on males. The capacity of non-Athenian females for independent action is recognized in [Dem.] 59.46, where the alien Neaira is judged to be 'her own mistress' (*auten hautes kyrian*).[27]

The volunteer

One of the main distinctions between acts liable to legal action in English law is that between 'crimes' and 'torts'. Though the distinction is not absolute (since in some cases at least the same act can be construed as either crime or tort), essentially a crime is an offence against society, and it is usually pursued by the civil authorities, while a 'tort' is the infringement of the interests of an individual, and legal action is taken by the individual (though the individual will normally be represented by a member of the legal profession).[28] The Athenians were aware of distinctions between different kinds of actionable conduct. Again there were overlaps, but the most significant distinction in Athenian law was between public actions (*dikai demosiai*), those which were felt in some way to impinge on the interests of society as a whole, and private actions (*idiai dikai*), which were the concern of the individual whose interests were affected.[29] But this distinction, though important for the specific forms of procedure, had no significance for the relative roles of individual and state. In Athens we find few traces of the elaborate mechanism of state intervention which we find in the English system. With few exceptions, all legal actions are brought by the individual. To a large extent, anyone pursuing a wrong, against himself or society, was left to do the work which in modern states is usually done by official bodies.

This applies for instance to detection and investigation. Athens never had anything approaching a police force. Anyone wishing to obtain evidence against another would normally have to obtain that evidence for himself. This has important implications for some areas of the law, especially where habitual wrongdoers are concerned. The volunteer prosecutor was open to intimidation,[30] either by outright threats of a sort familiar from modern criminals or by the astute use of counter-prosecutions.[31]

The prosecution was likewise carried out by the individual (or by several individuals), unlike modern jurisdictions, where a public official or agency (such as the Crown Prosecution Service or the District Attorney) or their respresentative presents the case for the prosecution in court. In private cases only the alleged victim could take action, while in public cases prosecution was open to 'anyone wishing' (*ho boulomenos*) to initiate action.[32] But in either case, once the decision to bring action had been taken, it was for the individual to pursue the case. He would issue a summons, accompanied by summons witnesses (*kleteres*) to guarantee that the summons had actually been served, requiring the alleged perpetrator to present himself before the relevant official on a certain day. It was for the prosecutor to determine which law had been broken, and to copy the text of the law for presentation in court, since the panel of judges had no independent text of the laws available. This is a more difficult task than it seems at first sight, in the fifth century at least, for it was not until late in the century that the Athenians created a central collection of the laws. Before that time, it would be necessary to locate the relevant law and transcribe as necessary from the stone column which acted as the public text of the law. Even after the central collection was created, it is unclear how far it was kept up to date. As well as laws, the litigant (prosecutor or defendant) would need to assemble for himself such witnesses as were available[33] and ensure their presence in court. Although there were legal means available to the litigant to compel a reluctant witness to give evidence,[34] the onus was on the litigant to make use of the relevant procedure; there was apparently no mechanism for the presiding magistrate or the judges to compel appearance. In the fourth century, the litigant's role with reference to witness testimony increased. Although it was normal in the fifth and early in the fourth century for witnesses to give evidence in person, from the late 380s it became the rule that witness testimony was submitted in writing; a text drafted by the litigant was read out in court by the clerk and confirmed by the witness, whose role now was to take public responsibility for the testimony.

Once the case came to court, it was normally presented by the litigant in person. But his role did not stop with the presentation of the case. The system relied on the natural hostility of competing litigants to monitor and check abuse. It was for the litigant to pursue cases of false testimony on the part of his opponent's witnesses; to do this he had to declare his intention to bring an action for false witness (*dike pseudomartyrion*) before the judges had cast their vote on the case in question. If the case against the witness succeeded, the litigant adversely affected by his testimony would obtain damages. It is noteworthy that false testimony was for the most part treated as an offence against the individual litigant (since it was a private action), not against the city, though repeated misconduct of this sort was clearly felt to impinge on the public domain, since three convictions for false testimony brought loss of citizen rights. In the case of disputes about property, the successful litigant was entitled to enter into possession unimpeded. If he was opposed, he could bring an action for ejectment (*dike exoules*). Again, the system relies on the volunteer.

It is particularly in the area of the public action that the volunteer becomes important. As was noted above, the most significant procedural distinction between public and private actions was that, while in private actions only the alleged victim could prosecute, in public actions the right to prosecute was open to the volunteer. In some types of public action however it was evidently felt that an inducement was necessary, and so rewards were offered for successful prosecutors. In *phasis*, an action available largely against various kinds of financial misconduct, the successful prosecutor received half the fine imposed on the defendant or the sum raised by confiscation of property. The procedure of *apographe* allowed an individual to draw up a list of the property of a public debtor or someone allegedly holding property belonging to the state with a view to having the goods sold to cover the sum due to the state; if the list was contested a court hearing would follow; the successful volunteer obtained as his reward a portion of the sum realized from the sale.[35] By the middle of the fourth century at least the laws made it a punishable offence for an alien to contract or feign marriage with a citizen. An alien convicted under this law was liable to be sold into slavery, and to have his or her property confiscated and sold;[36] the successful prosecutor again received a portion of the proceeds.

The existence of these incentives indicates that the Athenians were aware of the limitations of a system based on the volunteer. That they were needed is indicated by a significant fact noted by Osborne:[37] although public actions were open to 'anyone who wished', in practice we find that public cases are usually brought by the victim (where there is a victim) or by a political enemy of the accused. People were evidently reluctant to become embroiled in cases which did not concern them directly. This is hardly surprising. The panel of judges in a public trial was larger, and the time available for the presentation of the case longer; as a result the whole experience must have been intimidating. In addition, there were substantial penalties attending on conspicuous failure in public cases. Anyone who either dropped the case[38] or failed to obtain 20 per cent of the votes cast was subject to a fine of 1,000 drachmas (the equivalent of several years' pay for a labourer), and in certain circumstances at least lost the right to bring the same kind of action again.[39]

In view of the substantial financial incentives on offer, it might be thought that the Athenians would approve of, or at least tolerate, those who resorted to law for reasons of profit. In fact, although the legal system relied on the personal and political grudges and feuds and on the greed of the volunteer for its operation, the Athenians were in general hostile to any trace of professionalism in relation to the courts. Particular animosity was felt for the *sykophantes*, an untranslatable term (frequently transliterated as 'sykophant' because of the lack of a neat modern equivalent) implying a mixture of the sharp lawyer, the blackmailer, the hireling prosecutor and the unscrupulous pleader, anyone in short who for personal advantage or profit manipulated the legal system.[40] The courts were seen as a last, not a first, resort, and litigation was to be avoided where possible. Hence the consistency with which speakers in court present themselves as having sought to avoid litigation, and as being unfamiliar with and ill at ease in the courtroom. The scale of ignorance claimed by litigants is in fact inherently implausible. Six thousand Athenians served as judges, and they must have discussed their cases with relatives, as must individuals involved in trials as plaintiff, defendant or witness.[41] The courts were mostly adjacent to the agora; they had public areas for outsiders wishing to observe, and the tendency for Athenian males to do the shopping for the household (where it was not done by slaves) must have brought many into contact with trials, if only as observers. Certainly Aristophanes could confidently base a whole play, *Wasps*, on the courts in the expectation that a mass audience would appreciate the allusions. But the ideology of the ideal litigant as legal virgin (in private cases at least) persisted.

The Athenians believed however that they had become a very litigious society. In particular, as passages in comedy and oratory show, they believed theirs was a society in which sykophants were plentiful. This belief is perhaps best summed up by a passage in Aristophanes' *Clouds* (vv. 206–8), where the hero Strepsiades is in conversation with a devoted pupil of Sokrates, who shows him a map of Greece. The student points to Athens on the map. Strepsiades says: 'What! I don't believe it; I don't see the judges in session.' In one respect the Athenians were right. Political changes in the fifth century meant that the courts now dealt with political cases which would not previously have come before the mass panels. In addition, the Athenian insistence that the subject allies must send all capital cases to Athens for trial is represented by one source (admittedly hostile to the democracy) as bringing a great deal of legal business to Athens and a consequent stream of pay for the judges.[42] And some aspects of the Athenian system (in particular the requirements that the litigant execute judgment for himself in property cases and pursue cases of false testimony as private actions) meant that lawsuits could breed lawsuits. But it is likely that the level of political activity seriously distorted the picture for the Athenians. The difficulty of detection in the absence of a police force and the reliance on the individual (and the vulnerability of the individual to intimidation) probably meant that some kinds of (what we would call) criminal cases which loom large in our system were underrepresented in Athenian trials, with a consequent emphasis on property cases. The penalties attached to conspicuous failure in public actions probably meant that litigation of this sort was confined to a relatively small proportion of the population. In sum, therefore, the average Athenian may have been no more likely to find himself party to a lawsuit than his modern counterpart.

THE TRIAL

The presentation of the case

As I have already observed, the role of the individual included the presentation of the case in court; the litigant was expected to represent himself, unlike most systems with which we are familiar, in which the case is conducted by professional lawyers. The ideology of the amateur pervading the Athenian system prevented any development along these lines. It was possible for a litigant to introduce one or more supporting speakers (the term for such a supporter was *synegoros*) to address the panel on his behalf. Usually however such speakers merely follow and reinforce the main speech rather than replacing it. Only rarely do we find the *synegoros* effectively presenting the case, and then (ostensibly at least) because of special circumstances, such as youth and inexperience (Lys. 32, [Dem.] 59) or poor command of Greek (Dem. 36). In general it seems that the judges would not warm to a litigant who shrank from speaking for himself.

The accuser spoke first. Both sides presented their case in the form of a linear and continuous speech, interspersed with evidence in the form of witness statements, laws, contracts, wills and other documents. The emphasis was thus placed firmly on the litigant's version of events and presentation of argument, with depositions and other evidence playing a supplementary and confirmatory rather than a primary role as in our courts. Given the opportunities for distortion where the litigant speaks uninterrupted and is free to evade, expand or contract issues according to his immediate needs, this mode of presentation strikes us as flawed. But continuous speech was so firmly established as the means of persuasion in Greek public life that to the Athenians it must have seemed both natural and inevitable.

In order to manage the business of the courts, strict time limits were imposed on legal hearings. Time limits were imposed according to the type of case and sum at issue rather than the specifics of the individual case. A panel would normally try four private cases in a day; in contrast, only one public case might be tried by a given panel in a single day.[43] Equal time was allowed to prosecution and defence. The time was controlled by the *klepsydra* or water clock, a crude but very effective device consisting of a water-filled container with a hole at the bottom and a hole near the rim to ensure that the contents did not vary. The length of a speech was measured in the number of water clocks allocated to it.[44] The hole at the bottom was stopped with a bung, which was removed when the litigant began to speak. Once the last water clock was empty the litigant had run out of time. The bung was inserted for evidence (witnesses, laws, etc., though not for supporting speakers) in private cases, though not in public cases. Presumably an experienced speaker or speechwriter could gauge the length of a speech accurately.

Evidence

In his treatise on rhetoric (*Rhetoric* 1355b35–56a4), Aristotle divides the means of persuasion (*pisteis*) into two kinds: artful or artificial (*entechnoi pisteis*), which he defines as the means of persuasion which are produced by rhetoric, and artless or inartificial (*atechnoi pisteis*), which consist of the factual support available in a given situation. Under this heading he includes witness testimony (*martyria*), oaths (*horkoi*), evidence extracted under torture (*basanos*), law (*nomos*), and contracts (*syngraphai*). The documentary evidence was assembled by the litigant and read out during his speech at intervals of his choosing by the clerk of the court. Here I am concerned solely with factual evidence from individuals.

Witnesses played an important role in the Athenian system. Athens throughout the classical period relied on word of mouth in many areas of formal activity where we would expect documentation. In the general absence of official documentation (there were no birth or marriage certificates or registers), much greater emphasis was placed on the testimony of witnesses. During the fifth century, witnesses in court deposed in person, but early in the fourth century this procedure was abandoned and witnesses merely presented themselves in court to confirm a written deposition drafted by the litigant for whom they appeared. The witness had relatively little room for manoeuvre. It was not open to him to deny the truth of a deposition. He could take an oath of denial (the *exomosia*) stating that he did not know the alleged fact or that he had not been present. Otherwise he could only attest the deposition or risk the penalty attached to failure to appear.[45] The use of written depositions also precludes the possibility of testing evidence in court; there was no opportunity to cross-examine a witness. Hearsay evidence was not admissible, though an exception was made with reference to the words of the dead. A special arrangement (called *ekmartyria*) was made in the case of potential witnesses who were ill or away from Athens at the time of the trial. The witness deposed to a third party, who then appeared in court to confirm that the witness had given the evidence offered in court. An example of this can be seen at Isaios 3.19. The witnesses we meet in the orators tend to be closely associated with the litigant for whom they appear. We in contrast are more inclined to believe a witness who is unconnected with the participants. Given the nature of the cases which survive (which usually involve disputes in which the parties could ensure the presence of witnesses at crucial stages), this is hardly surprising; but it is difficult to believe that the material which survives is so unusual that our perception would be dramatically altered if we had significantly more speeches available. It has been suggested that part of the reason for the emphasis on witnesses known to the parties is a desire on the part of those responsible for state justice, who are remote from the events and issues in question, to obtain an impression of how those who are in a position to observe events at close quarters evaluate those events. It has also been suggested that the role of the witness in classical Athens was primarily to offer support to the speaker for whom he appeared.[46] An extreme form of this view[47] assumes that witnesses are expected to lie routinely and that the factual content of their evidence does not interest the judges. There is no reason to doubt that witnesses *do* offer moral support and that the identity, status and public record of a witness are set to the credit of the litigant. But it would be a mistake to suppose that the factual message is of no interest. Witnesses are *always* called to attest a fact, never merely to state their support; and there are penalties for (proven) false testimony. And there is no real reason to believe that Athenians were more prone to give false evidence than moderns.

Special rules applied to evidence from slaves. Since chattel slavery was normal throughout Greece, and since slaves were a constant presence, both indoors and in the outside world (carrying out chores unsupervised,[48] accompanying their masters, or working semi-independently[49]), it must often have happened that a slave held a key piece of information for the resolution of a dispute. For the evidence of a slave to be used formally in court, it had to be extracted under torture. The reasons for this have been disputed; it has been suggested that a source of pressure is needed to counterbalance the hold over a slave exerted by the master, or that the aim of the process is to impose a degree of risk on the slave comparable with the fear of prosecution for false testimony which hung over the free witness, or again that the imposition of torture marks an important difference of status between slave and free. It may be that more than one factor was operative. The normal procedure where the evidence of one or more slaves was desired was for one of the parties to issue a formal challenge to his opponent either offering his own slave or slaves for examination under torture or demanding that his opponent hand over his slave or slaves for examination. Examples can be found in [Dem.] 59, Ant. 1, Dem. 54 and Dem. 37. Surviving speeches assert both the reliability and the unreliability of such evidence, and they are equally divided on the direction of any bias in a slave's testimony, sometimes asserting that slaves favour and sometimes that they hate their masters.[50] Not surprisingly, the arguments for and against the reliability of such evidence reflect the situation and rhetorical needs of the speaker. The cool estimation of the practical value of slaves' evidence can be seen from a fact which has often been noted: that while challenges to torture are common in the orators, there is no single surviving case in which such a challenge is carried out. Either they are declined (as in Ant. 1.6, 8) or, if they are accepted, a pretext is discovered to prevent the torture from going ahead (as in Dem. 37.39f.). This does not of course mean that no such torture ever took place. But unless the surviving speeches are completely unrepresentative of Athenian practice torture was rarely applied in ordinary forensic contexts. The challenges however are not otiose. Formal challenges refused by one's opponent could be used in court as evidence of the opponent's lack of faith in his case, and so formed part of a general strategy of seizing the moral high ground.

Judgment

Once both sides had delivered their speeches the judges queued to cast their vote. In 'assessed cases'[51] the verdict was followed by a short speech in which the parties put forward their penalty assessment. Voting involved the use of two different tokens, one for the accused and one for the accuser, and two urns, one for the token reflecting the judge's preference and one for the 'spoiled' vote. There was no opportunity for deliberation, though judges would have an opportunity to discuss the case with their immediate neighbours while queuing to vote (as well as during the hearing, since there was no attempt to impose silence on the panel). As a result the panel's vote reflected the sum total of individual decisions rather than a genuinely collective decision.

FORENSIC ORATORY

Modes of argument

It was pointed out above that the presentation of the case was by continuous speech interrupted only by supporting evidence, unlike most modern systems, where the structure of the trial is based on examination of each piece of evidence or testimony in turn by both sides. The content of the speeches themselves is somewhat surprising when viewed from the perspective of the modern courtroom. As well as statements of (alleged) fact and arguments in support of the litigant's case we find attempts (often explicit) to arouse in the judges emotions which will incline them to vote for the speaker and attempts to present the speaker as a man of moral worth and the opponent as someone devoid of moral scruple. As a result, we find in Athenian courtroom speeches many allegations irrelevant to the main issue. Only in the Areopagos (where the procedural rules forbade statements *exo tou pragmatos*, 'outside the issue') was any serious attempt made to exclude such material, and even there, as Lys. 3 shows, the effect was to check 'irrelevance' rather than to exclude it completely. The inclusion of such material is in line with ancient rhetoric, which acknowledges that the character of the participants in a dispute and the emotional response of the hearer have an important role to play in the task of persuasion alongside argument. Three other factors also favoured the introduction of statements 'outside the issue'. The first was the stress laid in Greek rhetoric on argument from probability (that is, from general tendencies to specific instances); the importance of this mode of argumentation will have reinforced the commonsense assumption that the plausibility of specific statements about an individual can be assessed with reference to his or her established patterns of behaviour. The second is the limitation of a system based on the volunteer prosecutor. Given the difficulty of detection and the potential for intimidation within such a system,[52] an habitual malefactor might find himself only rarely in court.[53] The third was the limited flexibility open to the judges. If they wished to show leniency to a defendant they believed to be guilty, or to withhold success from a prosecutor whose motives or behaviour they considered suspect, they could only register this desire by voting for acquittal or conviction, or (in 'assessed' cases only) by choosing the more lenient of the penalties proposed. It was therefore necessary not only to project a character which invited trust but also to present oneself as deserving the judges' goodwill in order to ensure that any inclination on the part of the judges to be swayed by factors outside the issue counted in one's favour.

But over and above any practical reasons for the inclusion of such material, the most important factor is cultural. Whereas most modern systems surround the lawcourt with artificial rules and barriers designed to treat the individual case in isolation, the Athenians viewed the trial within the lives of the parties, the judges and the community as a whole.

The professionals

The Athenian distrust of professionalism or even expertise in legal matters prevented the rise either of the jurist as an overt adviser on law or of the professional pleader. It was in fact illegal to act as supporting speaker for payment. However, professionalism still entered the Athenian legal system during the fifth century. The fifth century was an age of technical development and radical thought, and one important aspect of this change was the growth of rhetoric, the art (*techne*), as Aristotle puts it, of finding the means of persuasion available in any given situation.[54] Training in rhetoric formed an important aspect of the education offered by the sophists, itinerant intellectuals who travelled around Greece in the fifth century and after and who found in democratic Athens a ready market for their skills. The aspiring politician could attend the lectures of the major sophists, or purchase the sample speeches by the sophists which offered a template for the would-be speaker. The potential litigant could also adopt this course of action, but since for most people litigation was a unique or rare experience rather than a career, it was far more useful (if one could afford it) to obtain the advice and help of another kind of expert which flourished in the fifth century, the professional speechwriter (*logographos*, often anglicized as 'logographer'). The speechwriter would provide a speech to be delivered in court by the litigant, either from memory or from notes, ostensibly as the untutored thoughts of an ordinary citizen. Though the practice of writing speeches for pay was not illegal, there is evidence that public opinion was not favourable toward forensic speechwriters as a breed. Litigants accordingly never acknowledge the professional aid they have received. However, most of the speeches which have survived from classical Athens are compositions (of varying quality) by professional speechwriters intended for delivery in court.[55] They have survived because they were published at some point after the trial. There was therefore considerable interest in such speeches in Athens, both among potential litigants and among lovers of good oratory. The Athenian distaste for legal professionalism thus struggled with the equally Athenian enjoyment of a good speech.

THE AUTHORS FEATURED IN THIS BOOK

Discussions of the life and style of the Athenian orators and speechwriters can be found in G. Kennedy, *The Art of Persuasion in Greece*

(Princeton 1963) and M.J. Edwards, *The Attic Orators* (Bristol 1994); older but still of use is R.C. Jebb, *The Attic Orators from Antiphon to Isaeus* (London 1893, repr. 1962).

Antiphon of the deme Rhamnous was an active, if reclusive, politician, who is also reputed to have been the first of the professional speechwriters. He was tried and executed for his part in the oligarchy which briefly overturned the Athenian democracy in 411. His style is very dense, with individual words being loaded with meaning, and is rich in the various rhetorical devices (ultimately based on the concept of balanced phrasing) which were so popular in late fifth-century Athens. The remains of his output consist of speeches and rhetorical exercises written for real or imaginary homicide cases.

Lysias was a member of a rich metic family which fell foul of the unscrupulous oligarchic regime of the Thirty which ruled Athens for a brief and bloody period in 404/3 BC when his brother Polemarchos was executed and Lysias himself was forced to flee into exile. On the restoration of the democracy in 403 he prosecuted one of the Thirty, Eratosthenes (to be distinguished from the young victim in Lys. 1). It may have been the celebrity created by this incident which induced him to turn to speechwriting as a profession. He had died or retired by about 380 BC.

Isokrates was born in 436 and lived to the year of the battle of Chaironeia, 338 BC in which Macedon secured its mastery in Greece. He belonged to a well-to-do Athenian family. For most of his life he was a teacher of rhetoric rather than a speechwriter, and indeed in later life he sought to distance himself from the latter activity. He championed Philip and Alexander of Macedon, whom he saw as a means of uniting the Greeks against the Persian enemy. His style, which is not to everyone's taste, is finely honed, consisting of long and carefully wrought sentences and elaborate balance of clauses.

Isaios, like Lysias, was probably a member of the metic population. His speechwriting career began in the first half of the fourth century. He was allegedly a pupil of Isokrates and the teacher of Demosthenes. The surviving works are largely devoted to inheritance cases. He is very adroit at creating the impression of irrefragable proof by means which on closer inspection often utterly fail to convince.

Demosthenes, son of Demosthenes of the deme Paiania, was generally regarded in antiquity as the greatest of the canon of ten Attic orators established by the critics and editors working at Alexandria in the period after Alexander. He was born in the 380s, was politically active from the late 350s, and rose to prominence in the 340s. He is most celebrated for his vigorous opposition to the rise of Macedon. His first court appearance was for the prosecution of his guardians, who had misappropriated his inheritance. It may have been the notoriety arising from this precocious activity, together with the financial pressure caused by the depredations of his guardians, which encouraged him to turn to speechwriting.

Hypereides, born in 390, was another politician active in the anti-Macedonian cause. Originally allied with Demosthenes, he later (324) prosecuted him in the notorious 'Harpalos affair' (when Alexander's treasurer Harpalos defected to Athens with a vast treasure, part of which disappeared). He was executed in 322 after the abortive Athenian attempt to shake off the domination of Macedon. His style is remarkable for its vigour.

Apollodoros, son of Pasion, born in 394, has a precarious place among the Attic orators. An active politician and inveterate litigant (as well as a man of seasoned malice), he delivered a number of speeches which have survived under the name of Demosthenes, with whom he was at one time politically associated. Although scholars generally doubt that the speeches (or most of them at least) were delivered by Demosthenes, not everyone accepts the view of the present writer that Apollodoros himself composed them. Apollodoros' background was remarkable. His father, Pasion, was originally a slave who was freed and subsequently granted Athenian citizenship, eventually becoming one of the richest men in Athens.

NOTES

1 See A.R.W. Harrison, *The Law of Athens* (Oxford 1968, 1971), I, 21–4, for Athens. The sole source for the Spartan provision is Philo, *Special Laws* 3.22. D.M. MacDowell, *Spartan Law* (Edinburgh 1986), 82, expresses caution on the subject.

2 For a valuable discussion of our sources see S.C. Todd, *The Shape of Athenian Law* (Oxford 1993), 30–48.
3 See R. Thomas, *Literacy and Orality in Ancient Greece* (Cambridge 1992), 65ff.
4 Aristotle, *Ath. Const.* 4.1.
5 Aristotle, *Ath. Const.* 3.5.
6 Though not in the court scene depicted on the shield of Achilles in *Il.*18, ll.497 *et seq.*
7 Hesiod, *Works and Days*, 38f., 202, 248ff.
8 Aristotle, *Ath. Const.* 9.1.
9 MacDowell, *Law*, 32.
10 M.H. Hansen, *Eisangelia: the sovereignty of the people's court in Athens in the fourth century B.C. and the impeachment of generals and politicians* (Odense 1975), 19, argues that the procedure of *eisangelia* (a political process initiated before the Council of Five Hundred or the Assembly) was created by Kleisthenes. M. Ostwald, *Nomos and the Beginnings of Athenian Democracy* (Oxford 1969), 157ff., has suggested that the change in terminology for laws, from the older term *thesmos* to the term *nomos* which was normal in the classical period, was due to Kleisthenes.
11 Aristotle, *Ath. Const.* 9.1.
12 The frequency of recourse to this procedure can be seen from the fact that according to Aischines 3.194, the politician Aristophon boasted that he had been unsuccessfully indicted on a *graphe paranomon* seventy-five times. Even if this is an exaggeration, the fact that such a figure could be pulled out of the air is itself indicative of the usefulness of *graphe paranomon* as a weapon in the rivalry between political groups.
13 The involvement of the courts became more extensive with time. Aristotle (*Ath. Const.* 55.2) tells us that originally the Council, whose duties included the scrutiny of the Archons-elect and the Council-elect for the next year, had the right to reject candidates, but that by his own time rejected candidates could appeal to a court.
14 Aristophanes in *Wasps*, a play devoted to the legal system, represents the judges who make up the chorus as elderly men. Though this is clearly an oversimplification (as the play apparently acknowledges at ll.1114 *et seq.*), it does suggest that older men figured prominently among the panels, even if they did not make up the whole or even the majority.
15 See further, Harrison, *Law of Athens* II, 48, for the judge's oath.
16 Such a case was called an *agon atimetos*, literally 'unassessed contest/trial'.
17 Such a case was called an *agon timetos*, literally 'assessed contest/trial'.
18 See on this subject Todd, *Shape*, 134f.
19 Aristotle, *Ath. Const.* 53.3.
20 It appears that the number was always odd in public as in private cases, 501, 1001 etc., in order to avoid a tie, though there is evidence for cases in which an even number of judges voted (see Todd, *Shape*, 83 n.10), which means that abstention was either tolerated or impossible to prevent, or alternatively that where a judge fell ill or had to leave for any other reason the trial continued.

21 See in general V. Bers, 'Dikastic *thorubos*', in *Crux: essays in Greek history presented to G. E. M. de Ste Croix*, ed. P.A. Cartledge and F.D. Harvey (Exeter and London 1985).

22 So under the law cited at [Dem.] 59.52, which deals with cases where a husband divorces his wife without returning her dowry, legal action against the husband is taken not by the woman but by her *kyrios* on her behalf.

23 Thus in Ant. 1 the charge of murder is brought by the alleged victim's son against his stepmother and is answered not by the defendant but by her son, the prosecutor's half-brother.

24 As in Dem. 57.67 the speaker's male cousins appear, but the husbands of his female cousins. In Lys. 32 the author cleverly circumvents the rules by quoting a prolonged speech (real or invented) by the mother of the plaintiffs, thus creating the illusion that we actually have the woman present in court to testify. See Todd, *Shape*, 203.

25 See p. 12.

26 Hence at [Dem.] 59.26–7 Xenokleides, who was convicted of failure to serve on an expedition for which he was listed, is unable to appear as witness. This situation, in which a disfranchised Athenian had information of potential use in court, cannot have been unique. It seems that the possible problems for litigants were considered a price worth paying to maintain the status distinction between full and disfranchised citizens.

27 To the late twentieth-century reader this may appear to be an advantage enjoyed by metic females. It is however unlikely that Neaira and others like her would agree. Since access to the law depended on male connections, a woman without a protector was at a distinct disadvantage. Moreover, non-Athenian women lacked the status enjoyed by Athenian females.

28 This has not always been the case. D. Cohen, *Law, Violence and Community in Classical Athens* (Cambridge 1995), 5 n.2, points out that before the end of the nineteenth century prosecution by the individual was the norm in the English system.

29 For an interesting attempt to identify the discriminators between public and private actions, see Todd, *Shape*, 109ff.

30 For the opportunities for intimidation within the Athenian system see A.P. Dorjahn, *Classical Philology* 32 (1937), 341ff.

31 Examples are the prosecution of the speaker of Ant. 6 for homicide in response to his attempt to bring an action against a group of political figures, and the action brought by Phrastor in response to Stephanos' suit in [Dem.] 59. Counter-prosecution in classical Athens often resembles a poker game, since the purpose is often to compel an opponent to capitulate by raising the stakes. For more formal methods of blocking legal action, see the introductory remarks on Dem. 35 and Isai. 3.

32 Though some public cases could only be brought by citizens, such as the *graphe hybreos* (Dem. 21.47).

33 This was slightly less problematic than it seems, since the Athenians were in the habit of taking friendly witnesses with them when approaching any matter which might involve litigation. The principle is stated at Isai. 3.19, but is clearly visible from the identity of witnesses known to us. Only

where unforeseen situations arose (as in the assaults in Lys. 3 or Dem. 54) would chance bystanders be needed.

34 We have evidence for a procedure, called by moderns *kleteusis* (from the verb *kleteuein* used in ancient sources), whose precise mechanics are unclear but which probably involved proclamation by a herald. The penalty attached to this process was 1,000 drachmas. See Todd, *Shape*, 24f., with my demurrer, *Greek Orators VI. Apollodoros: Against Neaira. [Demosthenes] 59* (Warminster 1992), 25 n.38. At [Dem.] 59.28 I have hesitantly translated the verb *kleteuein* as 'subpoena' as the nearest modern equivalent, though the modern procedure of subpoena is quite different.

35 The precise portion is contested. See R.G. Osborne, *JHS* 105 (1985), 45.

36 The law is quoted at [Dem.] 59.16.

37 See Osborne, *JHS* 105 (1985), 52.

38 Since we find cases of people apparently dropping cases with impunity, the reality must be more complicated than the bland statement in the text. See Carey, *Greek Orators VI*, 114.

39 In some private cases at least there was a comparable penalty, the *epobelia*, consisting of one-sixth of the sum at issue, to be paid to the opponent. The difference of course is that in a private case the prosecutor's interests are directly involved.

40 For recent discussions of the sykophant, see R. Osborne and D. Harvey in *Nomos, Essays in Athenian Law, Politics and Society*, ed. P. Cartledge, P. Millett and S.C. Todd (Cambridge 1990), 83ff., 103ff.

41 See [Dem.] 59.110–11.

42 The source is the author of a treatise falsely ascribed in antiquity to Xenophon, usually labelled Pseudo-Xenophon nowadays or known almost affectionately as the 'Old Oligarch', [Xen.] *Ath. Const*. I.16.

43 Aristotle, *Ath. Const*. 67.1.

44 As a result, we find speakers occasionally using the word 'water' to mean 'time-allowance', as in [Dem.] 59.20, Dem. 57.61.

45 See n.34 above.

46 S.C. Todd, 'The purpose of evidence in Athenian courts', in *Nomos: Essays in Athenian Law, Politics and Society* (Cambridge 1990), 30f.

47 D. Cohen, *Law, Violence and Community in Classical Athens* (Cambridge 1995), 107ff., 166.

48 Like the slave who does the shopping in Lys. 1.

49 So apparently the slave Midas who caused all the trouble which led to the case against Athenogenes, p. 142.

50 Thus at Lys. 7.35 it is asserted that slaves are predisposed to give evidence against the master, while at Lykourgos *Leokrates* 30 it is assumed with equal confidence that they are likely to give evidence in his favour.

51 For the terms 'assessed' and 'unassessed', with reference to the fixing of penalty, see p. 7 and nn. 16 and 17.

52 See pp. 10–11.

53 Even if a man was regularly involved in litigation, the individual judge might encounter him only in the context of the specific trial, and the absence of a public record of judicial decisions meant that there was no other source of information about a person's career beyond that offered by his opponent.

54 Arist., *Rhet.* 1355b.

55 As a result the speeches do not provide a representative social sample from the court cases of the classical period. The characters we meet are for the most part drawn from the propertied classes. In this the speeches resemble most of our other sources of evidence for the ancient world.

1

HOMICIDE CASES

GENERAL

Homicide trials formed a distinct category in terms of legal procedure. According the *Constitution of Athens* (7.1) the only laws of Drakon retained by Solon were those dealing with homicide. Antiphon (6.2) emphasizes the antiquity of the homicide laws and insists that they have remained unchanged. It is conceivable that the laws had been subjected to adjustments between Drakon and the end of the fifth century, when they were reinscribed as part of a general revision of the laws, but there is no good cause to doubt the general impression we have of conservatism in this area of the law. The reluctance to change reflects the Greek conservatism in matters of religion, for homicide pollutes the perpetrator and anyone who comes into contact with him or her. The antiquity of the laws and the Athenian reluctance to meddle with them probably explains the fact that this, the most serious of crimes, was covered by a private action (though for obvious reasons the right to prosecute lay with the victim's family, whereas in ordinary private cases the victim alone had the right to sue) rather than by public action, as one would expect. The concept of public action (of prosecution by *ho boulomenos*) was created by Solon after Drakon's day. For the reader who wishes to explore homicide law in depth, D.M. MacDowell's *Athenian Homicide Law in the Age of the Orators* (Manchester 1962) is recommended; for the present it will be sufficient to adumbrate some of the distinctive features. The prosecution began with a proclamation in the agora instructing the alleged perpetrator to abstain from a number of religious and social activities, as being unclean (Ant. 6.35–6, [Dem.] 59.9). It proceeded more slowly than in other cases, with three preliminary hearings (*prodikasiai*) held in three separate months and the trial itself in the fourth. The trials made more extensive use of oaths than other cases, including (uniquely within the Athenian system) a compulsory oath from all witnesses to the effect that the accused had or had not committed the crime. They also had tight rules on relevance. Most strikingly perhaps, they were always held in the open air to prevent the judges from coming under the same roof as a polluted individual. The judicial panels were also distinctive. The most important homicide court, the Areopagos, consisted of ex-Archons, individuals with administrative and legal experience, and since the panel remained unchanged this effectively constituted an expert panel. The other courts were manned by the *ephetai*, fifty-one in number; these may have been selected from within the Areopagos, though this is far from certain. Another distinctive feature is the number of courts trying the same offence. The allocation of cases to courts depended on a number of factors, the status of the victim, the nature of the accusation and the nature of the defence.

CASE I: LYSIAS 1 – ON THE KILLING OF ERATOSTHENES

This speech was written for the defence of a man named Euphiletos (§16), who is accused of the deliberate killing of a young man named Eratosthenes. Both are otherwise unknown. He argues in his defence that he caught Eratosthenes in the act of sex with his wife. The killing was therefore legal. The case will have been heard by the Delphinion, the court which tried homicide cases in which the accused admitted the act but maintained that the killing was allowed by law. The date of the trial cannot be fixed with confidence. It could fall at any point between the probable start of Lysias' speech-writing career after 403 BC and his retirement or death some time around 380.

[1] I should value it greatly, gentlemen, if you would adopt the same attitude as my judges in this matter, as you would toward yourselves if you had been subjected to such treatment. For I am sure that if you were to have the same attitude to others as you do toward yourselves there would be nobody who would not feel indignant at what has taken place, but all of you would consider the penalties for those who behave in this way trifling. [2] And this would be the considered opinion not only here but in the whole of Greece. For this is

the only wrong for which both in democracy and in oligarchy the same redress has been given to the weakest against the most powerful, so that the lowest has the same rights as the highest; so firmly, gentlemen, do all mankind believe that this outrage is the most terrible. [3] Well, on the magnitude of the penalty I think you all are of the same mind, and that nobody is so lax as to think that those who are responsible for actions of this sort should obtain pardon or deserve light penalties; [4] but I think that what I must prove is that Eratosthenes seduced my wife and both corrupted her and disgraced my sons and insulted me by entering my house; and that there was neither any hostility between me and him apart from this, nor did I commit this act for money, to rise from rags to riches, nor for any other profit beyond the redress granted by the laws. [5] So then, I shall disclose to you the whole of my story from the beginning, leaving nothing out but telling the truth. For I see this as my only means of salvation, if I am able to tell you everything that happened.

[6] When I decided to marry, men of Athens, and I brought a wife into my house, during the early period my attitude was neither to annoy her nor to allow her too much freedom to do as she wished; I protected her to the best of my ability and kept watch as was proper. But when my child was born, from then on I trusted her and I placed all my property in her care, believing that this was the strongest bond of affection. [7] And to begin with, men of Athens, she was the best of all women; she was a skilled and thrifty housekeeper who kept careful control over everything. But when my mother died – [8] and her death has been the cause of all my troubles, for it was when my wife attended her funeral that she was seen by this man and eventually corrupted; he kept watch for the serving girl who used to go to market and passed messages and seduced her.

[9] Now first, gentlemen (this too I must tell you), I have a small house with two floors, with the upstairs and downstairs equal in size as far as the men's and women's quarters are concerned. When our baby was born, its mother nursed it. So that my wife would not run any risk going downstairs when she had to bathe him, I lived upstairs and the women below. [10] And this had become so normal that often my wife would go off downstairs to sleep with the baby, to give him the breast so that he wouldn't cry. And this went on for a long time, and I never once suspected, but was so gullible that I thought my own wife was the most decent woman in the city.

[11] After a time, gentlemen, I came home unexpectedly from the country. After dinner the baby cried and howled; he was being tormented by the maid on purpose to make him, because the man was in the house – afterwards I discovered all of this. [12] And I told my wife to go off and give the baby the breast to stop him crying. To start with she refused, as if she were pleased to see me back after a long absence. When I grew angry and told her to go she said: 'Oh yes, so that you can have a go at the serving girl here! You've groped her before too when you were drunk!' [13] I for my part laughed, while she stood up, went out and closed the door, pretending she was joking, and then turned the key. And I thought nothing of all this and suspected nothing, but went to sleep gladly, having come from the country. [14] When it was almost daylight, she came and opened the door. When I asked why the doors banged in the night, she said that the lamp by the baby had gone out and so she had got a light from the neighbours. I said nothing, and believed that this was true. But I thought, gentlemen, that she was wearing make-up, though her brother was not yet dead thirty days. Still, even so I said nothing about the matter but went off without a word.

[15] After this, gentlemen, time passed, and I remained in complete ignorance of my misfortunes. Then an elderly female slave came up to me; she had been sent secretly by a woman with whom Eratosthenes was having an affair – so I heard later. This woman was resentful and thought herself hard done by, because he no longer visited her frequently as before; so she kept watch until she found out the cause. [16] This female approached me near my house, where she was looking out for me. 'Euphiletos,' she said, 'don't think I've approached you through any desire to meddle. For the man who is insulting you and your wife is actually an enemy of ours. If you seize the girl who goes to market and works for you and put her to the test, you will discover everything. It is', she said, 'Eratosthenes of Oe who is doing this. Not only has he corrupted your wife but also many others; he makes a profession of it.'

[17] With these words, gentlemen, she went off, while I was immediately thrown into confusion; everything came into my mind and I was filled with suspicion. I reflected how I was locked up in my room, and recollected that the courtyard door and outside door banged that night, something which had never happened before, and that I thought my wife was wearing make-up. All this came into my mind and I was filled with suspicion. [18] I went home and told the serving girl to come to the market with me. I took her to the house

of one of my friends and told her that I had found out everything that was going on in the house. 'So,' I said, '*you* have two choices, either to be whipped and thrown into a mill and never have any release from miseries of this sort, or to tell the whole truth and suffer no harm but obtain pardon from me for your offences. Tell me no lies. Speak the whole truth.'

[19] As for her, to begin with she denied it and told me to do as I wished, since she knew nothing. But when I mentioned Eratosthenes to her and said that he was the man who was visiting my wife, she was amazed, supposing that I had detailed knowledge. At that point she threw herself at my knees, [20] and having received an assurance from me that she would suffer no harm she turned accuser, telling first of all how he approached her after the funeral, and then how she had finally served as his messenger and my wife was won over eventually, and the means by which his entry was arranged, and how at the Thesmophoria while I was in the country my wife went to the temple with his mother. And she gave me a detailed account of everything else which had taken place.

[21] When her whole story was told, I said: 'See that nobody in the world hears of this. Otherwise nothing I have agreed with you will stand. And I expect you to give me manifest proof of this. I don't need words, I want the action exposed, if it is as you say.' [22] She agreed to do this.

After this there was an interval of four or five days . . .* as I shall demonstrate with convincing evidence. But first of all I want to give you an account of what took place on the last day. I had a close friend, Sostratos, whom I met on his way from the country after sunset. I knew that having arrived so late he would find nothing he needed at home, and so I invited him to dinner. We reached my house and went upstairs and dined. [23] When he had eaten his fill, he went off while I went to sleep. Eratosthenes, gentlemen, came in, and the serving girl woke me at once and told me that he was in the house. Telling her to watch the door, I went downstairs in silence and left the house. I called on one man after another; some I didn't catch at home, while others, I found, were not even in town. [24] But I took as many as I could of those who were available and made my way back. We obtained torches from the nearest shop and went indoors – the door had been kept open by the serving girl. We pushed open the door of the bedroom. The first of us to enter saw

* Please note that ellipses indicate a gap in the Greek text.

him still lying beside my wife; those who entered after saw him standing naked on the bed.

[25] I knocked him down with a blow, gentlemen; I forced his hands behind his back and tied them, and asked him why he was insulting me by entering my house. He admitted his guilt, but begged and pleaded with me not to kill him but to exact money. [26] For my part I answered: 'It is not I who shall kill you but the city's law, which you broke, because you considered it less important than your pleasures. You preferred to commit a crime such as this against my wife and my children rather than obey the laws and behave decently.'

[27] So, gentlemen, that man paid the penalty which the law prescribes for those who commit such wrongs. He was not dragged in off the street, nor did he take refuge at the hearth, as these people maintain. How could he, when he fell down at once in the bedroom where he was struck, and I had bound his hands, when there were so many people in the room whom he could not slip past, and he had neither blade nor wood nor any other weapon with which to resist those who had entered the room? [28] No, gentlemen, I think you too are aware that people engaged in unjust plots do not accept that their enemies are telling the truth. By telling lies themselves and by such devices they stir up the hearers' anger against men who are acting justly. (*To the clerk*) Now first of all read out the law.

Law

[29] He did not dispute his guilt, gentlemen, but confessed it, and begged and pleaded not to die but offered to pay money. For my part I did not agree to his assessment. I considered that the law's authority was greater, and exacted the penalty which you believed most just when you imposed it for men guilty of such offences. Will my witnesses to these statements please step up.

Witnesses

[30] Please read out this law too from the column on the Areopagos.

Law

You hear, gentlemen, that it is explicitly decreed by the court on the Areopagos itself, which both by our ancestors and in our own day has been granted the right to try cases of murder, that a man is not to be convicted of murder if he exacts this punishment after catching a seducer with his spouse. [31] And the lawgiver was so convinced of the justice of this in the case of married women that he imposed the same penalty in the case of concubines, who are of less importance. Yet clearly, if he had had a harsher penalty in the case of married women, he would have employed it. As it is, unable to find a more severe penalty in their case, he determined that the punishment should be the same as in the case of concubines. Please read out this law too.

Law

[32] You hear, gentlemen, that he bids that if anyone forcibly shames a free man or boy, he is to pay double the damage, if a woman, in cases where killing is permitted, he is liable to the same penalty. So true is it that he considered that those who use force deserve a lesser penalty than those who use persuasion. For he condemned the latter to death, while for the former he doubled the damages, [33] in the belief that those who get their way by force are hated by their victims, while those who have used persuasion corrupt the women's minds to such an extent that they make other people's wives more loyal to themselves than to their husbands, so that the whole household is in their power and it is uncertain whose the children are, the husbands' or the seducers'. And so the lawgiver made death the penalty for them.

[34] So in my case, gentlemen, the laws have not only acquitted me of wrongdoing but have actually ordered me to exact this penalty. And it is up to you whether the laws are to have authority or to be of no account. [35] For in my opinion the reason all cities make their laws is so that on any issue on which we are in doubt we may go to them and determine what must be done. It is the laws which urge the victims in cases such as this to exact this penalty. [36] I urge you to show your agreement with them. If not, you will provide so much security for seducers as to encourage thieves too to claim that they are seducers. They will know well that if they offer this excuse and claim that this is their purpose in entering other people's houses, nobody will lay a finger on them. Everyone will know that the laws on seduction can be ignored, that it is your vote they need to fear. For this is the supreme authority in the city.

[37] And consider, gentlemen. They allege that I told the serving girl to fetch the young man that day. Personally, gentlemen, I should consider myself justified in using any means available to catch the man who had corrupted my wife. [38] For if words had been exchanged but no act had taken place and I told her to fetch him, I would have been in the wrong; but if the affair had been fully consummated and he had entered my house many times, and I used any means available to catch him, I should consider my action reasonable. [39] But note that this too is a lie. You will recognize this easily from the following facts. As I said before, gentlemen, my close friend Sostratos met me on his way from the country around sunset and dined with me, and when he had eaten his fill he went off. [40] Yet consider first of all, gentlemen, whether, if I was plotting against Eratosthenes that night it was better for me to dine elsewhere myself or to bring a dinner guest home. For in the latter case Eratosthenes would have been less likely to venture into the house. Then again, do you think I would have let my dinner guest go and leave me alone and unsupported, or ask him to stay, so that he could join me in taking revenge on the seducer? [41] Furthermore, gentlemen, don't you think I would have sent word to my associates during the day and instructed them to gather in the nearest of my friends' houses, instead of running around during the night as soon as I found out, without knowing whom I would find at home and who would be out? I went to Harmodios' house, and another's, who were out of town (I had no idea), and found that others were not at home, and made my way back taking all those I could. [42] Yet if I had known beforehand, don't you think I would have had servants ready and sent word to my friends, so that I could go in with the utmost safety myself (how could I know whether he had a blade too?), and take my revenge with the maximum number of witnesses? As it is, knowing nothing of what was to happen that night, I took along those I could. Will my witnesses to these statements please step up.

Witnesses

[43] You have heard the witnesses, gentlemen. Now consider the matter in your own minds, and ask if there has ever been any quarrel between Eratosthenes and me, apart from this. You will find none. [44] He did not persecute me with public charges; nor did he try to exile me from the city; nor did he bring private suits against

me; nor did he know any secret about me which I was so afraid someone would discover that I wanted to kill him; nor did I have any hope of receiving money from some source if I were to commit this act. For people sometimes plot each other's deaths for motives such as these. [45] Now, not only had no insult or drunken quarrel or any other dispute taken place; I had never even seen the man except that night. What conceivable reason could I have had to risk such a danger, if I had not received the most terrible wrong from him? [46] Then again, did I voluntarily summon witnesses to my impiety, when I could have ensured, if I was plotting wrongfully to kill him, that none of them would share my secret?

[47] In my opinion, gentlemen, this was not a private punishment for my own sake but for the whole city. For people who act in this way, once they see the prizes set up for such offences, will be less likely to commit them against others, if they see that you are of the same mind. [48] Otherwise, it is far better to expunge the established laws and make others which will impose the punishments on men who protect their own wives and grant full immunity to men who wish to offend against them. [49] This is far more just than for the citizens to be ambushed by the laws; these bid anyone who catches a seducer to treat him as he chooses, but it turns out that the trials are far more dangerous for the victims than for those who disgrace other men's wives contrary to the laws. [50] For I now find my person, my property, everything else, in danger, because I obeyed the city's laws.

The individual right to self-help, that is to take legally sanctioned action without recourse to the courts, persisted in certain contexts in the classical period. Among them was the punishment of the seducer (Greek *moichos*). Where a free male found another male having illicit sex with a woman under his protection and control, he had a range of options: he could prosecute by *graphe*; he could hold the guilty party prisoner and extract a ransom; he could subject him to physical degradation; he could even (where certain close female relatives at least were concerned) kill. The defence under Athenian law is to be distinguished from modern concepts such as diminished responsibility or *crime passionnel*. The defence is not that the killer lost control but that he carried out a lawful execution. From Euphiletos' understandably sketchy account of the prosecution case, it seems that the dead man's relatives argue that Eratosthenes was not taken in illicit sex but was enticed to the house by the serving girl (and perhaps dragged in at the last moment), and therefore presumably that there was some other motive for the killing than that advanced by Euphiletos. From Euphiletos' strenuous denial that he sent for Eratosthenes, it would appear that his right to take action was, if not negated, at least compromised if he had in any way connived in the seduction. The prosecution also claim that Eratosthenes had taken refuge at the hearth before he was killed. Since the hearth was sacred, the killing in these circumstances would be sacrilege. Though irrelevant to the question of the validity of Euphiletos' defence, the allegation if accepted by the judges would prejudice them against Euphiletos.

In factual terms, in order to secure his acquittal, Euphiletos needs to demonstrate that he killed Eratosthenes in the circumstances and for the reasons he claimed. That the dead man was a seducer and was taken in the act seems to be proved conclusively by the many witnesses whom Euphiletos took with him on the night in question. He also attacks the notion that there could have been any other reason for killing Eratosthenes. From his confidence on this score we may perhaps conclude that the prosecutors are hard pressed to find a plausible motive for homicide. They may however be closer to the truth with their allegation that Eratosthenes was enticed into the house. Euphiletos produces a body of testimony from people whom he visited on the night in question, and who were unavailable, and an argument from probability that this lack of preparation refutes the claim that Eratosthenes was tricked. However, one is struck both by the convenient neatness of this evidence for unpreparedness and by the striking disparity between, on the one hand, his advance instructions to the maidservant to give him visible proof and the efficiency with which he set about his activities on the fateful night and, on the other, his avowed failure to ascertain in advance the movements of his friends against the likely need for their assistance.

However, the most significant means of gaining credence for his account is the characterization of Euphiletos by Lysias. This was a technique in which Lysias excelled. Here the speechwriter creates for his client a personality whose accuracy we cannot assess with confidence but which is so convenient for Euphiletos' line of defence that one suspects that it is determined more by strategic considerations than by any resemblance to the historical Euphiletos. Lysias presents us with a trusting, even naive, individual (an archetypal cuckold), who seems incapable of the kind of deception alleged by his accusers. As well as bolstering Euphiletos' version of events, this characterization also commands the sympathy of the hearer. Eratosthenes in contrast, though he never emerges as a distinct personality, is presented as the arch-seducer, a threat to society. In order to strengthen the defence, Lysias also obscures the range of procedures available against seducers. He creates the illusion that killing Eratosthenes was an inevitable course of action; in fact, as was observed above, the aggrieved male had a number of options, not all violent.

CASE II: ANTIPHON 1 – ACCUSATION OF POISONING AGAINST THE STEPMOTHER

The present speech was written for the prosecution of a woman accused of causing the death of her husband by poisoning. The allegation is that she tricked another female (probably a slave) into administering the poison. The dead man had been married twice. The prosecutor is his son by his first marriage; the accused is the second wife, and her defence is presented by her son by the dead man, half-brother to the accuser. Although it has been doubted, it is likely that the charge is *bouleusis* of homicide. *Bouleusis*, literally 'planning', is used more broadly in the Athenian system to mean 'encompassing', including perhaps incitement, and accordingly can be applied both to intentional and to unintentional homicide. The accuser in the present case alleges *bouleusis* of intentional homicide. Cases of *bouleusis* were tried at the Palladion. The date cannot be determined for certain.

[1] Young as I am and inexperienced still in lawsuits, I am in a terrible dilemma in this matter, gentlemen; I must either fail to proceed against his killers despite my father's injunction or if I do proceed I must start a quarrel with those I least should, my paternal half-brothers and their mother. [2] The course of events and my opponents themselves have compelled me to undertake this action against the very people who would by rights have acted as both the dead man's avengers and as the prosecutor's allies. As it is the reverse has happened. For these very people turn out to be the adversaries and the killers, as I and my written indictment state. [3] I urge you, gentlemen, if I demonstrate that their mother by design and forethought is our father's killer, and has been caught before now in the act of contriving his death, not just once but on several

occasions, first of all avenge your laws – these you have received from the gods and from your ancestors, and you apply the same standards as they when voting for conviction; secondly avenge the dead man; and at the same time rescue me, for I am left all alone. [4] For you are my nearest kin. The ones who should by rights have acted as the dead man's avengers and as my allies have proved to be the dead man's killers and have become my adversaries. What allies is a man to seek, where else will he go for refuge, except to you and to justice?

[5] I am amazed at my brother. Whatever does he mean in appearing as my opponent? Does he think that piety consists in not abandoning his mother? Personally, I think it far more impious to abandon the vengeance due to the dead man, especially as his death was unplanned and unintentional on his part, while the murder was deliberate and intentional on hers. [6] And he cannot claim that he knows for certain that his mother did not kill our father. For he refused the one source of sure knowledge, from torture, while he welcomed sources which could not provide information. Yet he should have been eager, and this was the substance of my challenge, to investigate what really happened. [7] For if the slaves did not support me, he could have offered a vigorous defence against me based on certain knowledge and his mother would have been rid of this charge. But where he refused to put the facts to the test, how can he possibly have knowledge of matters he refused to ascertain?

[8] What defence will he offer, I ask myself. For he was well aware that torture meant she could not be saved; he thought her salvation lay in refusing the torture. They believed that the facts could be suppressed by this means. So surely his oath that he knows for certain cannot be true, if he refused to obtain sure information when I was willing to use the fairest test, the torture, in this matter? [9] For to start with I offered to put to the torture his slaves, who knew that this woman, their mother, had also plotted earlier to kill my father with drugs, that my father had caught her in the act and that she made no denial beyond claiming that she was administering them not to kill him but as a love potion. [10] This was my reason for wishing to put them to the test in this way. I put accusations against this woman in writing and invited my opponents themselves to act as questioners in my presence, so that the slaves would not be forced to answer questions put by me; instead I was satisfied if the questions in my document were used. (And it is right that this should count as evidence for me, that I am pursuing my father's

killer properly and justly.) And if they gave negative or contradictory answers, the torture was to compel them to expose what had been done; for torture will make even people suborned to tell lies speak the truth.

[11] Yet I am certain that if they had come to me and offered to hand over their slaves as soon as they were informed that I was proceeding against my father's killer, and it was I who refused to accept, they would be advancing this very fact as their strongest evidence that they are innocent of the murder. As it stands, as I am the one who though willing to act as questioner myself invited them to carry out the torture in my place, it is surely right that this same fact should count as evidence that they are guilty of the murder. [12] For if my opponents had offered to hand them over for torture and I had refused, they would have counted it as evidence. So this same fact should count for me, since I offered to put the matter to the test and they refused to hand them over. I think it appalling that they are trying to induce you not to convict them when they did not see fit to judge their own case by handing their slaves over for torture.

[13] So on this issue it is quite clear that they shrank from obtaining certain knowledge of the facts. They knew that the crime which would come to light would be laid at their door, and so they wanted to leave it in silence, untested. I am certain you will not, gentlemen. You will expose it.

So much for this point. However, I shall try to give you an account of what really took place. May justice be my guide.

[14] Our house had an upstairs room, which Philoneos used to occupy whenever he was in town. He was a decent man, a friend of my father. He had a concubine, whom he intended to put in a brothel. My brother's mother discovered this and befriended her. [15] Having ascertained that Philoneos intended to treat the woman badly, my mother sent for her and on her arrival told her that she too was being badly treated by our father. If the woman was ready to follow her instructions, she claimed that she was able to regain both Philoneos' affection for the woman and my father's for herself. She would devise, the other would obey. [16] Then she asked her if she was willing to carry out her instructions, and the woman promised, straight away, I imagine.

Subsequently, as it happened, Philoneos had a religious ceremony to Zeus of Possessions to perform in Peiraieus, while my father was on the point of sailing to Naxos. Philoneos thought it an excellent idea both to accompany my father to Peiraieus, as a friend of his, and to entertain him after making the sacrifice. [17] Philoneos' concubine went along for the sacrifice. When they were in Peiraieus, Philoneos sacrificed, of course. And when he had completed the sacrifice, the female wondered how to administer the drug to them, before or after dinner. And as she considered the matter she concluded that after dinner was better; she was also acting on the instructions of this Klytaimestra, my brother's mother. [18] The full account of the dinner would be too longwinded for me to tell and you to hear. I shall try to give as brief an account as I can of the rest, of how the poison was administered. After dinner, naturally, since one was sacrificing to Zeus of Possessions and entertaining the other, and one was about to go on a voyage and was dining with a close friend, they made a libation and offered incense for their future. [19] And while Philoneos' concubine was pouring the libation for them – as they offered prayers which would never be fulfilled, gentlemen – she poured in the poison. Thinking she was being clever, she gave more to Philoneos in the belief perhaps that if she gave him more she would win more affection from him – she had no idea that she was my stepmother's dupe until disaster struck – while she poured less in our father's drink. [20] They for their part after pouring their libations took their final drink, holding in their hands their own killer. Philoneos died at once on the spot; our father was afflicted with a sickness from which he died after twenty days. For this the assistant who carried out the act has the reward she deserved, though she was not to blame – she was put on the wheel and then handed over to the public executioner; the guilty party, the one who planned it, will soon have hers, if you and the gods will it.

[21] Note how much more just my plea is than my brother's. I urge you to avenge the dead man, who is the victim of an irreparable wrong. For the dead man my brother will offer no request, though he deserves your pity and support and vengeance for having his life taken in a godless and inglorious manner before his time by the last people who should have done this. [22] His plea will be for the murderess, a plea which is unprincipled, unholy, which deserves neither fulfilment nor attention either from the gods or from you; he will seek with his plea ⟨to induce you not to convict her for her crimes⟩ though she could not induce herself not to devise them.* But you must give your support not to those who kill but to the

* Please note that angle brackets denote wording which is a modern edition to the text.

victims of deliberate murder, especially at the hands of the last people who should have killed them. It is now up to you to come to the right verdict on this case; you must do so.

[23] He will plead with you for his mother, who is still alive, who killed the dead man in such a reckless and godless manner, to prevent her from paying the penalty for her crimes – if he can persuade you. But I plead with you for my dead father, to ensure that at all costs she will pay it. It was precisely to ensure that wrongdoers pay the penalty that you became judges and were given this title. [24] My purpose in speaking for the prosecution is to ensure that she pays the penalty for her crimes and I avenge our father and your laws; for this reason it is proper that you should all support me, if I am speaking the truth. His purpose in acting as her supporter is the opposite, to ensure that the woman who ignored the laws does not pay the penalty for her crimes. [25] Yet which is more just, that someone who has murdered intentionally should pay the penalty or not? Who is more deserving of pity, the dead man or the woman who killed him? Personally, I think it is the dead man. This would be more just and more pious of you in the sight of gods and men. I urge now that just as she destroyed him without remorse and without pity, so she should be destroyed by you and by justice. [26] For she deliberately inflicted death of her own free will, while he suffered it unwillingly and by force. Certainly by force, gentlemen; he was about to set sail from this territory, and was being entertained by a friend of his. She however in sending the drug and ordering it to be given to him to drink killed our father. How can you or anyone else see fit to show her pity or consideration, when she did not see fit to pity her own husband but destroyed him ruthlessly and shamefully?

[27] So then, it is more proper to feel pity for involuntary suffering than for intentional and deliberate wrongs and offences. She killed him without respect or fear for gods or heroes or men; by the same token, if she were destroyed by you and by justice, if you were to show her no consideration or pity or respect, her punishment would be completely just.

[28] I am amazed at the impudence of my brother's attitude, in swearing in my mother's defence that he knows for certain that she has not committed this act. How can he know for certain when he was not present? People plotting to kill those around them do not devise their plans in front of witnesses but as furtively as they can so that no-one in the world knows. [29] The victims of their plots

are completely ignorant until disaster strikes and they recognize the ruin which has befallen them. Then if they are able, if they have time before they die, they summon their friends and relatives and call them to witness; they tell them the identity of the killers and solemnly instruct them to take vengeance for the crime against them – [30] as my father instructed me, his son, during his last pitiable illness. If they cannot reach them, they write down a statement and call their servants to witness and reveal the identity of the killers. This is what my father did; he revealed all this and gave his instructions to me, young as I still was, not to his slaves.

[31] For my part, I have told my tale and given my support to the dead man and the law. It is for you to consider the rest for yourselves and to vote in accordance with justice. I think that the gods below also take an interest in the victims of wrongdoing.

The central facts are straightforward enough. The speaker's father died not long after a friend, Philoneos, with whom he had dined. According to the speaker, he believed himself to have been poisoned. Philoneos' mistress, who was probably a slave, confessed under torture to administering poison, apparently in the belief that she was giving Philoneos a drug which would restore his desire for her. The speaker claims that his father imposed a solemn injunction (Greek *episkepsis*) on him, stating that he was the victim of murder and instructing him to pursue the killer. §30 seems to suggest that the speaker was very young at the time, and it may be that a substantial interval has intervened since the father's death, perhaps the interval needed for the speaker to reach the age of majority and so be able to prosecute (there was no time limit, *prothesmia*, in homicide cases).

There is no real reason to doubt the broad outline of ascertainable events provided by the speaker, and one can readily see why the son of the first marriage might welcome the chance to prosecute his stepmother. The problem resides in the imputation of guilt to the stepmother; there is in fact a striking lack of evidence to incriminate her. Even if we accept that Philoneos and the speaker's father were poisoned (and not merely the victims of food-poisoning or some other natural cause) and that Philoneos' mistress had administered a fatal drug (and did not simply confess to a non-existent crime to be rid of the torture), the speaker's father could do nothing more than express his suspicions. Whether he even suspected his second wife is not made explicit by the speaker; this may be a deliberate evasion of a weak point. The woman who was tortured evidently did not incriminate the stepmother, or we should have expected to hear more of her confession; as it stands the narrative takes us to her death and then the speech abruptly changes tack, moving from narration to argumentation. With such a lack of solid evidence, the speaker is forced to rely on emotional appeal (sympathy for himself, forced to take such an action while so young, pity for his dead father, abhorrence for the monstrous woman who killed him, likened to Klytaimestra §17) and especially on the inference to be drawn from his stepbrother's refusal to agree to the torture of slaves who might have helped determine what actually happened. The general difficulty in obtaining any evidence may explain the surprising absence of witnesses in this speech, though one would have expected at least to have heard from the doctor who attended the dead man.

CASE III: ANTIPHON 5 – ON THE KILLING OF HERODES

The present case arises out of the death of an Athenian named Herodes. He and the speaker, Euxitheos, a native of Mytilene in Lesbos, were sailing from Mytilene to Thrace when they were compelled by bad weather to put in on the coast of Lesbos. To pass the time more comfortably, they boarded another boat, which offered cover from the rain, and engaged in a drinking bout. During the night Herodes left the boat (one would imagine, though we are not told, to answer a call of nature) and never returned. After a fruitless search, Euxitheos continued his voyage. Relatives of Herodes then conducted their own investigation. They tortured two men, one of whom (who was certainly a slave) incriminated both himself and Euxitheos in the killing of Herodes, the other (alleged by Euxitheos to be free) exculpated Euxitheos. A further search of the vessel where the drinking party took place revealed a note incriminating Euxitheos. Blood was found, but proved to be animal blood from a sacrifice. Herodes' relatives then killed the slave. Euxitheos has now been summoned to face prosecution in Athens. However, the case is not a regular homicide trial; instead of charging Euxitheos with intentional killing, the accusers have subjected him to the procedure of *endeixis* (denunciation) as a *kakourgos*. *Kakourgos*, literally 'wrongdoer' (translated in the present volume by 'felon'), was not as one might suppose a generic term for lawbreakers but referred to a class of criminals whose crimes were mainly against property; they included burglars (*toichorychoi*), muggers (*lopodytai*, literally 'clothes-strippers') and thieves (*kleptai*), and were liable to summary arrest and (if they confessed) execution by the officials known as the Eleven. The trial is therefore heard not by the Areopagos but by an ordinary judicial panel. The date cannot be fixed with precision; certainly it is later than 428, the date of the revolt of Lesbos from the Athenian Empire, when the speaker was still a boy (§75), but not too long after, since he is still a young man. But since Lesbos is still subject to Athenian control, the speech must predate 412, when the island joined the general revolt of Athenian subject-states which flared up after the destruction of the Athenian expeditionary force in Sicily. A date between 420 and 412 would serve. A detailed commentary on this important speech can be found in M. Edwards and S. Usher, *Greek Orators I. Antiphon and Lysias* (Warminster 1985).

[1] I could have wished, gentlemen, that my powers of speaking and experience of affairs were equal to my misfortune and the evils which have befallen me. As it is I have more experience of the latter than is fair, while in the former I am more deficient than is safe. [2] For when I had to suffer physical mistreatment along with this unjust charge I had no experience to aid me, while now that I have to secure my safety with a truthful account of what happened, my lack of ability as a speaker damages my case. [3] Many people before now who were inadequate as speakers have failed to win credence with the truth and have been ruined by it through their inability to prove it, while many able speakers have won credence with falsehood and have been saved by it, because they lied successfully. As a result, of necessity anyone who lacks experience of litigation is at the mercy of the arguments of his accusers rather than the facts and the reality of what took place.

[4] So my request to you, gentlemen, will not be that made by the majority of defendants, that you give them a hearing, a sign that they distrust themselves and have judged you guilty in advance of bias. For it is proper that before a jury of good men, people on trial should be granted even without asking the same hearing which the prosecutors received without asking. [5] My request to you is this, that you bear with me if I make some mistake in speaking and conclude that it is an error of inexperience rather than injustice, and if I make an effective point that my success is due to truth rather than cleverness. It is not right either that someone whose actions are

wrong should be saved by words or that someone whose actions are right should be ruined by words. For a word is a fault of the tongue, while an act is a fault of the mind. [6] And it's inevitable that a man whose life is in danger will make some errors. Of necessity he will have his mind not only on his words but also on his fate; for anything that is still uncertain depends more on chance than on foresight. It's inevitable that this will cause considerable anxiety for the individual at risk. [7] Personally I observe that even experienced litigants speak much worse than usual whenever they are in jeopardy, but are more successful when they are involved in an issue which brings no risk. My request, gentlemen, which accords both with law and with piety, is fair both to you and to me. As to the charges, I shall answer them point by point.

[8] First of all I shall demonstrate to you that I have been brought to trial here in a highly unlawful and violent way. Not because I would try to evade the democratic court – since I should entrust my life to your vote even if you were not bound by oath and there was no law on the matter, such is my confidence that I have done no wrong in this matter and that you will reach a just verdict – but so that the prosecutors' violent and unlawful conduct may count as an indication of their general case against me. [9] To begin with, though I have been denounced as a felon I am on trial for murder, an experience without precedent in this country. That I am not a felon and am not subject to the law on felons my opponents themselves have attested. For the law deals with thieves and muggers, but they have not shown that any of this applies to me. So as far as concerns my arrest they have made my acquittal by you the most lawful and just decision. [10] They maintain that murder itself is a great felony, and I agree that it is one of the greatest, as is sacrilege and betrayal of the city. But there is a separate law laid down for each of them. To begin with, they have ensured that my trial is held in the very place from which other defendants in trials for homicide are barred by public proclamation, in the agora. Again, they made a penalty proposal, when the law is laid down that the killer pays with his life; this is not for my benefit but for their own convenience, and in the process they have allowed the dead man less than the penalty established in the law. Their motive you will discover later in my speech. [11] Furthermore, as I think you all know, all the courts try cases of homicide in the open air, with the specific aim of ensuring that the judges do not come into the same building as men whose hands are unclean and the prosecutor does not share

a roof with the killer. But you have disregarded this law and done the opposite of the rest. And you should have sworn the most serious and solemn oath, calling down destruction on yourself and your kin and your household, that your accusation would concern itself solely with my guilt on the actual charge of homicide; as a result even if I were guilty of many crimes I would not have been convicted except on the charge itself, nor if I were responsible for many good deeds would I have been saved by them. [12] But you disregarded this and invented laws for yourself. You accuse me without oath; your witnesses give evidence without oath, when they should have taken the same oath as you and should testify against me with their hands on the sacrificial victims. And then you ask the judges to convict on a charge of murder, putting their trust in witnesses who are not under oath, whose credibility you have removed by disregarding the established laws; you think that they should hold your contempt for law more important than the laws themselves.

[13] You say that I would not have stayed if I had been set free, but would have absconded, as though you had forced me to enter this country against my will. Yet if it had been of no concern to me to be barred from this city, it would have been all the same to me to refuse to come when summoned and let the case go by default, or to have the right to leave the country after making my first defence speech; that right is open to everyone. But on your own initiative you are striving to deny me alone the right which is available to every other Greek, making a law to suit yourself.

[14] Yet I think everyone would agree that the laws which have been enacted to deal with these matters are the most noble and sacred of all. The fact is that they are the oldest in this land; moreover, their content and application have remained the same, the surest sign that laws are well made; for time and experience reveal imperfections to mankind. So you should not determine whether or not your laws are good according to the prosecutor's statements but decide on the basis of the laws whether or not the prosecutors' speeches present the case to you in an honest and lawful way. [15] So then, the laws on homicide are excellent, and nobody has ever dared to interfere with them. You alone have had the audacity to make yourself legislator in order to debase them; you have disregarded the laws and seek to destroy me unjustly. Your illegal behaviour is my best testimony; you were well aware that there would be no-one who would testify against me having taken that oath.

[16] Then again, you did not arrange for a single and conclusive trial on the issue, like someone confident in his case, but you left room for dispute and further argument, as though you would not trust even these judges. So I gain no advantage even if I am acquitted in this court, but you can claim that I was acquitted as a felon but not on the charge of murder, while if you convict you will demand my death as one found guilty of murder. What more monstrous scheme could there be than this, if you have achieved your ends by convincing the judges once, while if I am acquitted once the same danger awaits me? [17] In addition, gentlemen, I was imprisoned with a disregard for the law without parallel. Though I was ready to provide three guarantors in accordance with the law, they contrived to deprive me of the opportunity. No other foreigner who offered to provide guarantors has ever been imprisoned, though the officials responsible for felons are bound by this same law. And so I alone was deprived of the protection of this law, which is open to everyone else. [18] For it was to their advantage firstly that I should be as badly prepared as possible by being unable to handle my own affairs, and secondly to have me suffer physically, so that my physical suffering would make my friends more ready to testify falsely for my opponents than to tell the truth for me. They have inflicted, both on me personally and on my family, a disgrace which will last my whole life long.

[19] So I face this trial sorely deprived both of your laws and of justice. Nonetheless, as far as this situation allows I shall attempt to prove my innocence, though it is difficult to disprove all at once false accusations which have been devised over so long a period. For one cannot protect oneself against attacks which one has not foreseen.

[20] I set sail from Mytilene, gentlemen, in the same boat as this man Herodes, whom they say I killed. We were sailing to Ainos, I to visit my father (who happened to be there at that time), Herodes to arrange the ransom of slaves with some Thracians. The slaves he was due to release were on board, and the Thracians who were to pay the ransom. I shall present you with the witnesses to these facts.

Witnesses

[21] Such was the motive for his voyage and mine. As it happened, we encountered a storm, which forced us to put in at a part of the

territory of Methymna. There the boat was moored to which Herodes moved, the one in which they claim he was killed. First of all note this, that what happened was due more to chance than to any choice of mine. There is nothing to indicate that I persuaded the man to sail with me; rather, he made the voyage on his own initiative for his own business. [22] Nor can it be shown that I sailed to Ainos without good reason, or that we put in at this spot deliberately; we were forced to. Nor again was the move to the other boat due to any scheme or trick; rather, this too was through necessity. The boat in which we were sailing was undecked, the one to which we moved had a deck; we moved because of the rain. I shall present you with witnesses to these facts.

Witnesses

[23] After we moved to the other boat, we had a drinking session. It is certain that Herodes left the boat and did not return, while I did not leave the boat at all during that night. The next day, when the man did not appear, I was as active as the others in searching for him, and I as much as any of the others thought it a strange business. And it was I who was responsible for a messenger being sent to Mytilene; he was sent on my suggestion. [24] When nobody else was willing to go, none of the others on board nor any of those who were sailing with Herodes, I was ready to send my own servant; yet I would surely not knowingly send someone who could inform against me. And when the man, despite being searched for, was not found either in Mytilene or anywhere else, and all the other ships were setting sail, I too sailed away. I shall present you with witnesses to these facts.

Witnesses

[25] These are the facts. Consider now the probabilities. Firstly, before I set sail for Ainos, while the man was missing, nobody at all accused me, though my opponents had already heard the news; otherwise I would not have sailed off. But for the time being the truth of what had happened was too strong for an accusation from them; besides, I was still around. It was when I sailed off and they had carefully conspired to lay this plot against me that they brought their accusation.

[26] They allege that the man was killed on shore and that I struck him on the head with a stone, I who never left the boat at all. And though their knowledge is precise on this point, they can offer no plausible explanation of the manner of his disappearance. It's likely, obviously, that it would have happened near the harbour, since the man was drunk and he had left the boat at night; for probably he would not have been in control of himself, nor would there have been a plausible pretext for anyone trying to lead him a long way away at night. [27] But though a search was held for Herodes for two days both in the harbour and away from the harbour no eyewitness was found nor blood nor any other sign. Still, I shall accept my opponents' version, even though I offer the witnesses to show that I did not leave the boat; but even if I really did leave the boat, it was inconceivable that the victim could have been disposed of unobserved, unless he had gone a long way from the seashore. [28] But he was thrown into the sea, they say. In what boat? Evidently the boat was from the harbour itself. Then how is it that it wasn't found? And it was to be expected that there would be some trace in the boat of a man killed and thrown overboard at night. As it stands, they claim to have found traces in the boat in which he was drinking, the one he left, though they accept that the victim was not killed there. As to the one from which he was thrown into the sea, they did not find either the boat or any trace. I shall present you with the witnesses to these facts.

Witnesses

[29] When I had sailed off to Ainos and the boat in which Herodes and I had been drinking arrived at Mytilene, first of all they came on board the boat and searched it, and when they found the blood they claimed that this was the spot where Herodes was killed. But when this proved impossible and it was clear that the blood belonged to the sheep, they abandoned this version and seized the men and put them to the test. [30] And the one whom they put to the test on the spot said nothing incriminating about me; it was the one whom they put to the test days later, whom they had kept in their own custody for the intervening time, who was won over by them and told lies against me. I shall present witnesses to these facts.

Witnesses

[31] The testimony has shown how much later the man was tortured. Observe now the way in which the torture has been carried out. As to the slave, probably my opponents promised him freedom, and it was in their power to end his suffering; he was doubtless induced to lie by both these reasons, in the hope that he would win his freedom and the desire to be rid of his immediate torture. [32] I think you are aware that people undergoing torture tend to favour those who have the most control over the torture, and say whatever is likely to gratify them. Their release lies with these people, especially if the victims of their falsehoods happen to be absent. If it was I who ordered him to be racked for failing to tell the truth, perhaps this in itself would have deterred him from telling lies against me. As it is, the prosecution were both torturers and assessors of what was to their advantage.

[33] Well, as long as he thought he had some hope of getting something by lying about me, he maintained the same story. But when he realized he was going to be killed he told the truth and said that he had been induced by my opponents to lie against me. [34] Though he had tried falsehood and subsequently told the truth, neither course helped him; they took the man and killed him, the informer on whom they rely in prosecuting me. Their behaviour is the opposite of others. Other men give money to informers if they are free men and free them if they are slaves; these men rewarded the informer with death, though my friends forbade them to kill him before my return. [35] Evidently they had no use for his person, only his words. Alive the man would have exposed their plot when put through the same torture by me; dead he deprives me, through the destruction of his person, of the chance to prove the truth, while I am being destroyed by his lying words as though they were true. Please call the witnesses to these facts.

Witnesses

[36] In my opinion they should have provided the informer in person here and convicted me. This is how they should have conducted their case, by presenting the man here and inviting me to put him to the test rather than kill him. Come now, which of his statements will they use, the earlier or the later? Which of them is true, his statement that I did the deed or his denial? [37] If one is to

decide the matter on the basis of probability, the later statement is clearly more true. For he lied with a view to his own advantage, but when his lies were destroying him he thought that by telling the truth he might be saved. He had nobody to defend the truth; I, for whom the truth of his second statement was an ally, was not actually present; but there were people to obscure the facts to prevent his earlier lying statement from being converted to the truth. [38] Other men who are informed against abduct the informers and do away with them; my prosecutors, the very ones who seized the man and were investigating the case, have done away with the man who informed against me. Now if it was I who had done away with the man or refused to hand him over to them or sought to evade any other test, they would have relied on this as their most convincing proof in the matter and this would have been their most telling evidence against me. As it is, since they were the ones guilty of evasion when my friends challenged them, this should be evidence on my side against them that the accusation which they made is untrue.

[39] Furthermore, they also claim that under torture the man admitted to being my accomplice in the killing of Herodes. I for my part declare that this is not what he said; he said that he led me and Herodes from the boat, and that once I had killed Herodes he helped to lift him and put him into the boat and then threw him into the sea. [40] But bear in mind that to start with, before he was put on the wheel the man continued to tell the truth and exonerate me until extreme pressure was applied. But when he was put on the wheel, at that point he yielded to the pressure and falsely accused me in his desire to escape the torture. [41] And when the torture stopped he no longer maintained that I had done anything, but with his last words expressed pity for me and for himself as men being destroyed unjustly, not to curry favour with me (how could that be, when he had falsely accused me?) but confirming under pressure from the truth that his original statement was correct.

[42] Then again, the other person, who was sailing on the same boat and was present throughout and in my company, when subjected to the same torture confirmed the truth of the first and the later statements of the other (he exonerated me from first to last), but contradicted the statement which the other made on the wheel under pressure rather than for its truth. For the slave said that I left the boat and killed Herodes and that he helped me to remove the dead body, while this man denied outright that I left the boat. [43] Probability too is on my side. Surely I am not so pathetic as to plan

to murder Herodes alone, to prevent anyone knowing – for this was where all the risk lay – but arrange witnesses and accomplices once the deed was done. [44] And according to the prosecution account the man was killed near the seashore and the boats. But can it be that though being killed by just one man he neither cried out nor attracted any attention either from the people on shore or from those on the boat? And indeed sound can be heard over a greater distance at night than by day, on a shore than in a city; moreover, they state that people were awake when the man left the boat. [45] Furthermore, though he was killed on shore and put into the boat, there was no trace of blood or anything else in the boat; yet he was murdered by night and put in the boat by night. Do you think that a person engaged in such an act could have scraped off the traces on the shore and washed away those on the boat, when he would have found it impossible by day, in full control of himself and unafraid, to obliterate them completely? How can this be plausible, gentlemen?

[46] What you should bear in mind especially – and do not be angry with me if I make the same point repeatedly; I am in great danger, and any point which you grasp correctly is my salvation, while any point on which you are cheated of the truth is my ruin. Let nobody remove from your minds the fact that they killed the informer and made absolutely sure that he did not come to court and that I had no opportunity on my arrival to take the man and put him to the test, [47] though this would have been to their advantage. Instead they bought the man and on their own initiative they killed him, the informer, without any decree from the city, though he was not the dead man's murderer. They should have kept him in custody or given him up on surety to my friends or handed him over to your officials, and his fate should have been put to a vote. Instead you yourselves condemned the man to death and killed him, though no city even has the right to put anyone to death without the permission of the Athenians. You expected this jury to be judges of his statements but appointed yourselves judges of his actions. [48] Yet even slaves who kill their masters, if they are caught in the act, are not put to death by the actual relatives; the relatives hand them over to the officials according to your ancestral laws. For if it is possible to give evidence for a slave against a free man for his murder and for the master, if he sees fit, to prosecute for murder on behalf of his slave, and the jury's vote has equal authority over the killer of a slave and the killer of a free man, there should have been

a vote on *his* fate too; he should not have been put to death without trial by you. So it would be far more just if you were on trial rather than myself being prosecuted unjustly by you as now.

[49] You should also use the statements of the two men, gentlemen, to determine where justice and probability lie. The one who was a slave made two statements; at one point he said that I had committed the crime, at another he denied it. The free man however has not yet to this day said anything incriminating against me, though he was subjected to the same torture. [50] It was not open to them to influence him like the other by offering him freedom. And he preferred to take his chance with the truth and suffer whatever he had to; he too recognized his own advantage, that he would be spared the rack once he said what they wanted. So who is more deserving of belief, the man who maintained the same story throughout or the one whose story changed from one moment to another? But even without torture of this sort people who maintain the same story about the same events are more reliable than those who contradict themselves. [51] And the two statements of the slave favour both parties equally; his assertion of my guilt favours the prosecution, his denial favours me. Likewise the statements of the two individuals, for one affirmed my guilt while the other denied it throughout. Assuredly an equal balance counts for the defendant rather than the prosecutor, just as when the votes are equal in number the advantage is with the defendant rather than the prosecutor.

[52] Such was the outcome of the torture, gentlemen, on which the prosecution rely when they claim that they know full well that the man was killed by me. Yet if I were conscious of guilt and had actually committed such a crime, I would quite simply have done away with the two persons, since I had the power to take them off to Ainos with me or to send them across to the mainland instead of leaving behind potential informers against me who were aware of my guilt.

[53] They claim they found a note on the boat which I intended to send to Lykinos, informing him that I had killed Herodes. Yet what need was there to send a letter when its bearer knew the secret? So the accomplice could have given more reliable information in person, and there was no need to conceal the facts from him; for one would be most likely to send in writing information which the bearer could not know. [54] Then again, in the case of a lengthy matter one would of necessity put it in writing because the

messenger could not remember the message due to its length. But this was a short message: 'the man is dead'. Bear in mind furthermore that the note contradicted the slave under torture and the slave contradicted the note. Under torture he said that he personally killed Herodes, though the letter when opened revealed me as the killer. [55] Which should one believe? Initially they did not find the note when searching the boat; they found it later. They had not yet fabricated this scheme. It was only when the first of the two to be tortured had nothing to say against me that they dropped the note in the boat to give them ground to impute the blame to me. [56] But once the note had been read out and the second man to be tortured failed to corroborate the note it was no longer possible to suppress what had been read out. If they had expected to induce the man to lie against me at the start they would not have fabricated the contents of the note. Please call witnesses to these facts.

Witnesses

[57] Now what motive did I have to kill the victim? There was no hostility between us. The prosecution have the audacity to allege that I killed the victim as a favour. And who has ever committed such a crime as a favour? No-one, in my opinion. Anyone contemplating such an act must feel great hostility, and there must be many indications of the plan he is devising. But there was no enmity between Herodes and me. [58] Well then perhaps I was afraid of an attack like this from him? For a man might be driven to do this from some such cause. But I had no such fear of him. Did I then expect to gain money by killing him? But he had none. [59] No, I could more plausibly attribute this motive to you, and with truth, that you are trying to kill me for money, than you can ascribe it to me for killing him. And it would be more just for you to be prosecuted successfully for murder by my relatives for causing my death than I by you and Herodes' relatives. I can give clear proof of your intent against me, while you are attempting to destroy me by an argument without foundation.

[60] So I say to you that I personally had no motive to kill the man. But I must also, it seems, offer a defence for Lykinos, not just for myself, to show their accusation against him is equally unreasonable. So I state before you that his position with reference to Herodes is the same as mine. He had no means of gaining money for killing Herodes; nor was there any danger to be escaped by

Herodes' death. [61] The most convincing indication that Lykinos did not desire his death is this. He had the opportunity to bring Herodes to trial on a very dangerous charge and use your laws to destroy him, if he had some grudge against him; he could have both achieved his private ends and won the gratitude of your city if he had proved his guilt. But he chose not to; he made no attack on Herodes. Though he would have been facing a more honourable risk. . . .

Witnesses

[62] But it seems on that occasion he let Herodes off, yet when there was inevitably a risk both for him and for me he plotted against him, despite the fact that his discovery would have deprived me of my homeland and deprived himself of religious and secular rights, and everything else which is most important for mankind. Yet again, even if Lykinos really did want him dead (to accept the prosecution's argument), when he was reluctant to kill with his own hand, could I ever have been induced to commit this act in his place? [63] Why? Because I was more fitted to face physical danger and he to pay for the risk I ran with money? Not a bit of it. He had no money, but I did. Quite the reverse: he would more readily have been induced by me in all probability than I by him, since he could not even secure his own release when he was late paying a debt of seven mnai; it was his friends who had him released. Indeed, this is the strongest indication of my relationship with Lykinos, that he was not such a close friend that I would have obeyed his every order. It cannot be supposed that, while I did not pay seven mnai for him when he was in prison and in discomfort, I took on such a dangerous enterprise and killed a man because of him.

[64] I have shown to the very best of my ability that I am not guilty of this charge and nor is he. But the prosecution make much of this point, that Herodes has disappeared. Perhaps you too are eager to hear more on this point. If I am to guess, the matter concerns you and me in equal measure. For you are no more guilty of the deed than I am. If they must have the truth, let them ask one of the perpetrators. He would be their best informant. [65] As one who did not do it, this is the fullest answer I can give: I did not do it. The man who did it can most easily give the facts, or, if he cannot give the facts, offer a plausible account. Those who commit crimes find

an excuse for their villainy while committing it. The innocent man finds it difficult to offer a guess about the unknown. In my opinion each one of you, if he were asked something on which he is ignorant, could say no more than that he does not know. And if asked to speak at greater length I think you would be at a complete loss. [66] Do not then place me in a quandary in which you would yourselves be at a loss. And do not demand that my acquittal should depend on my ability to make a good guess; let it suffice that I have proved my innocence of the charge. My innocence consists not in discovering how he disappeared or has been killed but in my having no motive at all to kill him. [67] I know from hearsay that it has happened before now either that the victims or that the killers were not found. It would not be right if their associates were to be held to blame. Many people before now have been held to blame for the acts of others and have been killed before the truth of the matter was discovered.

[68] For instance, to this day the killers of Ephialtes, your fellow citizen, have not been found. If someone had insisted that his associates should guess who the killers of Ephialtes were, or failing that be liable for murder, it would not be fair on his associates. Moreover, the killers of Ephialtes did not attempt to dispose of the body; nor by so doing did they take the risk of exposing their crime, as the prosecution say I did in making no-one my accomplice to the killing, only to the disposal.

[69] Again, not long ago a slave less than twelve years old tried to kill his master. And if he had not taken fright when the master cried out and fled leaving the knife in the wound, but had had the nerve to stay, everyone in the house would have been killed. For nobody would have thought that the boy would ever have dared to do this. As it happened he was seized and subsequently incriminated himself.

Again, your Hellenotamiai, when accused falsely, as I am now, of theft, were put to death out of anger rather than reason, all but one; and the truth was discovered subsequently. [70] This one man – they say his name was Sosias – had been condemned to death but had not yet been executed. Meanwhile it was revealed how the money was lost and the man was set free by your Assembly, though he had already been handed over to the Eleven; but the others had all been killed, though they were completely innocent. [71] The older among you know this from memory, I think, the younger men from hearsay, like me.

So it's a good thing to rely on time to test the truth of a matter. It may be that the way Herodes died will also become clear in time. So do not discover the facts afterward, when you have killed an innocent man. Decide carefully in advance, and not in anger and prejudice; for there could be no worse advisers than these. [72] It's inconceivable that an angry man could reach a sound judgment. Anger corrupts the organ of deliberation itself, the mind. The succession of day on day is a great force for turning a mind from anger and discovering the true course of events.

[73] Rest assured that I deserve more to be pitied by you than punished. Punishment is appropriate for the unjust, pity for those who are unjustly placed in danger. Your power to save me justly should always prevail over the desire of my enemies to destroy me unjustly. For delay still allows you to inflict the awful fate which they are urging, while haste does not allow sound judgment from the outset.

[74] I must also offer a defence of my father. Though more properly he should offer a defence for me, as my father. He is much older, old enough to know my affairs; I am much younger, too young to know of his actions. If my opponent were on trial and I were giving evidence against him on matters of which I had no firm knowledge but knew of from hearsay, he would complain that I was harming him. [75] As things stand, he is forcing me to offer a defence about events before my time which I know from hearsay; but he sees no harm in this. Still, as far as my knowledge allows, I shall not betray my father when he is being criticized unjustly in your court. Though I may go wrong and fail to give a sound account of matters where his actions were sound. Nonetheless, the risk must be run.

[76] Before the revolt of Mytilene, he always demonstrated his loyalty to you by his actions. And when the city as a whole made the unwise decision to revolt and misjudged your resolve, he was forced to join the whole city in folly. Now, his attitude to you remained the same, but he was no longer free to demonstrate his loyalty towards you. It was not easy for him to leave the city; he had sufficient pledges there to keep him, in the form of his children and his property. But in remaining he had no power to oppose the city. [77] But since you punished those responsible for this act (and my father was not found to be one of these) and granted the rest of the people of Mytilene the right to live in their own city, there has been absolutely no misconduct from him, no failure in any of his duties;

neither city, yours and Mytilene, has lacked any public service, but he serves as chorus producer and pays his taxes. [78] And if he prefers to live in Ainos, it is not in an attempt to withhold any of his duties toward the state nor because he has become a citizen of another state (though I observe that others sometimes move to the mainland while others reside among your enemies and bring suits against you under treaty regulations), nor in an attempt to avoid you, the democracy, but because he hates the same people you do, the sykophants. [79] It is not right that my father should be punished individually for actions which he committed along with the city as a whole and from compulsion rather than choice. For all the people of Mytilene that mistake is a memory which will never fade. They exchanged great prosperity for great adversity, and saw their fatherland overthrown. As to their calumnies against my father as an individual, do not believe them. The whole conspiracy against me and him has been motivated by money. There are many factors which assist the sort who covet the property of others. My father is too old to help me, and I am far too young to be able to defend myself adequately. [80] So you must rescue me and not encourage sykophants to exercise greater power than yourselves. For if they come before you and get their way, it will be a demonstration that people must persuade *them* and avoid you, the democratic court. But if they come before you and are held to be crooks and get no profit, the credit and the power will be yours, as is right. So you must give aid both to me and to justice.

[81] All that could be shown by human proof and testimony you have now heard. But not least on issues like this you should also base your verdict on conclusions drawn from signs from the gods. Indeed, you place your faith above all in these for the safe conduct of the city's business, both in matters involving danger and those without danger. [82] In private matters likewise one should attach the greatest importance and trust to them. For I think you know that often before now men with unclean hands or some other pollution have embarked on a ship and destroyed along with themselves men who are pure in relation to the gods. Other people though not destroyed have faced the most extreme dangers because of such men. And often when attending a sacrifice men have been exposed as impure by preventing the sacrifice from taking place in the customary way. [83] In my case the opposite has happened in all these circumstances. All with whom I sailed have had excellent voyages. Whenever I attended a sacrifice, there is no single case where the

sacrifice was not entirely auspicious. I urge that these events should be accounted strong indications that the charge brought by the prosecution is not true. ⟨I shall present you with⟩ witnesses to these facts.

Witnesses

[84] This too I know, judges, that if the witnesses testified against me, to the effect that some unholy event had resulted when I was present on board ship or at a sacrifice, the prosecution would have used these facts as conclusive evidence and presented the signs from the gods as the clearest proof of their charge. As it stands, since the signs contradict their statements and the witnesses depose that my account is correct and their accusation untrue, they urge you to distrust the witnesses and say that you should trust their statements. And while the rest of mankind test words with facts, the prosecution try to discredit facts with words.

[85] I have answered all of the prosecution charges which I remember, gentlemen. I think it is also in your interest to acquit me. For the same verdict which saves me also accords with the laws and your oath. You have sworn to vote according to the laws, and I am not liable to the laws under which I was arrested, while a lawful trial is still possible for the acts of which I am accused. If one trial has become two, the prosecution are to blame, not I. But I'm sure that, when my fiercest enemies have contrived two trials of my case, you who are unbiased arbiters of justice will not prejudge me guilty of murder in this trial. [86] You must not, gentlemen. Leave some scope for time, with whose help those who seek the exact truth of events are most successful in finding it. For my part I would think it proper, gentlemen, that on such charges the case should be tried in accordance with the laws, but that in accordance with justice the issue should be tested as many times as possible. It would be judged all the better for this; for a plurality of trials is an ally of the truth but most inimical to prejudice. [87] Even a wrong verdict of homicide prevails over justice and truth. For if you convict me, I must abide by the verdict and the law even if I am not a killer and am not guilty of the deed. Nobody would dare to contravene the judgment, once passed, from confidence in his own innocence, or to refuse to abide by the law if conscious of his guilt. He must give way to the verdict in spite of the truth, or to the truth itself, especially if he has

no-one to avenge him. [88] For this very reason the laws, the oaths, the sacrificial pieces and the proclamations and all the other procedures in cases of homicide are very different from those in other cases, because it is of the utmost importance that the issues which form the subject of the trial are judged correctly. A correct verdict amounts to vengeance for the victim, but to convict an innocent man of homicide is a wrong and an act of impiety against both the gods and the laws. [89] And it is not the same thing for the prosecutor to make an unsound accusation and for you the judges to reach an unsound verdict. The prosecution charge has no effect; that rests with you and the trial. Any unsound judgment of yours in the actual trial cannot be referred elsewhere to correct the error.

[90] How then can you arrive at a sound verdict on the issue? By allowing my opponents to bring a prosecution when they have sworn the customary oath and me to make a defence on the actual charge. How are you to allow this? By acquitting me now. I shall not evade your judgment by this means; there too you will be the ones who vote on my case. If you spare me now you will be able on that occasion to do with me as you please, but if you destroy me there is no further opportunity to decide my case. [91] And indeed, if one had to make a mistake, it would be more consistent with piety to acquit unjustly than to destroy without justice. The first of these is just an error, but the second is actually a sin. So there is need of caution, when an irreparable action is in prospect. In a case which allows of reparation, the wrong is less even when people are influenced by anger and swayed by calumny; for one might change one's mind and still make a sound decision. But with irreparable actions the greater harm lies in changing one's mind and realizing one has made a mistake. Before now some of you have actually put men to death and then regretted it. But where you, the victims of deception, have regretted it, assuredly those who deceived you deserved to be put to death.

[92] Furthermore, one can forgive involuntary misdeeds, but not voluntary ones. An involuntary misdeed is an act of chance, gentlemen, but a voluntary one is an act of will. What could be more voluntary than if someone were to carry out immediately an act which he was considering? Furthermore, it is all the same whether one kills unjustly with one's hand or with a vote.

[93] Rest assured, I would never have come to your city if I were conscious of any such guilt. As it is, with my trust in justice, the most precious defence a man can have when he is sure he has

committed no impure action or impiety against the gods – for in circumstances such as this before now the spirit has saved the body when the latter had already given up, a spirit ready to endure because conscious of its own innocence; in contrast for the man with a guilty conscience this is his greatest enemy, for though the body is strong the spirit gives up in advance, in the belief that this has come about as the punishment for its sins. But I have come to you because I have no such guilt on my conscience.

[94] It is no surprise that the prosecution indulge in slander. That is their role, while yours is to refuse to be persuaded to commit injustice. If you are influenced by me, it is possible for you to have second thoughts, and the remedy is to punish me later. If you are influenced by them and do what they wish, there is no cure. Nor is there a long interval before you reach lawfully the verdict which the prosecution are trying to persuade you to reach unlawfully. The matter is not one for haste but for careful deliberation. For now act as surveyors of the case, later as judges; for now you can reach an opinion, later a decision, on the truth. [95] It is the easiest thing in the world to give false evidence against a man who is on trial for his life. If they can just persuade the jury for the moment to inflict the death penalty, vengeance is dead along with his life. For his friends will no longer incline to take vengeance for him once he is dead. And even if they want to, what profit is there for the dead man?

[96] So for now acquit me. In the trial for homicide my opponents will bring the case for the prosecution after swearing the customary oath, you will decide my case according to the established laws, and I shall have no ground to argue, if anything befalls me, that I was sentenced to death unlawfully. This is what I beg of you, without ignoring your pious duty or depriving myself of justice; in your oath lies my salvation. Respond to whichever of these arguments you choose, and acquit me.

The speech is an invaluable example of early logographic style. Especially interesting is the way, unlike his younger contemporary Lysias, Antiphon allows an allegedly nervous young man to speak in an elaborate manner at odds with his age and avowed inexperience.

As to content, it is impossible to do justice to so complex a composition in a brief survey. We may begin however by distinguishing different parts of the defence. The speaker begins by objecting to the procedure used against him; he then attempts both to rebut the charge and to cast doubt on the methods used to incriminate him;

finally he responds to an attack on his father, whom the prosecutors have sought to implicate in the revolt of 428.

The complaint against the procedure used against Euxitheos is difficult to evaluate. It is certainly surprising that the ordinary courts are used rather than the Areopagos. The references to *kakourgoi* which we meet elsewhere in the orators indicate that the term would not normally be understood as including murderers. However, it is unusual for Athenian laws to define offences in detail; if the law dealing with *kakourgoi* did not list all examples of this category of offender, then the prosecution were at liberty to rely on the etymology of the term rather than the generally accepted meaning and argue (though we cannot estimate the chances of success) that murderers were 'wrongdoers'. Certainly if the law provided an exhaustive list, and this list excluded killers, one might expect Euxitheos to tell us. One is also surprised to hear Euxitheos talk of a penalty proposal (§10) from the accusers, when the penalty for convicted *kakourgoi* was fixed at death, though this may reflect a rhetorical flourish by the prosecution rather than an obligatory part of the procedure. The choice of this procedure by the prosecutors is open to more than one interpretation. It could be that the lack of solid evidence to incriminate Euxitheos made them wary of facing the Areopagos; in addition, they may have felt that the appeal to prejudice against the rebels of Mytilene would be easier in a dikastic court than under the stricter rules of relevance applied in the Areopagos. Alternatively, it may be that they wanted to ensure that Euxitheos was executed. In trials for intentional homicide the accused had the right to withdraw into exile after the first set of speeches rather than face the possibility of conviction with the attendant death penalty. It is not clear whether, if a citizen of one of the subject states of the Athenian Empire exercised this option, he would be exiled from his home state or only from Athens; if the latter, it would be galling for the prosecutors to have him withdraw unpunished to his home. The same consideration might account for the fact that he was held in custody; though there is no reason to accept that this was in any way illegal, it is conceivable that it was a new departure at the time. But even if exile from Mytilene was an inevitable consequence of withdrawing from the trial, the prosecutors might find exile insufficient revenge. If, as the inclusion of the father in the opponent's speech suggests, the accusation reflects political rivalries within Mytilene, there may have been scores to settle between the Mytilenaean democrats who had betrayed the revolt to Athens and the oligarchs who initiated it. If, as has been suggested, Herodes' family were among the Athenian settlers sent out after the suppression of the revolt, they would have good reason to side with the enemies of Euxitheos. But the reader will readily see how tenuous the line of conjecture is becoming.

On the question of Euxitheos' guilt or innocence the jury is still out. The speech does not provide enough information for a plausible reconstruction of events on the night in question. Euxitheos is satisfied with undermining the case against him, and does not feel obliged either to prove that there was no murder or to offer an alternative suspect. It is not clear how much of his story the witnesses called in §24 corroborated. If they upheld his claim that he never left the boat on the night in question (as he insists in §27), he may well be guiltless. On the other hand, we do not know the relationship, if any, between Euxitheos and the witnesses. Nor is it clear whether the witnesses in §61 offer any support for his claim that he had no motive for murder. One would like to know more about the identity and the testimony of the two men who were tortured. Euxitheos maintains that the one who incriminated him was a slave, while the one who absolved him was free. Since it is in his interests to draw this distinction, we cannot be sure that it is accurate. The prosecution however does not seem to be more firmly supported than the defence. There is no body, and the note that was found incriminating Euxitheos after his departure (even if one does not accept his attempts to undermine this piece of evidence) looks a little too convenient to inspire confidence. The statements made under torture cannot formally be introduced in court, since the agreement of both parties was needed (and one of the individuals tortured was dead by the time of the trial anyway), though (as we see from the narrative in Lys. 1) informal use could always be made of the information extracted under torture in the course of narrative or argument.

The attacks on the career and character of Euxitheos' father are of course quite irrelevant from a modern standpoint. They may, however, have influenced the judges against him in court. Euxitheos maintains that his father was loyal to Athens. His undoubted wealth need not have inclined him toward the oligarchic cause, but it is conceivable that the prosecutors were telling the truth about him. The Athenians may not have succeeded in executing all of the ringleaders after the city capitulated.

CASE IV: ANTIPHON 6 – ON THE CHORISTER

The charge here is of *bouleusis* of unintentional homicide; the term *bouleusis* is explained in the introduction to Case II: Antiphon 1 (see p. 36). The present case arises from the Athenian system of wealth taxation. Except for war levies, the Athenians in general avoided direct taxation in money. They preferred to impose upon rich men the performance of a costly but visible public service (*leitourgia*, often anglicized as 'liturgy'), thus in effect harnessing for the democratic system the competition for honour between rich men. The speaker was serving as *choregos* ('chorus-producer') in the competition in the boys' chorus for the Thargelia (a festival in honour of Apollo), and as such was obliged to meet the expenses of the chorus representing his own and another tribe. One of the choristers has died, and the dead boy's family apparently allege that the death resulted from a potion administered on the speaker's instructions; there is no suggestion that the intent was to kill. The case will have been heard at the Palladion. The speech was delivered in 419/8 BC; for a résumé of the complex arguments for the date see K.J. Maidment, *Minor Attic Orators*, vol. I (repr. Cambridge, Mass. 1982), 235f.

[1] The happiest situation for a mortal, gentlemen, is not to face the danger of a capital charge, something one might include in one's prayers; or, if one really had to face the danger, that one should at least have the advantage (in my opinion the most valuable in such a situation) of having the clear conscience of an innocent man, so that if indeed some disaster were to strike it should come without crime or shame, from chance rather than criminal action. [2] I think everyone would agree that the laws which have been enacted to deal with these matters are the most noble and sacred. The fact is that they are the oldest in this land; moreover, their content and application have remained the same, the surest sign that laws are well made; for time and experience reveal imperfections to mankind. So you should not determine whether or not your laws are good according to the prosecutor's statements but decide on the basis of the laws whether or not their speeches present the case to you in an honest and lawful way.

[3] This trial is of the utmost importance to me, as the defendant and the one at risk. But I think that it is also very important for you the judges to reach a sound verdict in cases of homicide, most of all

because of the gods and for the sake of piety but also for your own sake. There is only one trial for such a charge, and a wrong verdict prevails over justice and truth. [4] For if you convict a man, he must abide by the verdict even if he is not a killer and is not guilty of the deed, and be barred by law from the city, its sanctuaries, gatherings and sacrifices, the most significant and most ancient aspects of human life. Such is the law's power to constrain that, even if a man kills someone under his control who has nobody to avenge him, through fear of custom and the gods he cleanses himself and will avoid the activities prescribed in the law, in the hope that this will give him the best chance of security. [5] For the greater part of human life rests on hope. And by committing impiety and offending in matters of religion a man will deprive himself of hope itself, the greatest blessing for mankind. And nobody would dare to contravene the judgment, once passed, from confidence in his own innocence, or to refuse to abide by the law if conscious of his guilt. He must give way to the verdict in spite of the truth, or to the truth itself, even if the victim has no-one to avenge him. [6] For this very reason the laws, the oaths, the sacrificial pieces and the proclamations and all the other procedures in cases of homicide are very different from those in other cases, because it is of the utmost importance that the issues which form the subject of the trial are judged correctly. A correct verdict amounts to vengeance for the victim, but to convict an innocent man of homicide is a wrong and an act of impiety against both the gods and the laws. And it is not the same thing for the prosecutor to make an unsound ⟨accusation and for you the judges to reach an unsound⟩ verdict. The prosecution charge has no effect; that rests with you and the trial. Any unsound judgment of yours in the actual trial cannot be referred elsewhere to correct the error.

[7] My attitude to my defence is quite different from that of my accusers to the prosecution. They claim that they are bringing the action for motives of piety and justice, but the whole case for the prosecution has been marked by calumny and deceit, the most unjust course of action which is humanly possible. Their aim is not to establish my guilt and take their revenge justly, but to create prejudice and punish me with exile from this country even if I am innocent. [8] In contrast, I think it right to begin by replying on the actual subject at issue and giving you a full account of events; I shall then be happy to answer the other accusations made by the prosecution, if that is your wish. I think the account will be to my

credit and advantage and to the shame of those who accuse and insult me. [9] For it is monstrous, gentlemen, that when it was open to them to expose any offence by me against the city, either as chorus producer or in any other activity, convict me and thereby both take vengeance on an enemy and benefit the city, none of them was ever able to prove any offence, great or small, on my part against you, the democracy; but in this trial, though they are prosecuting me for homicide and the law holds that the prosecution must direct itself to the main issue itself, they conspire against me with fabricated claims and slanders about my conduct toward the city. To the city all they grant for any wrong against it is an accusation in place of revenge, while they claim for themselves personal satisfaction for the wrongs they say the city has suffered. [10] Accusations such as this deserve neither gratitude nor credence. For the prosecutor is not making the accusation in a context in which the city could have obtained satisfaction for any wrong it had received, a course of action which deserves the city's gratitude. And a man who directs his accusation against issues other than those on which his prosecution is based in a case of this sort deserves not trust but distrust. I'm fairly confident of your attitude, that you would neither convict nor acquit a man on any other ground than the main issue. This accords with piety and justice. So this is where I shall begin.

[11] When I was appointed chorus producer for the Thargelia and was allocated Pantakles as chorus trainer and the tribe Kekropis as well as my own, I carried out my duties with the utmost care and fairness. First of all, I set up a training area for the chorus in the most suitable part of my house, the same place where I trained the chorus when I was chorus producer for the Dionysia. Then I assembled the chorus with the utmost care, without fining anyone or exacting sureties by force or incurring the hatred of anyone. But as if the business was entirely agreeable and convenient for both parties, I made my demands and requests, and the parents readily and willingly sent their sons.

[12] When the boys arrived, initially I was too busy to be there and supervise. As it happened I was involved in a dispute with Aristion and Philinos, and I was concerned, after bringing the impeachment, to present a sound and just case to the Council and the rest of the Athenians. So my personal attention was directed to this issue, and I appointed Phanostratos, a fellow demesman of the prosecutors there and my relative by marriage (I married my daughter to him), to take care of any needs of the chorus, and ordered him to

take the best care he could. [13] In addition to him I appointed two men, Ameinias of the tribe Erechtheis, who had been voted by his tribesmen to recruit the chorus and see to the tribe's needs on each occasion, whom I considered reliable, and . . . of the tribe Kekropis, who used to recruit for this tribe regularly. The fourth was Philippos, whose job was to make purchases and pay out such sums as instructed by the trainer or any of the others, to ensure that the production for the boys' chorus was as efficient as possible and that they did not want for anything because I was busy.

[14] This was the arrangement for my service as chorus producer. And if I am lying in any of this by way of an excuse, my prosecutor can refute any point he wishes in his second speech. For it's the truth, gentlemen. Many of these bystanders have detailed knowledge of all this, and they can hear the oath officer and are paying attention to my reply. And I would like them to feel that I am a man who respects oaths, and that I persuaded you to acquit me by telling the truth.

[15] First of all I shall demonstrate to you that I did not order the boy to drink the potion or force him or give it to him, and that I was not even present when he drank it. And my purpose in insisting on this point is not to exonerate myself and place the blame on someone else. No indeed, I blame no-one, except fortune, which is responsible, I think, for the deaths of many other mortals. And neither I nor anyone else could prevent her from befalling each man according to his destiny. ⟨And I shall present you with witnesses to these facts.⟩

Witnesses

[16] Testimony has been given on the main issue as I promised. You should use it to examine the oaths sworn by my opponents here and by me and decide which is more truthful and more honestly sworn. My opponents here swore that I killed Diodotos, that I prompted his death, while I swore that I did not kill him either with my own hand or by prompting his death. [17] They base their accusation on the principle that the person who ordered or forced the boy to drink the potion or gave it to him is liable. In contrast, on the basis of this very accusation I can demonstrate that I am not liable. I did not order or force him or give the potion. Moreover, I add a further point to theirs, that I was not even present when he drank it. If they say anyone who ordered the boy to drink

is guilty, then I am not guilty; I gave no order. If they say that anyone who forced him is guilty, I am not guilty; I did not force him. And if they say the man who gave the potion is to blame, I am not to blame; I did not give it. [18] Anyone can make lying accusations at will; each individual has this power. But to make something take place which did not happen or an innocent man guilty, that in my opinion does not depend on the prosecution's assertions but is a matter of justice and truth. In the case of murders planned and committed in secret, where there are no witnesses, the decision must be based on the actual speeches of accuser and defendant; one must follow the arguments closely and suspect each nuance, and vote on conjecture rather than firm knowledge of the facts. [19] But in a case where even the prosecution admit firstly that the boy's death was not intended or planned, secondly that every act took place in public and in front of many witnesses, men and boys, free and slave, from whom the identity of the guilty party, if any, could be clearly established and, if an innocent man were accused, the truth could be proved most effectively . . .

[20] It is worth bearing in mind, gentlemen, both the attitude of my opponents and the way they approach the issue. From the very first their behaviour towards me has been quite different from my behaviour towards them. [21] Philokrates here presented himself at the court of the Thesmothetai on the day of the boy's funeral and asserted that I caused the death of his brother in the chorus by forcing him to drink a potion. When he made this claim, I presented myself before the court and told the judges that Philokrates was not representing the law fairly in accusing and slandering me before the court when I was about to bring suits against Aristion and Philinos the next day and the day after that, and that this was his reason for making these statements. [22] But I added that his slanderous accusations could easily be proved false. There were many people who knew the facts, free and slave, young and old, in all more than fifty people, who knew what had been said and done with regard to the drinking of the potion, indeed all the facts.

[23] This was what I said in the court, and I challenged him there and then, and again on the following day before the same judges. I told him to take as many witnesses as he wished to those who had been present (and I gave him the name of each), and question and test them, the free men in the manner fitting for free men, who would have told the truth about the incident for their own and for justice's sake; as for the slaves, if he thought they gave a truthful

answer to his questions, well and good; if not, I was ready to hand over for torture all my own slaves, and if he demanded anyone else's slaves, I agreed to persuade the owner to hand them over to him to be tortured in any way he pleased. [24] Although I issued this challenge and made these points in the court, where both the judges themselves and many private citizens were present to witness, my opponents would not accept this fair offer either right then or at any subsequent time. They were well aware that this would not have provided them with proof against me but me with proof against them that their charge was unjust and untrue.

[25] You know, gentlemen, that compulsion is applied with the greatest force and effectiveness which is humanly possible, and the resultant proof of where right lies is most certain and reliable, when there are a great number of free men who know the facts and a great number of slaves, and it is possible to compel the free men by extracting an oath or a word of honour, which are the most binding and serious commitments for free men, and the slaves with other pressures, which force them to tell the truth even if by speaking out they condemn themselves to death. For actual is stronger than future compulsion for everyone.

[26] So then I challenged them to all these procedures; and it was open to them to learn the facts from all the sources a mortal man should use to discover where truth and right lie, and there was no excuse left to them. I, the accused, the guilty party as they maintain, was ready to offer them the fairest means of proving my guilt, while they, the accusers, who claim to be the victims, were themselves the ones who refused to prove the existence of any wrong done to them. [27] If I were the one who refused a challenge from them to identify those who had been present, or if I were reluctant to hand over servants in response to a request from them or evaded any other challenge, they would regard this very fact as the surest proof that the charge against me was true. So since my opponents were the ones who evaded the means of proof in response to my challenge, surely it is only fair that this should count as evidence against them, that their accusation against me is false.

[28] I also know this much, gentlemen, that if the witnesses who were present were testifying against me, the prosecution would regard these very people as utterly convincing and would represent the witnesses against me as the most reliable proof. But when these same men testify that my statements are true and theirs are false, they instruct you to disregard the witnesses who testify in my

favour and claim that you should trust their own assertions, though if I made such statements without witnesses they would accuse me of lying. [29] But it is bizarre that the same witnesses would be reliable if testifying for them but are to be regarded as unreliable when testifying for me. And if there had been no witnesses there at all and I were presenting witnesses, or if I were presenting not those who were there but other people, it would be reasonable to believe the assertions of the prosecution over my witnesses. But when they admit that witnesses were there and I am presenting them, and from the very first day both I myself and all the witnesses have undeniably made the same statements which we now make before you, what other means than these, gentlemen, should one use to make the truth credible and false statements incredible? [30] If a man were to give you a verbal account of the facts without providing witnesses, one might say that his version lacked the support of witnesses. Again, if he were to provide witnesses but could not offer inferences to corroborate the witnesses' account, one could say much the same if one chose. [31] Now *I* am presenting you with plausible arguments, witnesses who corroborate my arguments, facts which corroborate the witnesses, and inferences based on the facts; moreover, I offer in addition two most significant and convincing arguments, the fact that the prosecution are refuted both by their own account and by mine, and that I am absolved of guilt both by the prosecution and by myself. [32] For in refusing to prove any wrong they had suffered in response to my offer to be examined regarding their accusations, evidently they absolved me and they testified against themselves that their accusation was quite unjust and untrue. Now if in addition to my own witnesses I offer my adversaries themselves as witnesses, what further means, what other proof, must one have to be acquitted of the charge?

[33] Now, I think that what I have said has demonstrated that you would be right to acquit me, gentlemen, and that you are all aware that this charge does not apply to me. But with a view to giving you further information I shall continue my speech and prove that my prosecutors there are the most perjured and irreligious men alive and deserve not only my hatred but yours as well and that of the rest of the citizen population for bringing this suit. [34] The first day, when the boy died, and the next day when his body was laid out, not even my prosecutors themselves saw fit to accuse me of any crime in this affair but passed time in my company and conversed with me. It was on the third day, when the boy's

funeral took place, that they were won over by my enemies, began preparing a charge and issued the proclamation imposing on me the legal bars. Who were the individuals who influenced them? Why were they so keen to exert this influence? This too is something I must tell you.

[35] I was about to prosecute Aristion, Philinos, Ampelinos and the undersecretary of the Thesmothetai, who was party to their thefts, on the impeachment charge I laid before the Council. The facts were such that they had no hope of acquittal – such was the nature of their crimes. But by persuading my opponents to register the charge and issue the proclamation imposing the legal bars they thought they would be saved and rid of all their troubles. [36] For the law is that once someone is charged on a homicide case he is subject to these bars. I should have been unable to pursue my prosecution when so barred, and if I, who impeached them and knew the facts, failed to pursue the case they would easily secure their acquittal and avoid paying you the penalty for their crimes. I was not the first victim of a device such as this from Philinos and the others; they had done the same thing before to Lysistratos, as you have heard yourselves. [37] At that point my prosecutors were keen to register the charge against me at once the day after the boy was buried, before the house was purified and the rites demanded by custom had been carried out, choosing the very day on which the first of the criminals was due to be tried, to prevent me from proceeding against any one of them and exposing their crimes to the court. [38] But then the King-archon read out the laws and showed them that there was insufficient time to register the charge and issue the necessary summonses, and I took the people who had devised this scheme to court and had them all convicted, with the penalty which you all know. My prosecutors were thus unable to provide them with the assistance for which they had been paid. At that point they approached me personally and my friends and requested a compromise; they were ready to make reparation for the wrongs they had done. [39] Under the influence of my friends I came to terms with them on the Akropolis in front of witnesses who effected a settlement between us by the temple of Athene. Subsequently they spent time in my company and conversed with me in the temples, in the agora, in my house, their own and everywhere else. [40] Finally – in the name of Zeus and all the gods! – this man Philokrates personally stood with me on the rostrum in the Council chamber in full view of the Council and touched and spoke to me, calling

me by name as I did with him. And the Councillors were shocked to learn that I had been the object of a proclamation by these people imposing the legal bars, when they had seen them in my company conversing with me the day before.

[41] Please consider the following, gentlemen, and use your memory. For I shall not just use witnesses to prove my case but also you will easily see that I am telling the truth from the very acts of my opponents. Firstly, their allegations against the King-archon and their claim that it was because of his partisanship for my cause that he refused to register their action are evidence against themselves that they are not telling the truth. [42] The King-archon would have been obliged, once he registered the action, to hold three preliminary hearings over three months and bring the action to court in the fourth month, as has happened now. But there were just two months left of his period of office, Thargelion and Skirophorion. He would not have been able, evidently, to bring the action to court within his own term; it is impossible to pass on a homicide case, and no King-archon has ever passed on such a case in this country. So since he could not bring the case to court or pass it on, he did not see fit even to register it in contravention of your laws. [43] The clearest sign that he has not wronged them is the fact that Philokrates here, who was in the habit of shaking down and persecuting other officials undergoing audit, did not come to the audit sessions to make accusations against this King-archon, though they claim his conduct has been monstrous and immoral. What firmer indication could I give you that he was not wronged either by me or by the King-archon?

[44] But when the current King-archon entered office, though it was open to them for thirty days in succession from the beginning of the month of Hekatombaion to register their suit on any day they chose, they never did. And again in the month of Metageitnion from the very first day it was open to them to register on any day they chose, but even then they had not yet done so, but they let twenty days of this month too go by. So the sum total of days during the term of the current King-archon on which they could have registered but did not was over fifty. [45] Everyone else who finds that the period of office of the King-archon is insufficient ⟨registers the charge as early as he can under the next King-archon⟩. But my opponents, though they know every law, though they could see me serving on the Council and entering the Council-chamber – and in the Council-chamber itself there is a shrine of Zeus of the

Council and Athene of the Council, where the Councillors as they enter make prayers; I was one of them, and it was no secret that I did the same, and entered all the other temples with the Council, and offered sacrifice and prayer on behalf of this city, that I had served as a President for the whole of the first prytany but two days, that I made offerings and sacrifices on behalf of the democracy, that I put questions to the vote and advanced opinions on the matters of the utmost importance and concern to the city. [46] Though they were present in the city, though they could have registered their action and barred me from all these activities, they did not see fit to register. Yet there were two motives strong enough to jog their memory and make them think, if they really had been wronged: their own interests and those of the city. Why then did they not register their action? Because they were associating and conversing with me. They were in my company because they did not consider me a killer, and this was their reason for not registering their charge; they did not believe I killed the boy or that I was liable for homicide or that I had anything to do with the business.

[47] What human beings could be more ruthless or contemptuous of the law? Though they could not convince themselves, they expect to convince you of this; though by their actions they voted for acquittal, they urge you to vote for conviction. And the rest of mankind use facts to test assertions, while these men seek to use assertions to discredit facts. [48] If I had offered no other statement or demonstration and provided no witnesses, but had proved just this, that these people made accusations and issued proclamations when paid to attack me, but when there was nobody to pay associated and conversed with me, to hear only this would be enough for you to acquit me and regard them as the most perjured and irreligious men in the world. [49] Is there an action they would not bring, a court they would not deceive, an oath they would scruple to break, when in the present case, after accepting thirty mnai from the Providers, the Sellers, the Executors and their undersecretaries and getting me ejected from the Council-chamber, they have sworn such solemn oaths? All this because when I was one of the Presidents I discovered that they were guilty of unscrupulous and criminal conduct and brought them before the Council and urged that it must investigate and pursue the case. [50] Now the guilty parties and the middlemen with whom the money was deposited have paid the penalty for their misdeeds, and the facts have come to light, so that the prosecution will find it difficult to deny the truth even if they want

to; such is the outcome. [51] So what court would they hesitate to deceive? What oaths would they scruple to break, these utterly unholy men, when knowing that you are the most pious and upright judges in Greece they have still come before you with the hope of tricking you if they can, after swearing such solemn oaths?

Antiphon 6 is a mine of information on homicide procedure. In particular, it is to this speech that we owe our knowledge both of the designedly cumbersome procedures for homicide, with three preliminary hearings (*prodikasiai*) in three separate months and the trial in the fourth and of the implications for the timing of legal actions – that is, that since the King-archon's term lasted only one year and the same King-archon had to see a homicide case through to the end, cases could not be accepted after the eighth month of the year.

In answering the case against him, the speaker begins with some weighty observations on the seriousness of the charge and of its consequences and on the impropriety of the use of a homicide case to attack a political enemy instead of a trial directed specifically to alleged political offences. He returns to this theme at the end and tries to expose the political motives behind the trial.

As to the main charge, the details of the allegation do not emerge very clearly. As in speeches 1 and 5, Antiphon presents a spare narrative, providing only such information as is absolutely necessary. It appears however that one of the choir took a potion; one would naturally suppose (though it is nowhere stated, since it would not help the speaker's case to display a detailed knowledge of events leading up to the death) that it was medicinal and was connected with his service in the choir. The potion was believed to be the cause of his death. The speaker distances himself from the whole process. His narrative makes clear that because of the political trial he was conducting he delegated responsibility for the chorus, and he offers witness testimony to prove that he not only did not make the boy drink the potion but was not even present at the time (§15). He offers no alternative suspect, presumably because the man to whom he delegated his responsibility was a kinsman. He also places heavy emphasis on his challenge to the opponents to obtain information from the large number of people, free and slave, who were actually present. The vagueness of his account leaves one unsure whether his subordinates (if they did give a potion to the boy) were acting on his instructions.

The speech sheds an interesting light on the use of the courts for political purposes. The speaker argues that the prosecution for homicide was intended to prevent him from prosecuting a group of politicians. Irrespective of the truth of his claim, the fact that he can make it indicates that such things were considered entirely possible within the Athenian political arena (for another such case see [Dem.] 59.9–10). Politics in Athens was played for very high stakes, with substantial rewards (in terms both of potential for earnings, in the form of gifts from interested individuals and groups, and of prestige) and enormous penalties for failure (from huge fines through exile to death), meted out usually through political trials decided by democratic juries. Though the original intention to block a specific prosecution was frustrated by the King-archon's refusal to accept the case (§§41–2), the prosecutors persisted; if the speaker is right to claim that the root cause is political, it may be that his opponents now wish both to avenge themselves and to remove the speaker from the political scene by having him exiled. Antiphon wrote a speech for the prosecution to which the speaker refers, that of Philinos; the speaker is thus not merely a casual client of Antiphon but a political associate.

This speech is also informative on the informal procedures available for blocking legal action. There were in existence formal means of checking a legal move by an opponent, the *diamartyria* (for which see the introduction to Case IX, Isaios 3, p. 109) and the *paragraphe* (for which see the introduction to Case XIII, Demosthenes 35, p. 150). But in addition it was always possible to use counter-prosecution (either by oneself or by an agent) to intimidate or otherwise thwart an opponent. In the present case, in addition to the prospect of intimidation, the ban imposed on those accused of homicide would have prevented the speaker from entering a court.

2

ASSAULT AND WOUNDING

CASE V: LYSIAS 3 – REPLY TO SIMON, A DEFENCE

This speech concerns a case of intentional wounding (*trauma ek pronoias*), an offence which fell under the jurisdiction of the Areopagos. This fact, together with the severity of the penalty and the procedural similarities between wounding and homicide trials, support the contention of our speaker (§41) that wounding was regarded as attempted murder, as does the fact that the speaker of Lysias 4 (another wounding case, not included in this collection) argues as though he were charged with attempting to kill, not merely knowingly wounding, his alleged victim. Accordingly one is not surprised to find that there appears to have been no action for accidental wounding. Although scholarly opinion has traditionally viewed *trauma* as a private case all the evidence indicates that, unlike homicide, wounding was covered by a *graphe*, a public action. It appears to have been distinguished from battery (*aikeia*) and outrage (*hybris*) by the use of a weapon. The unnamed defendant is (as the opening makes clear) into middle age; he is evidently a man of substance, as the reference at the close to public services (*leitourgiai*) indicates. His opponent Simon is otherwise unknown. The date of the speech can be fixed broadly by the reference to the battles of Corinth and Koroneia near the close. Both battles were fought in 394.

[1] Though I know many appalling things about Simon, Council, I would never have expected his audacity to reach the point where he would bring a charge, as though he were the victim, relating to acts for which he should himself be punished, and come before you having sworn such an important and solemn oath. [2] Now, if any

other judges were going to decide my case, I should find the risk very frightening; for I observe that sometimes the effect of fabrications and accidents is such that the result often surprises those on trial. But coming before you I hope to receive just treatment. [3] What I most resent, Council, is that I shall be compelled to speak to you about matters which so embarrassed me that I tolerated mistreatment to avoid having them widely known. But since Simon has placed me in this difficult situation, I shall tell you the whole story without concealment. [4] And I ask, Council, that if I am guilty you show me no mercy; but if on this issue I prove that I am not guilty of the acts to which Simon swore, and in general if it becomes clear that my feelings for the lad display a folly inappropriate to my age, I ask you to think no worse of me; for you know that desire is common to all mankind, but the best and most decent man is the one who is capable of bearing his misfortunes with the most decorum. All my efforts to achieve this have been blocked by this man Simon, as I shall prove to you.

[5] We both fell in love with Theodotos, a Plataian youth, Council. And I tried to win his affection by treating him well, while Simon thought that with violent and lawless behaviour he would force the boy to do whatever he wanted. It would take too long to tell all the mistreatment Thoeodotos has received from him. But what I think you should hear is his offences against me personally.

[6] Discovering that the boy was with me, he came to my house at night, drunk, broke down the doors and went into the women's quarters, when my sister and my nieces were there; and they have lived such a decent life that they are embarrassed to be seen even by their relatives. [7] Such was his violence that he refused to go until the passers-by and the people who came with him, shocked at his conduct in entering the presence of orphaned young girls, made him leave by force. And so far from regretting his outrageous conduct, he found out where we were dining and did the strangest thing, something quite incredible, unless one happened to know the man's madness. [8] He called me from indoors, and when I came out he immediately tried to strike me; when I resisted, he stood at a distance and pelted me with stones. He actually missed me, but hit Aristokritos, who had come with him to see me, with a stone and split his forehead open.

[9] Personally, Council, though I thought myself appallingly treated, I tolerated it through embarrassment at my unfortunate situation, as I have already said. I preferred to forgo satisfaction for

these wrongs rather than to be thought a fool by my fellow-citizens, in the knowledge that, while these events would be thought consistent with the villainy of this man, my sufferings would excite mockery from many of those who habitually resent it if anyone in the city tries to be a useful citizen. [10] I was so unsure how to cope with this man's contempt for legality, Council, that I decided it would be best to go away from Athens. So taking the boy along (I have to tell the whole truth) I left the city.

When I thought that enough time had elapsed for Simon to forget the youth and regret his former misconduct, I came back. [11] I went off to Peiraieus. But Simon noticed at once that Theodotos was back and was at the house of Lysimachos, who lived near the house which Simon had leased, and he summoned some of his friends. They passed their time dining and drinking; they had set watchers on the roof so that when the boy emerged they could drag him in. [12] At this juncture I came back from Peiraieus, and while passing I called in at Lysimachos' house. After a short interval we came out. Drunk by now, our opponents jumped on us. Some of Simon's companions refused to join in his misbehaviour; but Simon here, Theophilos, Protarchos and Autokles began dragging the boy off. He however threw off his robe and took to flight. [13] As for me, thinking Theodotos would escape and that my opponents would turn back in shame as soon as they encountered people – with these thoughts I went off in another direction; I was so keen to avoid them, and I thought that all I had experienced at their hands a great misfortune. [14] And at this point, where Simon says the fight took place, none of them or us had his head cut open or suffered any other injury, as I shall prove by presenting those who were there as witnesses.

Witnesses

[15] The testimony of those who were there has shown, Council, that Simon was the offender and that he plotted against us, not I against him. After this the boy took refuge in a laundry, and they rushed in together and began to drag him off by force, while he yelled and called for witnesses to his protests. [16] A large number of people ran up and expressed disapproval of the affair, saying that these acts were appalling; but they ignored the comments and when Molon the fuller and some others tried to protect the boy they beat them severely. [17] By now they were in the vicinity of Lampon's

house, when I came upon them, walking along on my own. I thought it would be appalling and disgraceful of me to stand by while the youth was assaulted in so lawless and violent a manner; so I took hold of him. When asked why they were subjecting him to such unlawful treatment, my opponents refused to answer but let go of the young man and began to hit me. [18] A fight ensued, Council, in which the boy was pelting them and fighting for his life and these people were pelting us and still beating him drunkenly, while I was defending myself and the passers-by were all of them assisting us as the victims, and in this confusion we all had our heads split open.

[19] As for all the others who joined Simon in his drunken violence, as soon as they saw me after this, they asked me to forgive them, as the ones who behaved intolerably and not the victims. And from that day to this, though four years have elapsed nobody has ever brought any complaint against me. [20] But as for this man Simon, the cause of all the trouble, for most of the time he kept his peace through fear for himself; but when he saw me lose some private suits arising from a challenge to exchange property, he began to despise me and with the impudence you see embroiled me in a trial of such a serious nature. To prove the truth of my story, I shall present you with those who were there as witnesses.

Witnesses

[21] You have heard what happened both from me and from the witnesses. I could wish, Council, that Simon's attitude was the same as mine, so that you could hear the truth from both of us and decide with ease where justice lies. But since he has no respect for the oaths he swore, I shall try to correct the lies he has told you.

[22] He had the audacity to state that he made an agreement with Theodotos and gave him three hundred drachmas, and that I schemed to detach the boy from him. But what he should have done, if this was the truth, was to summon the largest number of witnesses he could and deal with the matter legally. [23] But this man self-evidently never did anything of the sort, but assaulted and struck both of us, he came on a drunken visit, he broke down the doors and went by night into the quarters of free women. You should consider this conduct the firmest indication that he is lying.

[24] Observe how implausible his claim is. He assessed his whole property at a value of two hundred and fifty drachmas. Now it

would be remarkable if he hired a male lover for more money than he actually possesses. [25] But his impudence is such that he is not content to lie merely about this point, the payment of the money; he actually says that he has been repaid. But surely it's inconceivable that at that point we would commit offences of the sort he has charged us with, in an attempt to deprive him of the three hundred drachmas, and pay back the money precisely when we had out-fought him, without obtaining formal release from his charges and when under no compulsion? [26] No, Council, all this is a calculated fabrication by him; he says he gave the money so that he will not seem guilty of intolerable conduct in daring to treat the lad so outrageously when there was no compact between them, and he pretends to have been repaid because it is obvious that he never made a formal complaint about money or made any mention of it whatsoever.

[27] And he claims that he was beaten and left in a terrible condition by me at his own door. Yet it is certain that he pursued the boy more than four stades from his house without any injury, and he denies this though more than two hundred people saw it.

[28] He says that we came to his house with shards of pottery and I threatened to kill him; and this indicates intent. In my opinion, Council, it is easy to tell that he is lying, not only for you who regularly consider such matters but for the rest of the world as well. [29] Who could find it credible that with full intent and deliberation I came to Simon's house in the daytime, with the lad, when there was such a large number of people gathered there, unless I was so deranged as to wish to fight alone against large numbers? Besides which, I knew that he would be delighted to see me at his door, since it was he who used to come to my house and force his way in, and who had the impudence to search for me without any consideration for my sister and my nieces, and finding out where I happened to be at dinner called me out and hit me. [30] And at that point, it seems, I kept my peace to avoid notoriety, regarding his criminality as my misfortune, but when time had passed, I then (according to him) became eager for notoriety!

[31] If the boy had been at his house, it would make some sense for him to lie to the effect that I was compelled by desire to behave somewhat more foolishly than usual. As it stands, the boy would not even talk to him, but hated him more than anyone in the world, while it was with me that he was actually staying. [32] So which of you finds it credible that, when I had earlier made a voyage away

from the city taking the boy with me, to avoid fighting with Simon, once I arrived back I took him to Simon's house, where I was likely to have the most trouble? [33] And when scheming against him did I come so ill-prepared that I had summoned neither friends nor servants nor any other person, except for this child, who could not have helped me, but would be able to disclose under torture any offence I committed? [34] Was I so stupid that when scheming against Simon, instead of watching for an opportunity to catch him alone, at night or in daylight, I went to the very place where I was sure to be seen by the largest number of people and beaten up, as though my intent was against myself, to ensure that I received the maximum humiliation from my enemies?

[35] Furthermore, Council, you can easily tell from the fight which took place that he is lying. Once the boy realized what was happening, he threw off his robe and took to flight, and these people followed him, while I went off by another route. [36] But who should one hold responsible for what happened, the ones who ran away or the ones who tried to catch them? I think it's obvious to all that people who fear for their safety flee and people who wish to cause harm pursue. [37] And it's not the case that though this is the probability what actually happened was different. They seized the lad on the street and were dragging him off by force; I came along, and I did not touch them but took hold of the boy, while they were dragging him off by force and beating me. This has been attested for you by those who were present. So it is intolerable if it is to be believed that I am guilty of intent in matters where these people have in reality behaved in such an appalling and lawless way.

[38] Whatever would have happened to me, if the reverse of this had happened, if accompanied by many of my friends I had met Simon, fought with him and beaten him, then pursued him and having caught him I tried to drag him off by force, if as it is when he has behaved like this I find myself facing a trial of such seriousness, in which I stand to lose my fatherland and all my possessions?

[39] The most important and clearest indication is this. The man who has been wronged and schemed against by me, as he claims, could not bring himself to bring a charge before you for four years. Other people, when they are in love and are robbed of the object of desire and are beaten up, grow angry and attempt to take revenge at once, while this man does it ages afterwards.

[40] I think, Council, that I have given adequate proof that I am not to blame for what happened. But my attitude to quarrels over

matters like this is such that, though I have suffered a great many other outrages from Simon and had my head split open by him, I could not bring myself to take legal action against him. I thought it preposterous that just because we had been in competition with each other for a lover one should try to have people exiled from their homeland.

[41] Then again, I did not think that intent applied to a wound unless the person inflicting it wanted to kill. For who is so foolish as to spend a long time planning to wound one of his enemies? [42] Clearly our legislators did not see fit, just because people happened to injure each other's heads in a fight, to punish them with exile from their fatherland. In that case they would have exiled a good many people. No, it was for those who having planned to kill people wounded them and failed to kill that they made the penalties so severe. They believed that they should be punished for acts which were planned and intended; if they failed, the deed had still been done as far as their action was concerned. [43] This is a decision you have often reached before now in the matter of intent. For it would be bizarre if, whenever people received a wound as a result of drunken rivalry or horseplay or an insult or a fight over a mistress, for incidents which everyone regrets when they come to their senses, you are to make the penalties so severe and awful that you exile some of the citizen body from their homeland.

[44] One thing especially amazes me about his character. I don't think that the same nature is capable of both love and malicious litigation; the former belongs to simpler souls, the latter to the most unscrupulous. I wish it was possible for me to give proof of this man's criminality in your court from the rest of his conduct, so that you would realize that it would be far more just for him to be on trial for his life than to place others in danger of losing their homeland. [45] Most of it I shall omit. But I shall mention a fact which you should hear and which will be an indication of his audacity and impudence. In Corinth, after arriving too late for the battle against the enemy and the expedition to Koroneia, he fought with Laches the taxiarch and struck him; and though the whole citizen body took part in the expedition, he was deemed thoroughly undisciplined and wicked and alone of the Athenians he was formally dismissed by the generals.

[46] There are many other tales I could tell about him, but since it is not allowable in your court to speak outside the main issue, please bear this in mind. It was they who entered our home by

force; they who pursued; they who tried to drag us by force off the street. [47] Remember this and vote for what is just. Do not allow me to be exiled unjustly from my fatherland, for which I have faced many dangers and performed many public services; I have never been responsible for any harm to it, nor has any of my ancestors, but for much benefit. [48] So in justice I should be pitied by you and other men, not only if any of the things Simon wants were to happen to me but also because I have been forced as a result of events like this to face a trial of this nature.

The case arises out of a dispute between two rivals for the affections of a youth named Theodotos. The dispute obviously has a long history. The speaker (§5) traces it back to vindictive jealousy on Simon's part because the boy preferred the speaker's kindness to Simon's abusive treatment. Simon for his part appears to be arguing (§22) that he had a sexual contract with the boy and that the speaker induced the boy to breach this arrangement. The speaker's evasiveness on the subject suggests that Simon may be telling the truth on this point. The rivalry has erupted into violence, and Simon is prosecuting the speaker for allegedly wounding him. The speaker claims that Simon laid an ambush for the boy and that the speaker and the boy were innocent victims. Simon claims that the speaker came to his house and threatened to kill him.

The case for the defence relies heavily on a tapestry of contrasting characterization woven by Lysias. Noteworthy is the use of the preliminary narrative in §§5–10, tracing the prehistory of the dispute, to create a vivid impression of Simon in preparation for the main narrative. Simon emerges as consistently drunken, violent and lawless. In contrast, the speaker is a mild-mannered individual, painfully embarrassed at the strength of his passion, unbecoming in a man of his years, and eager to avoid trouble at all costs. As in Lysias 1 (Case I), the characterization effects an implicit argument: could a man as retiring as the speaker be an aggressor, and could a man as violent as Simon be an innocent victim of aggression? So powerful is this contrast that it is only on reflection that we notice that the speaker is our sole source for this characterization. The speaker also, by emphasizing that similar quarrels have taken place before and stressing the triviality of the cause, and by presenting the fight in question as a confused and slightly comic affair, seeks to present the incident as a petty squabble unworthy of the attention of the Areopagos. In the same vein he presses the definition of *trauma* as attempted murder (§§41–3), a charge which in the seriousness both of allegation and punishment is disproportionate to the activity which engendered it. In the process he distorts the legal position on wounding with intent. He treats intent as though it necessarily involved premeditation in the fullest sense. In fact, the presentation of wounding, both in Dem. 54.18–19 (Case VI) and [Dem.] 40.32 (not in this collection), as arising out of an escalating quarrel would suggest that intentional wounding was treated as attempted homicide even if it occurred in the heat of the moment.

Is the speaker guilty? We may reasonably accept that witness testimony supports the claim that Simon and his gang pursued the boy through the streets. Clearly Simon is no innocent victim of violence. But there are two features of the defence which leave one dissatisfied (in the study, though possibly not in the lawcourt on the day). Instead of arguing bluntly that he at no time wounded him, the speaker is content to give us a blurred impression of a confused street fight in which everyone received some injury (§18). In view of this evasion it is difficult to resist the conclusion that Simon was actually injured (how seriously it is impossible to guess). The other suspicious feature is the presence of the speaker and the boy in the vicinity of Simon's house on the day in question. If the retiring personality he projects is real, it is surprising to see him taking such a risk. This lends some support to Simon's version. The interval between alleged offence and prosecution suggests that Simon has been waiting for an opportunity for revenge.

Little detail emerges about Theodotos, the cause of the quarrel, in all this; the mention of the possibility of his being questioned under torture (§33) suggests that he may have been a slave.

This text is also interesting for the light it casts on Athenian attitudes to homosexuality. It was common for grown males to form erotic relationships with pubescent youths (as in the present case), and this is the normal expectation for homoerotic relationships. Although by no means all Athenian writers approve of the practice, there is a broad acceptance that such desires are normal, as can be seen from the fact that the speaker's embarrassment at the opening concerns the strength of his passion, its unseemliness for one of his age, and the situations into which it drew him, rather than the gender of the love object. Likewise, at §43 he sets his quarrel on the same level as fights over mistresses (*hetairai*, courtesans slave or free). Attitudes to, and the etiquette of, homosexuality are however complex, and the reader interested in pursuing the issue further will find an admirable discussion in K.J. Dover, *Greek Homosexuality* (London 1978).

CASE VI: DEMOSTHENES 54 – AGAINST KONON FOR BATTERY

We have here a private action for battery (*aikeias dike*). A young man named Ariston claims to have been the victim of an unprovoked attack by a middle-aged man named Konon. Although he has brought a private case, Ariston notes that he could have brought a public action for outrage (*graphe hybreos*). The nature of these actions is discussed in the brief essay at the end of the speech. Both plaintiff and defendant appear to be people of substance, to judge by both the reference to public services (*leitourgiai*) at the close and the fact that Konon's associates (§7) include Spintharos, whose father Euboulos was one of the most successful politicians in fourth-century Athens. The date of the action can be fixed by the reference in §3 to garrison duty at Panakton two years before the trial. Demosthenes speaks at 19.326 of an expedition to Panakton in 343, and tells us that during the Sacred War (355–346) no such expedition had been necessary. It is far from clear that the expedition mentioned in Dem. 19 and the guard duty mentioned here are the same kind of operation; nor can we exclude the possibility that Demosthenes is exaggerating. But the evidence such as it is would suggest a date of 357 or 343 for the incidents narrated and 355 or 341 for the hearing. It is difficult to choose with confidence. The association of Konon with the son of Euboulos, whose faction Demosthenes was attacking by the late 350s on the ground of its failure to check the rising power of Macedon, suggests that Demosthenes may have accepted the case from political motives. Unfortunately, even if true, this conjecture does not help for dating, since Demosthenes was still struggling (though more successfully) with this faction in the late 340s. However, since by 341 Demosthenes was one of the leading political figures, he is less likely to have needed, or to have been free, to take on a speechwriting brief. So a date in the 350s seems marginally more likely.

[1] I was outrageously assaulted by this Konon, judges, and placed in such a serious condition that for a long time neither my family nor any of the doctors expected me to pull through. So having

recovered my health and survived against expectation I have brought this suit for battery against him. Though all the friends and relatives whom I consulted declared that his acts rendered him liable to summary arrest as a mugger and indictment for outrage, they advised and encouraged me not to take on a task beyond my abilities nor to be seen bringing a complaint beyond my years for the injuries I suffered. So this is what I have done, and under their influence I have brought a private suit, though I would prefer most of all, men of Athens, to bring him to trial on a capital charge. [2] This you will all understand, I am sure, when you hear what I have suffered. Though the outrage committed then was terrible, the defendant's appalling conduct since then has been every bit as bad. I urge and beg all of you alike, firstly to give a favourable hearing to my account of my sufferings and secondly, if you think I have been wronged and treated unlawfully, to help me as justice demands. I shall give you a full and detailed account of events as briefly as I can.

[3] Two years ago I went out to Panakton, when we were assigned to garrison duty. The sons of Konon here had a tent near us, though I wish they hadn't. For that was the origin of the hostility and clashes between us. I shall tell you how it came about.

These people used to spend the whole day drinking, beginning immediately after the midday meal, and they continued to do this all the time we were on garrison duty. As for us, we behaved outside the city exactly as we used to do here. [4] So when the time came for the rest to have dinner, they were already engaged in drunken games. Most of it they directed at our servants, but finally against us personally. They claimed our servants annoyed them with the smoke when they were preparing food and took every remark as an insult. So they beat them, emptied their chamberpots over them, and urinated on them; there was no kind of disgraceful or outrageous act which they omitted. Though we saw all this and were vexed, initially we remonstrated with them; but when they mocked us and refused to stop, we went and told the whole story to the general, all of my mess together, not myself alone. [5] Though he abused them roundly and reproached them, not only for their disgraceful treatment of us but also for their entire conduct in the camp, so far from desisting or feeling ashamed, as soon as it grew dark they immediately rushed into our tent that evening; they began by insulting us but finally threw some punches at me. And they raised such a noisy uproar around the tent that the general and the taxiarchs came with some of the other soldiers; it was these who prevented us from suffering some irreparable injury, or indeed inflicting it in response to the drunken violence of these people.

[6] Now that the matter had gone so far, when we returned here, as one would expect, there was anger and hostility between us. But good heavens, I did not think it necessary to sue them or to make an issue of any of the events; no, I simply decided for the future to be careful and avoid them and to have no dealings with people of that sort.

First of all, I wish to provide the depositions relating to the statements I have made, and then to show you the treatment I have received from Konon himself; then you will realize that the very man who should have criticized the original offences has himself taken the lead in committing far more serious crimes.

Depositions

[7] These are the events I chose to ignore. Not long afterwards I was walking in the agora one evening, as was my habit, together with Phanostratos of Kephisia, one of my contemporaries, when this man's son Ktesias came up, drunk, in the vicinity of the Leokorion, near Pythodoros' premises. On catching sight of us he shouted out, and after talking to himself as a drunk would, so that one could not catch what he was saying, he went off up to Melite. It turns out they were drinking there (as we learned later) at Pamphilos the fuller's place, Konon here, a man named Diotimos, Archebiades, Spintharos son of Euboulos, Theogenes son of Andromenes, and many others. All these Ktesias roused up and set off to the agora.

[8] As it happened, we were returning from the shrine of Persephone and were once more walking roughly opposite the Leokorion, when we encountered them. When we closed with them, one of them (someone unknown to me) fell upon Phanostratos and held him down, while Konon here, his son and the son of Andromenes attacked me and to begin with stripped me and then tripped me up and knocked me down into the mud; and they reduced me to such a state, by jumping on me and outrageously assaulting me, that they split my lip and closed up my eyes. They left me in such a poor condition that I could neither stand up nor speak. And as I lay there I heard them saying many dreadful things. [9] Much of it is abusive and I should hesitate to repeat some things in your court; but one thing which is evidence of his arrogance and an indication that he

was the leader in the whole business I shall tell you. He crowed in imitation of victorious cocks, and the rest urged him to flap his elbows against his sides by way of wings. After this I was carried home, unclothed, by passers-by; these people had gone off taking my robe with them. When I reached my door, there was shouting and yelling from my mother and her serving-girls, and with an effort I was eventually carried off to a bathhouse, where I was washed and shown to the doctors.

To prove the truth of these statements, I shall provide you with witnesses to the facts.

Witnesses

[10] As it happened, judges, Euxitheos of Cholleidai here, a relative of mine, and with him Meidias, who were coming back from dinner, came upon me when I was already near my home; they accompanied me as I was carried to the bath and were there when the doctor was brought. I was in such a weak condition that, to avoid my being carried the long distance home from the bath, those present decided to take me to Meidias' house for that night, and they did so. So then, take the depositions of these people also, so you will know that there are many people who know the sort of outrage I was subjected to by these men.

Depositions

Now take also the doctor's deposition.

Deposition

[11] At that point then my immediate condition from the blows I received and the outrage I suffered was such as you hear and all the people who saw me right then have testified to you. But subsequently the doctor said that he was not overly concerned for the swellings on my face and the cuts, but I was subject to persistent bouts of fever and severe and violent pains, especially of the sides and the pit of the stomach, and I was incapable of eating. [12] And according to the doctor, but for the fact that a very substantial spontaneous evacuation of blood occurred at a time when I was in great pain and already despaired of, I might even have died from suppuration. As it was, it was this that saved me, the evacuation of blood.

To prove that in this too I am telling the truth, and that I was subjected to illness such as to reduce me to a desperate condition, as a result of the blows I received from these men, read the doctor's deposition and that of the people who visited me.

Depositions

[13] So the fact that the blows I received were not slight or insignificant but that I found myself in extreme danger because of the outrageous behaviour and the violence of these people, and so the action I have brought is far less serious than they deserve, this has I think been made clear to you on many counts. And I imagine that some of you are wondering what on earth Konon will dare to say in reply to this. Now I want to warn you about the argument I am informed he has contrived; he will attempt to divert the issue away from the outrage of what was done and reduce it to laughter and ridicule. [14] And he will say that there are many individuals in the city, the sons of decent men, who in the playful manner of young people have given themselves titles, and they call some 'Ithyphallics', others 'Down-and-outs'; that some of them love courtesans and have often suffered and inflicted blows over a courtesan, and that this is the way of young people. As for my brothers and myself, he will misrepresent all of us as drunken and violent but also as unreasonable and vindictive. [15] Personally, judges, though I have been angered by the treatment I have received, my indignation and feeling of having been outraged would be no less, if I may say so, if these statements about us by Konon here are regarded as the truth and your ignorance is such that each man is taken for whatever he claims or his neighbour alleges him to be, and decent men get no benefit at all from their normal life and habits. [16] We have not been seen either drunk or behaving violently by anyone in the world, nor do we think we are behaving unreasonably if we demand to receive satisfaction under the laws for the wrongs done to us. We agree that his sons are 'Ithyphallics' and 'Down-and-outs', and I for my part pray to the gods that this and all else of the sort may recoil upon Konon and his sons. [17] For these are the men who initiate each other into the rites of Ithyphallos and commit the sort of acts which decent people find it deeply shameful even to speak of, let alone do.

But what's all this to me? I am amazed if any excuse or pretext has been discovered for use in your court to enable a man, if he is proved guilty of outrage and inflicting blows, to escape punishment. For the laws, quite the reverse, have provided even for pleas of necessity and sought to prevent them from turning into something more serious. For instance – I've had to find out and research this subject because of this man – there are suits for slander; [18] it's said that these take place so that people will not be led on to beat each other when insulted. Then again, there are suits for battery; I'm told that these exist to prevent anyone, when he is getting the worst of it, from retaliating with a stone or any other object of the sort, but to ensure that he waits for legal satisfaction. Again there are indictments for wounding to prevent murder from occurring when people are wounded. [19] The least significant, I think, the action for slander, has been provided for to avoid the ultimate and most serious offence, to ensure that murder will not be committed or people led on by degrees from slander to blows and from blows to wounds and from wounds to killing, but there should be an action for each of these acts laid down in the laws so that they are not judged by individual anger of whim.

[20] So this is what is in the laws. And if Konon says: 'We're a band of Ithyphallics, and in our love affairs we beat and strangle whoever we choose', will you laugh and let him off? I don't think so. None of you would have been seized with laughter, if he had chanced to be there when I was being attacked and stripped and outraged, when after going out in full health I was carried home, and my mother rushed out, and there was so much yelling and shouting at our house from the women, like that for a dead man, that some of the neighbours sent to our house to ask what had happened. [21] As a general rule, judges, in justice there should be no excuse or indemnity for anyone in your court such as to allow a man to commit outrage. But if it is open to anyone, it is proper that recourse to arguments of this sort should be reserved for people who commit any such act through youth, and in their case not to prevent them from being punished but so they face a lighter punishment than they should. [22] But when a man over fifty years old, and in the company of younger men, his sons at that, not only failed to dissuade or prevent them but has himself been ringleader and instigator and the vilest of all, what punishment could he suffer which would be adequate for his actions? In my opinion, not even death. Even if he had carried out none of the acts but had stood by while his son Ktesias committed the acts which Konon clearly has done, you would be right to hate him. [23] For if he has brought up

his sons in such a way that they feel neither fear nor shame to commit offences in his presence, offences at that which in some cases carry the death penalty, what punishment in your view could not reasonably be inflicted on him? For myself, I think that this is evidence that he did not respect his own father either; for if Konon personally had honoured and feared his own father, he would have demanded that his sons too honour and fear *him*.

[24] Please take these laws too, the law dealing with outrage and the one about clothes-stealers. For you will see that they are liable under both. Read it.

Laws

Konon's actions render him liable under both laws; he committed both outrage and clothes-stealing. And if we have chosen not to sue under these laws, though we would rightly be recognized as peaceful and reasonable, he is a criminal all the same. [25] Indeed, if anything had happened to me, he would have faced a charge of murder and the most terrible punishment. At any rate, in the case of the father of the priestess at Brauron, though it was agreed that he did not touch the dead man, the Council of the Areopagos exiled him because he urged on the man who struck the blow. And rightly so; for if bystanders instead of checking people attempting a wrongful act through wine or anger or any other cause actually incite them, there is no hope of escape for anyone who falls into the hands of men of violence, and it will be his lot to suffer outrageous treatment until they give up. And this is what happened to me.

[26] Now I want to tell you what they did when the arbitration took place. This too will show you their recklessness. They prolonged the time beyond midnight by refusing either to read out the depositions or to hand over copies and just taking our supporters one by one to the stone and making them take an oath, and drafting utterly irrelevant depositions, to the effect that this was his son by a mistress and that he had been treated in this way or that, behaviour which roused the disapproval and disgust of every person present, including finally their own.

[27] Anyway, when they tired and had had enough of this conduct, they issued a challenge aimed at causing delay and preventing the sealing of the jars, to the effect that they were willing to hand over for questioning about the assault some slaves whose names they wrote down. And now I think that much of their speech will be

on this subject. But in my opinion what you should bear in mind is that, if the purpose of their challenge was for the torture to take place and they had confidence in the justice of this point, they would not have issued the challenge when the decision was on the point of being made, at night, when they had no excuse left; [28] but at the start before the suit was lodged, when I was in bed ill, not knowing whether I would survive, and was telling all my visitors the identity of the man who struck me first and carried out most of the outrage inflicted on me, that was the time when he would have come at once to my house with many witnesses, that was the time when he would have offered to hand over the servants and invited members of the Areopagos along. For if I had died, they were the ones who would have tried the case. [29] If he was ignorant of all this, and if (as he claims now) though he had a valid argument to offer in this he made no preparations when facing a danger of this magnitude, at least when I was back on my feet and had summoned him, he would have shown himself willing to hand over the slaves at the first meeting before the arbitrator. He has done none of this. To prove that I am telling the truth and that the challenge was issued to cause delay, read out this deposition. This will make it clear.

Deposition

[30] Now on the subject of the challenge you should remember this, the time when he made the challenge, his evasive purpose in doing this, and the initial periods during which he has shown no desire to have this argument to support him, nor issued a challenge nor made any demand. So when all the facts were proved before the arbitrator as is happening now, and it was clearly demonstrated that he was guilty of the charges, [31] he entered a lying testimony and named as witnesses people whom I think you too will not fail to recognize, if you hear them: 'Diotimos son of Diotimos of Ikaria, Archebiades son of Demoteles of Halai, Chairetios son of Chairimenes of Pithe, testify that they were coming away from dinner with Konon and came upon Ariston and Konon's son fighting in the agora, and Konon did not strike Ariston.' [32] As if you would immediately trust them and would not work out the truth, that to start with neither Lysistratos nor Paseas nor Nikeratos nor Diodoros, who have explicitly attested that they saw me being beaten by Konon and stripped of my robe and subjected to all the other outrageous treatment I received, would have been willing to

give false testimony, as people unknown to me who turned up at the incident by chance, if they did not see me in this condition. Again, I myself would never, if I had not suffered this treatment at Konon's hands, have let off the men who on the admission of my opponents themselves beat me and elected to take action first against the one who never even touched me. [33] Why should I? No, the man who was the first to strike me and from whom I suffered the greatest outrage is the man I am suing, the one I hate and prosecute.

All of my claims are as you see true and patently so. But in his case, if he had not offered these witnesses he would have had no argument at all but would have found himself convicted in silence. But as drinking companions of his and partners in many acts of this sort they have naturally given false testimony. If it's to be this way, if people once abandon all shame and dare to give blatantly false testimony, and the truth brings no benefit, it will be intolerable.

[34] Oh, but they're not that sort of people. Yet many of you, so I believe, know Diotimos, Archebiades and Chairetios, the grey-haired man here, who in daylight assume a grim expression and claim to play the Spartan and wear short cloaks and thin shoes, but when they gather together and are in each other's company, leave no manner of evil or shameful deed undone. [35] And this is their splendid and spirited attitude: 'What, not give evidence for each other? Isn't this what confederates and friends do? What in the evidence he will bring against you is really to be feared? Some people say they saw him being beaten? We shall testify that he was never even touched. That he was stripped of his robe? We shall testify that they did this first. That his lip had to be stitched? We shall say your head was or some other part was fractured.' [36] But we actually provide the testimony of doctors. This is something they don't have, judges. Except for their own testimony, they will have no witness to offer against us. By the gods, I could not tell you the extent and nature of their readiness to commit any act in the world. But so you will know the sort of acts they go round committing, read out to them these depositions, and you, stop the water.

Depositions

[37] So then, when they break into houses and beat up people they meet, do you think they would scruple to give false testimony on a scrap of paper, men who have participated in viciousness, wickedness, unscrupulousness and outrage of this magnitude and

kind? For in my opinion at least all these qualities are found in the acts they commit. Yet there are other acts still more terrible committed by these men, but we should find it impossible to find all the victims.

[38] Now as to the most unprincipled thing I hear he intends to do, I think it better if I warn you. They say he intends to bring his children to the stand and swear on them, and to invoke dread and severe curses of a sort that someone who heard them announced them to us in amazement. Reckless acts of this sort are impossible to counter, judges. For the most decent people who would be least likely to tell any lie themselves are most easily deceived by such things. Nonetheless, one must base one's trust on a consideration of a man's life and character. [39] I shall tell you the contempt he feels for such concerns; I have been forced to discover it. I am informed, judges, that a certain Bakchios, who was condemned to death in your court, and Aristokrates, the man with bad eyes, and others of that sort including Konon here were comrades as young men and had the name 'Triballians'; and they used regularly to collect the offerings to Hekate and the testicles of the pigs used for purification before meetings and feast together, and to swear oaths and break them more casually than anything in the world. [40] So Konon, a man such as I describe, is not to be trusted on oath, not remotely, but the man who would not swear even an honest oath, and would not even dream of swearing on his children but would rather suffer anything in the world, and if he has to swears as custom dictates, is more deserving of trust than the one who swears by his children and is ready to go through fire. And I, who would more rightly be believed than you in every respect, Konon, was ready to swear this oath, not out of a readiness to do anything to escape punishment for wrongs I have done, as in your case, but for the sake of the truth and to avoid suffering additional outrage, since I had no intention of letting the case be lost by a false oath. Read out the challenge.

Challenge

[41] This is the oath I offered to swear, and I swear now by all the gods and goddesses, for your sake, judges, and that of the bystanders, that it is because I suffered at Konon's hands the acts for which I am now suing, and was beaten and had my lip split to the extent that it had to be stitched and I was outrageously assaulted

that I am bringing this action. And if my oath is honest, may much good befall me and may I never again suffer anything of the sort, while if my oath is false, may I myself perish utterly, and anything that is mine now or in the future. But my oath is not false, even if Konon says so till he bursts.

[42] So I urge you, judges, now that I have proved my case in full justice, and have given you a pledge in addition, that just as each of you would personally hate the perpetrator if he had suffered this, he should feel the same anger against Konon here on my behalf, and not regard as a private matter any such thing which might perhaps befall anyone. Whoever it befalls, you should give aid and grant justice, and hate people who in the face of their crimes are bold and impetuous and when put on trial are shameless and wicked and care nothing for custom or anything else in their efforts to escape punishment.

[43] But Konon will beg and weep. Now consider: who deserves more pity, the man who suffers what I have suffered at his hands, if I leave the court as a victim of further outrage, deprived of justice, or Konon, if he is punished? Is it more advantageous for each of you that people should be free to commit assault and outrage or not? I think not. Now if you acquit, there will be more of these people, but if you convict, there will be less.

[44] There is much I could say, judges, to show we have been useful citizens, both ourselves and our father during his life, serving as trierarchs and soldiers and doing our duty, and that neither Konon nor any of his family have been of use. But there is not sufficient time, and the case is not about these matters. Indeed, if in reality we were on our own admission even more useless and criminal than these people, we do not, I think, deserve to be beaten or subjected to outrage.

I don't know that I need say more. I think you understand all that has been said.

If no weapon was used, the victim of a violent assault had (in some circumstances at least) two options available, the private action for battery (*dike aikeias*) or the public action for outrage (*graphe hybreos*). Debate continues over the precise definition of *hybris* as a legal term. Although there is a widespread impression that *hybris* is primarily a religious term (denoting the pride which makes a mortal forget his place in the order of things), the word is most often used of dealings between human beings. It generally describes behaviour which is uncontrolled and which presupposes a desire to humiliate or at least a contempt for the rights and prestige of others. It could be applied to anything from mockery through verbal insult to physical assault, including rape. However, in law the term was narrower. The law on *hybris* quoted at Dem. 21.47 appears to cover action, not words. It is likely, moreover, that in legal contexts at least, though the law was imprecise (it appears to have begun: 'if anyone commits outrage [*hybris*] against someone . . .'), the offence was generally understood to cover physical violence. It is not clear what converted *aikeia* into *hybris*, but it may be suggested that where the speaker could argue that the assault was committed either with the intention of humiliating or with wilful disregard for the status of the victim then the action for outrage might succeed. In the present case the action of Konon in imitating a victorious fighting cock after beating Ariston could be held to prove either. In explaining his reasons for choosing the private action, Ariston naturally places the emphasis on modesty (a public action would require more boldness and greater legal experience than a young man should in this culture possess) and restraint. In the process he suppresses other motives. As was explained in the general introduction, the prosecutor in a public action faced serious penalties if he either dropped the case or failed to obtain 20 per cent of the judges' votes. In addition, since on most reconstructions *hybris* involved the state of mind or intention of the perpetrator it would be more difficult to prove than *aikeia*, for which the fact of striking first sufficed. Finally, if Konon were convicted in a public action for *hybris* any fine would go to the state, while the victor in a private action for *aikeia* stood to gain compensation.

The case against Konon is presented with remarkable force, and one's first impression is that Ariston's case is overwhelming. As to the assault itself, Ariston has good evidence from a doctor that he was severely beaten. That Konon was actually the perpetrator is suggested by Konon's behaviour at arbitration (for which Ariston has witness testimony); evidently Konon had difficulty assembling a case, and it appears that it was only when his situation was looking desperate that his associates gave evidence on his behalf. However, it is far from clear that the witnesses who carried Ariston home actually saw the attack; they may merely have found him lying beaten. It may be that the only witness on Ariston's side was his friend Phanostratos. From §§30–3 one has the impression that the deposition from Konon's friends attesting that Konon did not strike

Ariston swung the arbitration hearing in Konon's favour, which suggests that, guilty or not, he had numerically superior testimony.

Konon intends to argue that he came upon his son Ktesias fighting in the agora, and that instead of the life-threatening attack described by Ariston it was merely a fight between members of rival gangs. He may also be arguing (§26) that Ariston had in some way mistreated Konon, though this is far from clear. Ariston also claims that Konon intends to swear on the life of his sons (§38). The logographer's response to this is devastating. Konon's claim that Ariston and Ktesias are members of rival gangs is twisted into an admission that Konon is a member of such a gang. The attempt to make light of the incident is met with an insistence on its seriousness. The issue of gangs recurs in Ariston's response to Konon's proposed oath. The oath in question is far from unique. But Ariston presents it as unusual, and he undermines its effect further by representing Konon as belonging in his youth to a gang which (in a manner attested elsewhere among the smart young men of Athens in and after the age of the sophists) engaged in systematic affronts to religious sentiment; an oath from such a man is worthless. Above and beyond all this, characterization is used to great effect. As with Lys. 3 (Case V), which may have been Demosthenes' model, we are given a preliminary narrative ostensibly providing necessary background information but in fact presenting a characterization of the family of Konon (not, it should be noted, Konon himself) which both supports the main narrative (by offering a corroborative parallel) and predisposes the hearer towards the speaker's side on the main issue. The wilful and drunken violence attested there is of a piece with the alleged behaviour of Konon and his son on the night in question. In contrast, from his restrained opening, full of the modesty with the Athenians expected of youth, through to the end Ariston emerges as a moderate and decent young man. In fact, of course, Ariston is our only source for this view of him, both in camp and in general.

If Konon did assault Ariston, why did he do it? Ariston's account looks at first sight compelling. But in order to mount the attack on Ariston, Ktesias had to undertake a long walk from the agora up to Melite, and Konon had to return with him along the same route, not knowing whether Ariston would still be in the agora or not. This is of course entirely possible, but the behaviour of Konon and Ktesias makes more sense if Ariston on his first encounter with Ktesias had done or said something (he and Phanostratos outnumbered Ktesias) to provoke the attack. Ariston may not be quite the innocent he would have us believe. There may be some truth in Konon's presentation of Ariston and Ktesias as members of rival gangs.

CASE VII: ISOKRATES 20 – AGAINST LOCHITES

The present case concerns an alleged assault. As in Dem. 54 (Case VI) we have here the private action (*dike aikeias*); this is clear both from the opening, where the emphasis on the first to strike reflects the definition of the offence in the wording of the law, and the reference in §19 to what appears to be assessment of damages to be paid to the victim, which suggests the private suit. If this is a real speech, and not a rhetorical exercise in argumentation, it is incomplete; what survives is the proof section, the narrative being omitted. The speech postdates the restoration of the democracy. The rhetorical use made of experiences under the Thirty suggests that events are relatively recent; but memories were long; Aischines (2.78, not in this volume) could still capitalize on his father's loyalty to the democratic cause sixty years after the restoration.

. . . [1] The fact that Lochites struck me, and was the one who began the violence, has been attested to you by all who were present. You should not regard this offence as on a par with others, nor should the penalties for crimes against the person and those against property be the same. For you know that physical safety is of personal concern to all mankind and that it is with this end in view that we have made our laws, we fight for freedom, desire democracy, and carry out all the other activities in our lives. So it is reasonable for you to impose the most severe penalty on people who commit offences in an area which you consider of the utmost importance.

[2] You will find that our lawmakers also took physical safety especially seriously. First of all, this is the only offence for which they made both private and public actions exempt from the court deposit, so that each of us would be able to secure the punishment of wrongdoers to the best of his ability and according to his wish. Secondly, in the case of other suits the offender is liable to prosecution only by the victim in person, while in the matter of outrage, because the act is of public concern, it is open to any citizen to enter an indictment with the Thesmothetai and come into your

court. [3] So intolerable did they find the prospect of people striking each other that they even passed the law on slander, which orders those who use any of the prohibited insults to pay a penalty of five hundred drachmas. How severe then should the penalties be on behalf of people who have suffered physical mistreatment, when your anger for the sake of those who have merely experienced verbal insult is evidently so great?

[4] It will be amazing if you consider the people who were guilty of outrages under the oligarchy deserving of death but let off people who commit the same offences as they did under democracy. Rather the latter should in justice suffer a more severe punishment. For they are displaying their criminality more blatantly. If someone has the audacity to offend now, when it is not allowed, whatever would he have done when the people in control of the city were actually grateful to people who committed crimes of this sort?

[5] Perhaps Lochites will try to make light of the issue, ridiculing the charge and claiming that I suffered no injury from the blows and my arguments are more serious than the events merit. However, for my part, if his actions contained no element of outrage, I should never have come to court. As it is, I have come here to obtain satisfaction not for the general injury sustained from the blows but for the insult and the dishonour. [6] These are the things which should stir the greatest anger in free men and should receive the heaviest punishment. And I see that you, when you convict anyone for sacrilege or theft, do not base your assessment on the magnitude of the theft but condemn all to death alike and believe that people who attempt such crimes should receive the same punishment. [7] You should adopt the same attitude toward people guilty of outrage and consider not whether the injury they inflicted was not severe but whether they broke the law, and punish them not merely for what actually happened but for their character as a whole. [8] You should bear in mind that often before now trivial causes have been the cause of great misfortunes, and in the past some individuals have been driven to such anger by people who dared to strike them that wounds, deaths, exiles and the gravest disasters have resulted. The fact that none of this has happened is not due to the defendant; no, as far as his actions are concerned it has all come about, and it is due to chance and my character that no irreparable calamity has occurred.

[9] I think that the way for you to experience the anger which the issue warrants would be to consider in your minds how far this

offence exceeds the rest in seriousness. You will find that all other crimes harm a part of one's life, while outrage ruins the whole of one's affairs, that many households have been destroyed by it and many states devastated. [10] Why waste time speaking of the misfortunes of others? We ourselves have seen the democracy overthrown twice and been robbed of our freedom twice, not by people guilty of other kinds of criminality but by people who despised the laws and were willing to be the enemy's slaves and subject the citizens to wilful violence. [11] And the defendant is one of them. Even if he is too young to be part of the constitution in place then, still his character belongs to that regime. It was natures such as his which handed our power to the enemy, knocked down the walls protecting our land, and killed fifteen hundred citizens without trial.

[12] It is appropriate for you to remember those events and take vengeance not only on the ones who abused us at that time but also on those who now desire to reduce the city to that condition, and on those whom you expect to turn out evil more than on those who offended before, in so far as it is better to find a means of preventing future crimes than to punish those which have already taken place. [13] Do not wait for them to band together and seize an opportunity to offend against the whole city, but use any pretext on which they are handed over to you to take vengeance on them. Consider it a stroke of luck whenever you catch a man who has demonstrated the whole of his criminality in petty acts. [14] It would have been best of all if the wicked among mankind bore some mark to enable you to chastise them, before any of the citizen body is wronged. But since it is impossible to discover them before someone is harmed by them, at least when they are recognized everyone should hate such men and consider them public enemies.

[15] Bear in mind that risks to property do not apply to the poor, but we all alike are subject to assault on our persons. So when you punish people who take money, you benefit only the rich, but when you chastise those who commit outrage, you are helping yourselves. [16] So you must take trials such as this especially seriously, and in the case of transactions in general you should assess the penalty at the amount you think the prosecutor should get, but in the case of outrage you should assess a penalty whose payment will make the defendant desist from his current excesses. [17] If then you deprive of their property people who subject citizens to wilful abuse and if you hold the view that no penalty is sufficiently severe for people whose crimes are against the person but whose punishments are

financial, you will act in everything as befits fair judges. [18] For you will reach a sound verdict on the case before you, you will make the rest of the citizen body more disciplined, and you will make your own life safer. It is in the nature of sensible judges that in reaching a just verdict on the cases of others they simultaneously protect their own interests.

[19] None of you should think it proper to reduce the assessment in view of the fact that I am a poor man and one of the masses. It is unjust to exact lesser punishments on behalf of obscure victims than for the distinguished, or to consider poor men less worthy than rich. You would be treating yourselves with disdain if you held such a view about the citizen body. [20] Furthermore, it would be absolutely intolerable, if when the city is governed democratically we were not all to receive the same treatment, if we should see fit to hold office but deprived ourselves of our rights under the laws, if we were willing to die in battle for our country but when casting a vote we were to give an advantage to men of property. [21] If you will be advised by me, you will not take such a view of yourselves, and you will not teach young men to despise the mass of citizens, or think that trials such as this are the concern of others; no, each of you will cast his vote as though he were judging his own case. For those who dare to break this law which protects your persons are wronging all alike. [22] So if you are sensible you will encourage each other and mark your own anger on Lochites, in the knowledge that all men of his sort despise the established laws but think that judgments made here have the authority of law.

For my part, I have spoken on this matter to the best of my ability. But if anyone present can speak to my case, let him step up and address you.

In the absence of a narrative, even a conjectural reconstruction of the events at issue is impossible. We can however evaluate the strategies of the two sides. Inevitably we learn rather less about Lochites' line of argument, since it is not in the speaker's interests to give space to his opponent's case except to demolish it. The speech suggests that an important part of the defence case consists of making light of the injuries received. Since this line is taken by the speaker in Lys. 3 (Case V) and the opponent Konon in Dem. 54 (Case VI), this is evidently a standard (and potentially useful) approach, and the speaker is likely to be correct in anticipating Lochites' arguments.

The speaker retaliates by stressing the gravity of the offence. Two points are particularly worth noting. The first is the attempt to associate the opponent with the oligarchic coups which swept democracy aside twice in the closing years of the fifth century. Lochites himself is too young (§11) to have been politically active at the period in question, but the speaker links his attitude (of contempt for laws and for the citizen body) to that of the people who overthrew the democracy and ignored consitutional and legal restraints. His aim is to put the residual resentment against the oligarchs at the service of his prosecution of Lochites. He is also (in a manner typical of Athenian litigants) arguing that his case is not a purely private concern but is important for the city as a whole, including the judges. The second (and related) tactic of significance is his use of the concept of 'outrage', *hybris*. He has brought a private action for battery (*aikeia*) but he treats the assault as though he were conducting a public action for *hybris.* The aim is to exploit the strong emotions triggered by the concept of *hybris* and to present an implicit argument *a fortiori* (if Lochites is guilty of *hybris* he must be guilty on the lesser charge of *aikeia*).

3

SUITS CONCERNING PROPERTY

CASE VIII: LYSIAS 32 – AGAINST DIOGEITON

The speech against Diogeiton does not survive in its entirety. It owes its preservation not to the medieval manuscript tradition of Lysias but to the fact that it was cited by the critic Dionysios of Halikarnassos, who lived at Rome during the first century BC, as an example of Lysias' style. Dionysios quoted only part of the speech. It is a suit for impropriety in the conduct of the position of guardian (*dike epitropes*), and concerns the children of a man named Diodotos. Diodotos had married the daughter of his brother Diogeiton (a common occurrence) before heading off to war, leaving behind a will which made his brother guardian of his young sons and their sister. Diodotos never returned, and it is alleged that over a period of years Diogeiton systematically plundered the estate, while also failing to provide for Diodotos' widow and daughter (both of whom were subsequently married) the dowries anticipated by Diodotos. Under Athenian law an orphan (by which is meant a fatherless child) could on reaching the age of majority require from his guardian a full financial account for the period of the wardship, and could then sue if he believed that the estate had been managed in a dishonest manner. At least one of the boys is now of age, possibly both. The case for the prosecution however presented not by the older boy but by the husband of their sister, presumably because of the boys' youth. The date can be fixed fairly closely. Diodotos died on an expedition which can be dated to 410/9. The older boy came of age between seven and eight years later (§9; the Greek, counting inclusively, says 'in the eighth year'), that is in 403/2 or 402/1. Since Diodotos has been delaying the case, we may plausibly put the hearing in 402/1 or 401/400. There is a commentary on this speech, based on the Greek, by C. Carey in *Lysias: Selected Speeches* (Cambridge 1989).

[1] If the subject at issue were not of great importance, judges, I would never have allowed these people to bring the case before you. I consider it quite shameful to quarrel with one's family, and I am aware that it is not only the guilty parties whose reputation suffers in your estimation but also those who cannot tolerate losing out to their relatives. However, judges, since the plaintiffs have been defrauded of large sums of money and have appealed to me as their in-law because they have suffered grave mistreatment at the hands of the people from whom they least should, I have felt compelled to speak on their behalf. [2] I am married to their sister, the granddaughter of Diogeiton. After repeated requests to both sides I persuaded them to entrust the case to the arbitration of friends, since I thought it very important that no outsiders should know of their problems. But Diogeiton, though it was conclusively shown that he had the money, persistently refused to be influenced by any of his own friends but preferred to be sued, to move for the annulment of arbitration decisions and to face the most extreme risks rather than to do what was right and be rid of the plaintiffs' charges. [3] So I ask you: if I prove that the plaintiffs have suffered more shameful treatment by their grandfather as their guardian than anyone in the whole city has received from an outsider, help them as is right; if not, trust the defendant completely, and for the rest of time hold us in less esteem. I shall attempt to give you a full account from the beginning.

[4] Diodotos and Diogeiton were brothers, judges, by the same father and mother. They divided up their invisible property and held their visible property jointly. When Diodotos had made a substantial profit from trade, he was persuaded by Diogeiton to take the latter's only daughter in marriage. By her he had two sons and a daughter. [5] Some time later Diodotos was conscripted to serve as a hoplite under Thrasyllos. He called to him his wife, who was also his niece, and her father, who was his father-in-law and his brother, and grandfather and uncle to the children. Thinking that in view of these close bonds no-one had a stronger duty to do right by his children, Diodotos handed a will to him and five silver talents for his safe keeping. [6] He disclosed to him that there were seven talents and 40 mnai lent out on maritime loans, ⟨two thousand drachmas loaned out on property⟩, and two thousand owed in the

Chersonnesos. And he solemnly bound Diogeiton, in the event of his death, to give his wife in marriage with a dowry of a talent and to make her a gift of the contents of the bedroom, and to give his daughter in marriage with a dowry of a talent. He also left his wife twenty mnai and thirty Kyzikene staters.

[7] Having seen to this he left a copy of the documents in his house and went off to serve with Thrasyllos. After his death at Ephesos, Diogeiton concealed her husband's death from his daughter for a while, and collected the sealed documents which Diodotos had left behind, on the pretext that he needed these documents to collect the maritime debt. [8] When he finally revealed the death to them and they had carried out the customary rites, for the first year they lived in Peiraieus, where all the stores had been left. When this supply ran out, he sent the children to the city and gave their mother in marriage with a dowry of five thousand drachmas, one thousand less than her husband had given. [9] Over seven years later, when the older of the lads passed his scrutiny for manhood, Diogeiton called them to him and told them that their father had left them twenty silver mnai and thirty staters. 'Now, I have spent a good deal of my own money on your keep. While I was able to do so, I did not mind; but now I too am short of money. So as for you, now that you have passed your scrutiny and become a man, you must see to your needs for yourself.'

[10] On hearing this they went to their mother, shocked and weeping, and brought her along with them to my house. They were in a pitiful state, ejected miserably from their home, weeping and urging me not to stand by while they were robbed of their inheritance and reduced to beggary, treated outrageously by those who least should do so, but to help them for their sister's sake and their own. [11] It would take a long time to describe the extent of the grieving in my house at that point. But finally their mother implored and entreated me to arrange a meeting of her father and their friends. She said that even though she had previously not been in the habit of speaking in the presence of men, the magnitude of their misfortunes would compel her to tell the whole tale of their sufferings to us.

[12] I went and complained to Hegemon, who was now married to Diogeiton's daughter, I spoke to the rest of our circle of friends, and I demanded that Diogeiton submit to an investigation in the matter of the money. Initially he refused, but finally he was forced into it by his friends. When we met, the woman asked him what

state of mind induced him to adopt such an attitude toward the boys, 'when you are their father's brother and my father, both their uncle and their grandfather. [13] If you had no respect for any mortal,' she said, 'you should have feared the gods. For you certainly received five talents for safekeeping from Diodotos when he was setting sail. On this matter I am ready to stand my children beside me, both these ones and those I bore afterwards, and take an oath by them anywhere my father says. I am not so utterly lost, nor do I value money so much, as to die having perjured myself on the lives of my own children and deprive my father dishonestly of his property.'

[14] Furthermore, she demonstrated that he had taken receipt of seven talents and four thousand drachmas which had been loaned at maritime rates, and she showed the documents relating to these. She said that during the process of separation, when Diogeiton was moving away from Kollytos into Phaidros' house, the boys found a discarded book roll and brought it to her. [15] She demonstrated that he had received one hundred mnai which had been lent out at real estate rates, another two thousand drachmas and valuable furniture; and she said that the family received grain from Chersonnesos every year. 'And then did you have the nerve,' she said, 'when you had so much money, to claim that their father left behind two thousand drachmas and thirty staters, the very sums which were left to me and which I handed to you after his death? [16] And you saw fit to eject these boys, your own grandsons, from their own house dressed only in short cloaks, barefoot, without attendant, without coverlets, without robes, without the furniture their father left them, and without the sums of money he left with you to keep safe for them. [17] And now you are bringing up my stepmother's children in wealth and luxury (which is fine in itself), while you mistreat my sons; you have driven them without respect from their home and are keen to reduce them from riches to rags. And for acts such as these you show no fear before the gods nor shame before myself, who know the truth, nor loyalty to your brother's memory; you regard all of us as less important than money.'

[18] At that point judges, having heard the woman's long and dreadful tale, all of us who were there were so shocked by Diogeiton's conduct and her speech, as we saw what the boys had suffered, and thought of the dead man and how unworthy was the guardian he left in charge of his estate, and reflected how difficult it is to find someone to trust with one's property, that none of us

present, judges, was able to speak; weeping every bit as bitterly as the victims, we went out in silence.

First of all, will the witnesses to these facts please step up.

⟨Witnesses⟩

[19] I wish you to pay attention to his accounting, judges; then you will pity the young men for the magnitude of their misfortunes and conclude that this man deserves the anger of the whole citizen population. For Diogeiton creates such mutual suspicion in all mankind that in life and in death they have no more confidence in their closest relatives than in their most bitter enemies. [20] This man had the nerve to deny the existence of some of the money and having finally admitted to possessing the rest to declare receipt and expenditure of seven silver talents and four thousand drachmas for the upkeep of two boys and their sister in eight years. Such was his brazenness that, at a loss how to account for the money, he calculated five obols a day for food for two little boys and their sister; for footwear and clothing and the barber's shop he had not entered a monthly or annual figure but a sum total for the whole period of more than a silver talent. [21] For their father's memorial, though he spent less than twenty-five mnai from the declared sum of five thousand drachmas, he puts half of the latter figure down to himself and enters the other half against the boys. Again, he declared the purchase of a lamb for the Dionysia, judges, – and I don't think it unreasonable of me to include this point – at a cost of sixteen drachmas, and put down eight drachmas to the boys. This enraged us as much as anything. As you can see, judges, amid large losses sometimes the small ones cause just as much pain to the victims; they reveal the dishonesty of the wrongdoer all too clearly. [22] For the rest of the festivals and sacrifices he set down to them expenditure of over four thousand drachmas, and a vast number of other payments which were included in the total, as though the sole reason he was appointed guardian to the boys was to present them with sums, not sums of money, and reduce them from riches to absolute rags, and to ensure they would forget any ancestral enemy they might have and wage war on their guardian for defrauding them of their inheritance.

[23] Yet if he had wanted to deal fairly with the boys, it was open to him under the laws relating to orphans, which are applicable to anyone whether able or unable to act as guardian, to lease out the

property and be rid of a great deal of trouble, or to purchase property and support the boys from the income. Whichever of these courses he chose, they would have been as rich as anyone in Athens. As it stands, I think it was never his intention to make the extent of their property visible but to keep for himself what belonged to them; he thought his dishonesty should inherit the dead man's wealth.

[24] The worst thing of all, judges, is that this man, when he was serving as joint-trierarch with Alexis the son of Aristodikos, claimed that he had contributed forty-eight mnai, half of which he has charged to these boys who are orphans; yet the city has not only made orphans exempt when they are children, but has released them from all public services for a year even when they pass their scrutiny for manhood. But this man, their grandfather, illegally exacts half the cost of his own trierarchy from his daughter's children. [25] And he sent a merchant ship with a cargo worth two talents to the Adriatic. When he was sending it out, he told their mother that it was at the risk of the children, but when it returned safe and doubled the value, he maintained that the enterprise was his. Yet if he is to set down the losses as belonging to the boys but keep the money which comes back as his own, he will have no difficulty in finding sources of expense to enter in his accounts, and will find it easy to become personally rich from the property of others.

[26] To give you a detailed account, judges, would take a great deal of time. However, when after great difficulty they received the written account from him, I asked Aristodikos the brother of Alexis (Alexis himself was by now dead) in front of witnesses if he still had the account for the trierarchy. He said he did, and when we went to his house we found that Diogeiton had contributed twenty-four mnai to the trierarchy. [27] But Diogeiton had declared an expenditure of forty-eight mnai; so he has counted against the boys a sum equal to the whole of his outlay. But what do you imagine he has done on matters where no-one knew the facts and which he handled personally alone, when on business which was done through others, where it was not difficult to discover the facts, he had the nerve to tell lies and extract twenty-four mnai from his own grandsons? Will the witnesses to these facts please step up.

⟨Witnesses⟩

[28] You have heard the witnesses, judges. What I shall do is calculate for him on the basis of the amount which he finally admitted

to possessing, seven talents and forty mnai. I shall reckon in no income, but shall spend solely from the capital; and I shall suppose something without precedent in the city, an outlay of a thousand drachmas a year, a little less than three drachmas a day for two boys, their sister, an attendant for the boys and a maidservant. [29] In eight years the total is eight thousand drachmas. This leaves six talents from the seven and twenty mnai ⟨from the forty⟩. He cannot prove that he was robbed of this by pirates or that he lost it in business or that he has repaid debts . . .

The sums left by Diodotos on his death were (according to the speaker) as follows:

Left with Diogeiton (§5)	5 talents	
Invested in maritime loans (§6)	7 talents	40 mnai
Invested in the Chersonnese (§6)		20 mnai
Invested in real estate loans (§15)	1 talent	40 mnai
Left to Diogeiton's wife (§15)		28 mnai
Unspecified (§15)		20 mnai
Total	15 talents	28 mnai

The final figure is approximate, since the sum left to the widow (§15) was partly in the currency of Kyzikos, but the scale of the alleged estate can be gauged from the fact that property of three talents and over rendered a man liable to the liturgy system which served as the Athenian equivalent to wealth tax (see the introduction to Case IV, Antiphon 6 on p. 63). The accuracy of the figure cannot be determined with confidence, however, since for at least one major item (the five talents in cash entrusted to Diogeiton, §5) the only surviving witnesses were Diogeiton and the dead man's widow, and there is no reason to suppose that the account book supposedly found by the boys (§14) was comprehensive.

But although the scale of the estate is open to question, the fact of fraud seems inescapable. At least one (§27) and possibly more (depending on the nature of the witness testimony in §18) of his alleged frauds is authenticated by witness evidence, and the accounts rendered by Diogeiton (even if we allow for some exaggeration by the speaker) were patently implausible. On the other hand, the speaker ignores the fact that the period of Diogeiton's administration included the tail-end of the Peloponnesian War (culminating in the siege of Athens by Sparta and her allies) and the aftermath of oligarchy followed by civil war. Not all of the financial damage suffered by the orphans will have been due to Diogeiton's fraud.

The speech is exceedingly well crafted. A financial suit of this sort is by nature likely either to bore or confuse an audience. Lysias does not attempt to work through the accounts systematically but seizes a few items which exemplify Diogeiton's dishonesty. Particular attention is paid in the narrative to the characterization of Diogeiton. Lysias presents us with a plausible villain (even where he offers no corroborative evidence) by striving for consistency in the actions narrated. Diogeiton conceals the scale of the estate as he conceals his brother's death. He cheats on his daughter's dowry, as he cheats his wards by cunningly transferring to them the whole cost of sacrifice (§21), funeral monument (§21) or liturgy (§24, §26) disguised as half the cost. And he persistently avoids attempts to resolve the dispute (§2, §12). But perhaps the finest touch in the speech is the use of the widow, Diogeiton's daughter. As Todd has noted (*The Shape of Athenian Law*, 203), the quotation of the woman's speech to her father allows Lysias to circumvent to some degree one of the procedural limitations of the Athenian courts, the fact that women could not appear in any capacity. Yet Diogeiton's daughter is the only one (beside Diogeiton himself) who has personal knowledge of his depredations. The use of direct speech creates the illusion that we are actually hearing the woman herself. It also allows the speaker to achieve pronounced emotional effects while maintaining for himself the restrained personality appropriate to an individual embroiled in a dispute with kin.

CASE IX: ISAIOS 3 – ON THE ESTATE OF PYRRHOS [AGAINST NIKODEMOS FOR FALSE TESTIMONY]

There were in Athens two formal means of checking a legal move by an opponent. The older process, called *diamartyria*, consisted (as the derivation from *martys*, 'witness', suggests) of a formal affirmation of a fact which made a given action invalid. The affirmation stood, and the action in question was ruled out, unless the opponent brought an action for false testimony against the individual who made the assertion. The *diamartyria* declined in importance from the end of the fifth century (overtaken by the newer and more flexible *paragraphe*, for which see the introduction to Dem. 35 on p. 150F), and during the fourth century it remained in common use only in inheritance cases, where it was normally used to prevent

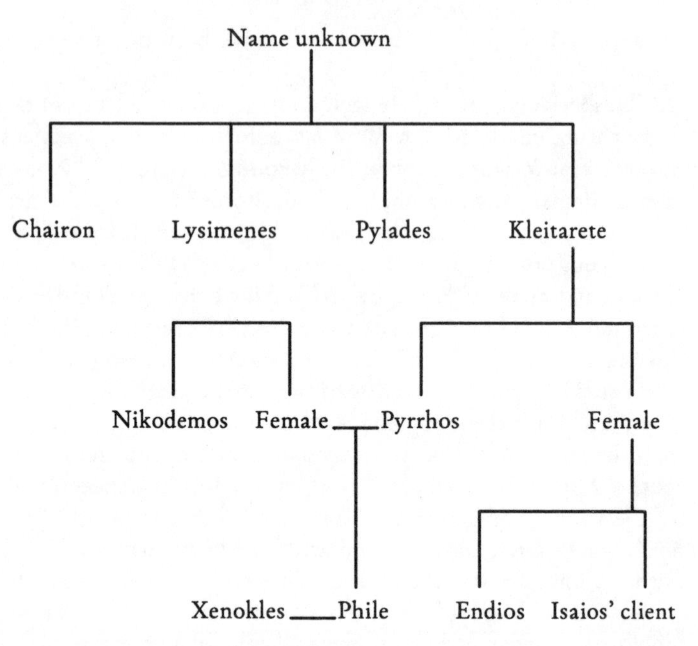

claims to an estate on the grounds that the dead man had left legitimate issue, to whom the estate would automatically go. The present case arises from a *diamartyria* lodged by claimants to the estate of Pyrrhos. The diagram makes the relationships clearer.

According to the speaker, his brother Endios had been adopted by their uncle Pyrrhos. Though his claim to the estate was not contested during his life, on his death the estate was claimed by Xenokles on behalf of his wife Phile. Xenokles issued an affirmation (*diamartyria*), that his wife was the legitimate daughter of Pyrrhos. He was successfully prosecuted for false witness by the speaker of Isai. 3, Endios' brother, who is claiming the estate on behalf of his mother, Pyrrhos' sister. At the trial for false testimony Xenokles was supported by Phile's uncle Nikodemos, who testified that he had given his sister, the mother of Phile, in marriage to Pyrrhos, so that Phile was the legitimate issue of Pyrrhos. Nikodemos too is now being sued for false testimony. The speaker's aim is probably to preclude further claims on behalf of Phile.

[1] Judges, my mother's brother Pyrrhos, who had no legitimate children, adopted my brother Endios as his son. After inheriting

Pyrrhos' estate Endios lived on for over twenty years, and during the long time he held the property nobody ever made a claim or disputed the inheritance with him. [2] But since my brother's death last year, Phile has come forward claiming to be my uncle's legitimate daughter, ignoring the last heir, and her representative Xenokles of Kopros saw fit to enter a claim to the estate of Pyrrhos, though Pyrrhos has been dead for over twenty years, and assessed the value of the estate at three talents.

[3] When our mother, who was Pyrrhos' sister, disputed the claim, the representative of the woman who had claimed the estate had the nerve to enter an affirmation that her brother's estate was not open to a claim from our mother because of the existence of a legitimate daughter of Pyrrhos, the original owner. We formally opposed the affirmation and brought into court the man who dared to enter it. [4] We proved conclusively that he had made a false deposition and won the case for false testimony in your court, and before the same judges we at once exposed this man Nikodemos as a man quite without shame for this deposition of his; he actually had the nerve to testify that he formally bestowed his sister on my uncle as his legal wife. [5] That his testimony was considered false in the previous suit is shown quite clearly by the conviction of the witness on that occasion. For if it was not believed that Nikodemos gave false evidence, clearly Xenokles would have left the court acquitted in the suit arising from his affirmation, and the woman he averred was the legitimate daughter would have become the heir to my uncle's property instead of our mother. [6] But since the original witness was convicted and the woman who claimed to be Pyrrhos' legitimate daughter abandoned her claim to the inheritance, it follows inevitably that Nikodemos' testimony was condemned at the same time. For it was for entering an affirmation on this very fact that Xenokles was tried for false witness to establish whether the woman claiming the inheritance was my uncle's daughter by a wedded wife or a mistress. You too will see this when you hear our sworn declaration and his deposition and the affirmation against which judgment was given. [7] Take these and read them out.

Sworn declaration, deposition, affirmation

It has been shown that Nikodemos was deemed there and then to have given false evidence. But it's right that his deposition should be refuted before you too, since you are about to reach a verdict on this same issue. [8] But first of all I wish to ask, with reference to this same point, what dowry he claims to have given, this man who has deposed that he gave his sister in marriage to the owner of an estate worth three talents; secondly whether the wedded wife left her husband while he was still alive or left his house after his death, and from whom he recovered his sister's dowry on the death of the man to whom according to his testimony he gave her. [9] If he could not recover it, is there any action for maintenance or for the actual dowry which he has seen fit to bring during twenty years against the man in possession of the estate? Is there a man alive before whom he ever during all that time made a complaint against the heir about his sister's dowry? I should like to ask this: why on earth was none of these actions taken when the woman involved was a formally married wife (according to his testimony)?

[10] Furthermore, did anyone else formally marry his sister, either any of the people who associated with her before our uncle knew her or those who had relations with her during his acquaintance with her or later after his death? For clearly her brother has given her on the same terms to everyone who has had relations with her. [11] If one had to list all of them, it would take not a little time. If you order me, I shall mention a few of them. But if some of you find it offensive to listen, as it is for me to speak about these matters, I shall present the depositions which were given in the previous suit, none of which our opponents saw fit to contest formally. Yet when they themselves have admitted that the woman was available to anyone who wanted her, how could one reasonably believe that the same woman was a formally wedded wife? [12] And in fact since they have not formally contested the depositions relating to this particular fact they have admitted it. When you too have heard the actual depositions, you will recognize that this man has blatantly given false evidence and that the verdict of those who judged the action, that since the woman's birth was irregular she had no right to the inheritance, was fair and lawful. Read them out; and you, please stop the water.

Depositions

[13] That the woman, whom this man has testified that he formally betrothed to our uncle, was a courtesan available to anyone who wanted her and not his wife has been demonstrated to you by the testimony of the rest of his relatives and his neighbours. They

have attested that, whenever the defendant's sister was at my uncle's house, she was the subject of many battles and serenades and a great deal of disorderly behaviour. [14] Yet I'm sure that nobody would have the nerve to go serenading married women. Nor do married women attend dinners with their husbands or think it proper to dine with outsiders, especially chance acquaintances. But still our opponents did not see fit to enter a formal protest against the man who attested this. To prove the truth of my statements, read the deposition to them again.

Deposition

[15] Read out also the depositions concerning the men who had relations with her, so the judges will know that she was a courtesan available to anyone who wanted her, and that she certainly bore no child by any other man. Read them out to the judges.

Depositions

[16] You should keep in mind the number of people who have attested to you that the woman whom the defendant has attested that he formally betrothed to our uncle was at the disposal of anyone who wanted her, and that there is no sign that she was formally betrothed to or lived in marriage with anyone else. Let's review the reasons one might imagine for such a woman being formally betrothed, to see if anything of the sort has occurred in the case of my uncle. [17] On occasion before now young men have conceived a passion for women of this sort, and unable to control themselves were led by their folly to damage themselves like this. What more reliable source of information could one have on this matter than the depositions of those who testified for our opponents in the previous trial and a consideration of the probabilities of the case itself? [18] Observe the sheer nerve of their assertions. The man who was about to betroth his sister (so he maintains) and connect her with an estate worth three talents, despite the importance of the business, alleged that a single witness, Pyretides, was present, and our opponents offered an absentee deposition from him at the previous trial. But Pyretides has not acknowledged this deposition, and denies that he deposed or that he knows whether any of it is true.

[19] Here is a clear indication that the deposition they provided was a blatant fraud. You all know that when we are approaching business which is foreseen, for which witnesses are needed, we usually take along our closest friends, those with whom we are on the most intimate terms, but in the case of unforeseen incidents which take us by surprise we all of us use any chance comers as witnesses. [20] And for the actual depositions we have to use as witnesses the people who were actually present, whoever they are. For obtaining an absentee deposition from people who are ill or are about to leave the country every one of us calls upon the most upright of the citizens and those best known to you, [21] and we all arrange the absentee deposition not in front of one witness or two but as many as we possibly can, to ensure that the individual who made the absentee deposition cannot subsequently deny the testimony, and to secure your trust more effectively by having a large number of decent men offer the same testimony. [22] Now when Xenokles went to our processing plant at the mine workings at Besa, he preferred not to rely on people who chanced to be there as witnesses to the eviction but brought with him from the city Diophantos of Sphettos (who spoke for him in the court hearing), Dorotheos of Eleusis, his brother Philochares and numerous other witnesses; he invited them along though the distance from here to there is nearly three hundred stades. [23] But when the betrothal of the grandmother of his own children was at issue Xenokles arranged an absentee deposition in Athens (so he claims); and it is certain that he invited none of his intimates along, but Dionysios of Erchia and Aristolochos of Aithalidai. Our opponents claim that they took the absentee deposition in the city in front of these two witnesses – a deposition of this sort in front of these individuals, whom nobody else would trust on any subject whatsoever. [24] Perhaps one could argue that the matter on which they claim to have obtained the absentee deposition from Pyretides was irrelevant or trivial, and so it's not surprising that they took it lightly. But how could this be? The action for false testimony against Xenokles turned on this issue, whether his wife was the daughter of a mistress or a properly wedded wife. Well then, if this deposition was true, would he not have thought it right to invite all his intimates along? [25] Yes indeed, in my opinion at least, if the claim was genuine. But one can see that it was not done like this, and that Xenokles took this absentee deposition in front of two passers-by, while Nikodemos here claims that he invited just one witness to accompany him when he

betrothed his sister to the owner of an estate worth three talents. [26] And the defendant alleged that Pyretides alone was there with him, though Pyretides denies it, while Lysimenes and his brothers, Chairon and Pylades, say they were present at the betrothal at the invitation of the man who was about to take in marriage a woman of this sort, though they were the groom's uncles. [27] It is for you now to determine whether the affair seems credible. In my opinion, considering the probabilities, it is much more likely that Pyrrhos would have wished to escape the attention of all his circle, if he was intending to undertake an agreement or an act unworthy of his family, than that he would have invited his own uncles along to witness a mistake of this magnitude.

[28] Another thing which surprises me is that no agreement was made that the giver or the recipient would hold the woman's dowry. Firstly, if any dowry was given, one would expect that the people who claim they were there would attest the fact. Secondly, if our uncle was led to contract the marriage by his passion for a woman of her character, clearly the man who was giving the woman in marriage was far more likely to make an agreement that he would personally hold the money for the woman, to ensure that the groom was not at liberty to get rid of his wife whenever he chose. [29] And it was to be expected that the man who was giving the woman in marriage would invite far more witnesses than the man who was marrying a woman of this character. For none of you is unaware of the fact that few such relationships last. Now the man who claims he gave her away maintains that he betrothed his sister to a man with an estate of three talents with a single witness and without any agreement on a dowry, while the uncles have attested that they were present when their nephew accepted in marriage a woman of this character without a dowry.

[30] These same uncles have attested that they were present on their nephew's invitation at the tenth-day ceremony for the person represented as his daughter. And what I find quite outrageous is the fact that the husband who laid claim to the paternal estate for his wife entered the wife's name as Phile, while Pyrrhos' uncles in claiming that they were present at the tenth-day ceremony attested that her father gave her the name Kleitarete after her paternal grandmother. [31] I'm surprised that a man who had been married for over eight years by now did not know his own wife's name. Moreover, he could not even discover it in advance from his own witnesses; and during all this time his wife's mother did not tell him

her daughter's name, nor did the uncle himself, Nikodemos. [32] No, instead of her paternal grandmother's name, if anyone really knew that her father gave her this name, her husband entered her name as Phile, when he was actually claiming her father's estate for her. Why was that? Was the husband's intention to deprive his own wife of her claim to the grandmother's name bestowed by her father? [33] Isn't it obvious, gentlemen, that the distant events which these people attest have been fabricated by them long after the claim to the estate was made? Otherwise it would not be the case that the people invited to the tenth-day ceremony (so they claim) for Pyrrhos' daughter, the defendant's niece, came to court with an accurate recollection from that day, whenever it was, that her father named her Kleitarete at the ceremony, [34] while the closest relatives of all, her husband, uncle and mother, did not know the name of the woman they say is his daughter. There's no doubt at all that they would know it, if the claim were true. But there will be time to discuss the uncles again later.

[35] Now as for Nikodemos' testimony, it is not difficult to determine on the basis of the laws themselves that he is clearly guilty of blatant false witness. If someone gives in a dowry a sum which has no value assigned to it, as far as the law is concerned, if the wife leaves her husband or the husband sends away his wife the donor cannot claim back anything which he did not evaluate as part of the dowry; so surely a man who actually claims that he gave his sister in marriage without making an agreement about the dowry is shown up as a patent liar. [36] What did he stand to gain from the betrothal, if it was open to the groom to send his wife away at will? And assuredly it would have been open to him, gentlemen, if he had not made a formal agreement that he would retain a dowry for her. I ask you, would Nikodemos have betrothed his sister to our uncle on these terms? When he knew that throughout her life she had been childless, and when the agreed dowry would become his under the law if anything were to befall the woman before she had children? [37] Does any of you consider Nikodemos so casual about money as to overlook any detail of this sort? I certainly don't think so. Again, would our uncle have seen fit to accept in marriage the sister of this man, who was indicted for non-citizenship by a member of the phratry to which he claims to belong and retained his citizenship by four votes? To prove the truth of my statements, read out the deposition.

Deposition

[38] Now this is the man who has testified that he betrothed his sister to our uncle without a dowry! Despite the fact that the dowry would become his if anything befell the woman before she had any children. Take now and read out these laws to them as well.

Laws

[39] Do you think that Nikodemos is so casual about money that, if the incident was real, he would not have paid minute attention to his own interests? Certainly he would, in my opinion, since even people who are bestowing their womenfolk as concubines always reach a prior agreement about the sums to be settled on the concubines. But Nikodemos, when he was about to betroth his own sister (so he claims) carried out only the legal requirements relating to the betrothal. This man, who for the small sum of money he desires to gain by addressing you is so keen to behave dishonestly?

[40] Now Nikodemos' dishonesty is known to the majority of you even without a word from me. So I have no lack of witnesses to every statement about him. But I wish first of all to make the following points to prove his complete unscrupulousness in the matter of this deposition. Tell me, Nikodemos: if you had given your sister formally in marriage to Pyrrhos, and if you knew that she had a surviving legitimate daughter, [41] how is it that you allowed our brother to claim the estate without also claiming the legitimate daughter, the one you claim our uncle left? Did you not realize that by the act of claiming the estate your own niece was being made a bastard? For anyone who laid claim to the estate was making the daughter of the man who left the estate into a bastard. [42] The same applies to Pyrrhos' act even earlier in adopting my brother as his son. For it is impossible for a man who dies leaving legitimate daughters to make a will or give any of his property to anyone without also bestowing the daughters. You will appreciate this when you hear the actual laws read out. Read out these laws to them.

Laws

[43] Do you think that the man who has testified to the betrothal would have allowed any such thing to take place? When Endios entered and pursued his claim, would he not have disputed the

claim on behalf of his niece and submitted an affirmation that her father's estate was not open to a claim from Endios? And indeed to show that our brother did lay claim to the estate and that nobody disputed his claim, read out the deposition.

Deposition

[44] When this claim had been made, Nikodemos did not dare to dispute his right to the estate nor to submit an affirmation that his niece was the legitimate surviving daughter of Pyrrhos.

[45] Now on the matter of Endios' claim one might offer a lying excuse; Nikodemos could pretend that they failed to notice, or he could accuse us of lying. Let's ignore the latter possibility. But when Endios was betrothing your niece to Xenokles, would you have permitted the daughter of the lawful wife of Pyrrhos to be given in marriage as though she was the daughter of a mistress? [46] Wouldn't you have brought an impeachment before the Archon alleging the mistreatment of the heiress, when she was being abused in this way by the adopted son and deprived of her father's estate, especially since these are the only actions which carry no risk for the prosecutor and it is open to any volunteer to protect heiresses? [47] For there is no fine attached to impeachments before the Archon, not even if the prosecutors obtain not a single vote cast, and there are no deposits or court fees required for impeachments. The prosecutors are free to impeach without risk to themselves, anyone who wants, while for anyone convicted on an impeachment the most severe penalties are applied. [48] So then, if his niece was our uncle's daughter by a formally married wife would Nikodemos have permitted her to be given in marriage like the daughter of a mistress? And when it took place, wouldn't he have brought an impeachment before the Archon alleging that the heiress was being abused by the individual who gave her in marriage like this? If what you have now had the nerve to depose were true, you would have sought vengeance on the guilty party there and then.

Or will you pretend that you failed to notice? [49] Didn't the dowry given with her alert you then? This very fact should have enraged you and induced you to impeach Endios, if he saw fit to retain for himself an estate worth three talents as though of right and to give away the legitimate daughter to another man with a dowry of a thousand drachmas. Wouldn't this have enraged Nikodemos and made him impeach Endios? Certainly it would, if his claim was true. [50] I doubt that either Endios in the first place or any other adopted son is so naive or so contemptuous of the established laws that when there is in existence a legitimate daughter to the man who left the estate he would give her to another and not to himself. For he knew full well that the inheritance of all their grandfather's estate belongs to the children born to the legitimate daughter. So then, knowing this, would a man hand his own property over to another, especially when it was worth the amount which our opponents have claimed? [51] Do you think that any adopted son would be so brazen or so foolhardy as to give a legitimate daughter in marriage with not even a tenth of her father's estate as her dowry? And when this happened, do you think her uncle would have allowed it, the very man who has testified that he gave her mother in marriage? I certainly don't think so. No, he would have laid claim to the estate and submitted an affirmation and brought an impeachment before the Archon, and taken any more robust action than these that was available. [52] So Endios gave the woman Nikodemos claims is his niece in marriage as though she were the daughter of a mistress. Yet Nikodemos chose neither to dispute the claim to Pyrrhos' estate with Endios nor to impeach him before the Archon for marrying off his niece as though she were the daughter of a mistress; he showed no resentment at the dowry which was bestowed on her, but simply allowed all this to take place. But the laws are precise on all these matters. [53] The clerk will firstly read to you once more the deposition concerning Endios' claim to the estate, then the one concerning the woman's betrothal. Read the documents to them.

Depositions

Now read out the laws also.

Laws

Now take this man's deposition too.

Deposition

[54] What clearer proof could one offer when prosecuting for false testimony than a demonstration based on the actions of the opponents themselves and all of your laws?

I have almost said all I have to say about Nikodemos. But consider too the husband of this man's niece, and see whether here too there is an indication that Nikodemos has given false evidence. [55] It has been shown by argument and testimony that he made the match and took her as his wife as though she was the daughter of a mistress. The truth of this testimony has been attested in practice by Xenokles himself over no short space of time. Obviously, if he did not receive her in marriage from Endios as though she were the daughter of a mistress, once he had children by his wife of the age his were, he would have claimed her father's estate against Endios on behalf of the legitimate daughter, [56] especially since he was prepared to deny that Endios' adoption by Pyrrhos had taken place. For he expressed denial when he was formally contesting the evidence of those who attested that they were present at the making of Pyrrhos' will. To prove the truth of my statements, the clerk will read to you the deposition which was made. Read it to them.

Deposition

[57] A further fact shows that they deny that Endios' adoption by Pyrrhos took place. They would not otherwise have ignored the last heir to the property and chosen to claim Pyrrhos' estate on behalf of the woman. For though Pyrrhos had already been dead for over twenty years, Endios died in Metageitnion last year, and they entered the claim for the estate at once, just two days later. [58] The law orders that claims for the estate be made within five years of the heir's death. So there were two proper courses open to Xenokles' wife, either to dispute the father's estate with Endios during his life, or on the death of the adopted son to lay claim to her brother's estate, especially if, as they claim, Endios had betrothed her to Xenokles as his legitimate sister. [59] For we are all fully aware that any of us may formally lay claim to the estates of brothers, but where there are offspring of legitimate birth none of them needs to enter a claim to the paternal estate. This is a matter which needs no discussion. For you and all the other citizens possess their own paternal property without having laid claim to it. [60] Now our opponents have become so reckless that they claimed that the adopted son did not need to make formal claim to what had been bequeathed him, while for Phile, who they claim is a legitimate daughter left by Pyrrhos, they saw fit to make a claim for her paternal inheritance. But, as I said before, in all cases where men leave legitimate children

of their own, those children need not lay formal claim to the paternal property. On the other hand, in all cases where men adopt by testament, these children must lay formal claim to the property bequeathed. [61] In the case of the former, since they are physical issue, nobody would contest the claim to the father's property, while in the case of adopted sons all the blood relatives see fit to dispute. So to prevent claims to the estate from any chance comer, and in case people dare to represent the estate as vacant and claim it, all adopted sons submit formal claims. [62] So none of you should think that, if Xenokles had thought his wife was legitimate, he would have put in a claim for her father's estate on her behalf. No, the legitimate daughter would have gone to her father's property, and if anyone tried to deprive her or oppose her by force, he would have been ejecting her from her father's property; and the man who opposed her by force would not only have found himself sued on a private charge but would have been the object of a public impeachment before the Archon and his life and all his property would have been at risk.

[63] But ahead of any intervention by Xenokles, if Pyrrhos' uncles knew that their nephew had left a legitimate daughter and none of us wanted to marry her, they would not have allowed Xenokles, a man without any connection at all with Pyrrhos, to marry and to keep a wife who belonged to them by virtue of birth. This would be bizarre. [64] Women who are given away by their fathers and live in marriage with their husbands (and who better to decide their fate than the father?), even women married like this, are open to claim by their nearest relatives under the law, if their father dies without leaving legitimate brothers to them; and often before now men in established marriages have been deprived of their wives. [65] Well then. If women given in marriage by their fathers are necessarily open to claim according to the law, would any of Pyrrhos' uncles, if she was a legitimate daughter left by Pyrrhos, have allowed Xenokles to marry and to keep the wife who belonged to them by virtue of birth, and to make him heir to an estate of this size in their place? [66] You should not imagine so, gentlemen. No mortal man hates his own advantage or thinks more of outsiders than he does of himself. So if they maintain that the woman was not open to claim because of Endios' adoption, and allege that this was their reason for failing to claim her, first you must ask them if they admit Endios was adopted by Pyrrhos even though they have formally contested the evidence of those who testified to that effect,

[67] and secondly why they chose to ignore the last heir to Pyrrhos' property and make a claim in defiance of the law. You should also ask them this: does any legitimate offspring see fit to enter a formal claim to his own property? These questions should be your response to their audacity.

That the woman *was* open to claim, if she really was a legitimate daughter of the deceased, one can discover most clearly from the laws. [68] For the law states explicitly that a man may dispose of his own property by will as he chooses, if he does not leave legitimate male children. If he leaves female children, he may dispose of the property along with them. So then, a man may give away and bequeath his property if it is with the daughters; but without including the legitimate daughters a man can neither adopt a son nor give any of his property to anyone. [69] So if Pyrrhos adopted Endios as his son without an arrangement for his legitimate daughter, the adoption would have been invalid under the law. If on the other hand he gave in marriage the daughter he left and this was a condition of the adoption, how could you, Pyrrhos' uncles, have let Endios claim Pyrrhos' estate without the legitimate daughter (if Pyrrhos had one), especially since you have testified that your nephew solemnly bound you to take care of this child? [70] I suppose, my good man, you may say that you failed to notice. But when Endios betrothed the woman and gave her in marriage, did you, the uncles, allow your own nephew's daughter to be betrothed to Xenokles like the daughter of a mistress? Especially when you claim that you were present when your nephew formally agreed to have this woman's mother as his wife according to the laws, and further that you were present by invitation at the feast on her tenth-day ceremony. [71] On top of this (and this is the monstrous part), though you claim that your nephew solemnly bound you to take care of this child, did you take such good care that you allowed her to be betrothed like the daughter of a mistress, and that despite the fact that she bore the name of your own sister, according to your testimony?

[72] From these arguments, gentlemen, and from the facts themselves, one can easily see how far these people surpass the rest of mankind in impudence. Why, if our uncle left a legitimate daughter, did he adopt my brother and leave him behind as his son? Could it be that he had other kin more closely related than ourselves, and that he adopted my brother as his son through a desire to deprive them of the opportunity to claim his daughter? But, since he had no legitimate issue, there is not and never has been anyone more closely

related than us, no-one at all. For he had no brother or brother's sons, and we were his sister's sons. [73] Well then, perhaps he might have adopted some other relative and granted him the estate and his daughter. But why should he have incurred the outright hostility of any of his relatives, when it was open to him, if he had really married the sister of Nikodemos, to introduce the female who has been represented as his daughter by her into his phratry as his legitimate daughter, leaving her to be claimed along with the whole estate, and solemnly instruct them to admit as his son one of his daughter's future children? [74] Obviously he would have known precisely in leaving behind an heiress that two alternatives awaited her: either one of us, his closest relatives, would formally claim the heiress and marry her, or, if none of us wanted her, one of these uncles who are now giving evidence, or, failing that, one of the other relatives would claim her under the laws with the whole property in the same way and have her as his wife. [75] So then, this is what he would have achieved if he had introduced the daughter to his phratry without adopting my brother as his son. But in adopting my brother and refusing to admit her to the phratry, he disinherited the bastard daughter, as he should, and left my brother the heir to his property. [76] And indeed, to prove that our uncle did not celebrate a marriage feast, and that he did not see fit to introduce to his phratry the woman alleged by our opponents to be his legitimate daughter, though this is a rule with the phratry, the clerk will read out the deposition of his fellow-phratrymen. Read it out; as for you, please stop the water.

Deposition

Now take the deposition showing that he adopted my brother as his son.

Deposition

[77] Now then, are you to consider Nikodemos' testimony more reliable than what amounts to depositions in absence from our uncle himself? Will anyone try to persuade you that our uncle had as his formally wedded wife a woman who had been available to anyone who wanted her? But you will not be convinced, so at least I think, unless he demonstrates the following to you, as I said at the

beginning of my speech. [78] Firstly what was the dowry when, as he claims, he betrothed his sister to Pyrrhos? Secondly, did the formally wedded wife appear before any Archon in order to leave her husband or his house, and from whom did he recover her dowry on the death of the man to whom he claims he betrothed her? Or if he demanded the return of the dowry unsuccessfully for twenty years, did Nikodemos ever bring any action for maintenance or for the actual dowry on behalf of the wedded wife against the individual in possession of Pyrrhos' estate? [79] In addition, let him also show to whom he formally married his sister either before or after Pyrrhos and whether she has had children by anyone else. Demand answers to these questions from him; and don't forget about the marriage feast in the phratry. For this is not the least important means of refuting his deposition. For obviously if Pyrrhos had been induced to marry her, he would also have been persuaded to hold a marriage feast for her in his phratry, and to introduce to the phratry the woman represented as his legitimate daughter by her. [80] And in his deme, as a man in possession of a property of three talents, if he was married, he would have had to feast the women at the Thesmophoria on behalf of his formally wedded wife and carry out the other public services in the deme appropriate to a property of this magnitude on his wife's behalf. You will find that none of these has ever taken place. The members of the phratry have testified for you. Now take also the deposition of his demesmen.

Deposition

The case for the prosecution of Nikodemos turns on the nature of the relationship between his sister and Pyrrhos. According to Nikodemos, he gave his sister formally in marriage to Pyrrhos. If so, her daughter Phile was Pyrrhos' legitimate daughter and so entitled to inherit his estate, which means that her husband Xenokles could claim the estate for her and administer it with a view to passing it on to her children in turn. If he is lying about the marriage, Phile is at most the illegitimate daughter of Pyrrhos and has no claim to anything beyond the *notheia* ('bastard's portion'), the bequest a man might make to illegitimate issue, which was limited by law at this period to a maximum of one thousand drachmas. Although Xenokles was convicted in the earlier trial, which would suggest that Nikodemos is lying, the defendant is supported by Pyrrhos' uncles, who attest that they attended the naming ceremony (*dekate*) for Phile shortly after her birth. This ceremony is closely associated, if not identical, with the *amphidromia*, the ceremony in which a child was admitted to its father's household (*oikos*). If Pyrrhos held the *dekate* for Phile, she was legitimate.

Isaios rains a series of repetitive hammer blows on the opposition, relying on arguments from probability to demonstrate that the marriage could not have taken place. He begins with the character of Nikodemos' sister, adducing witness testimony to show that her behaviour and treatment was that of a courtesan, not a wife. He emphasizes the fact (§18) that only one man, Pyretides attests the betrothal ceremony (*engye*). In a society without registers of births, marriages and deaths, the testimony of witnesses was of fundamental importance for the proof of facts for which we would adduce documentation. Hence this point is not without substance. But given the interval since the marriage, it is conceivable that Pyretides is the only surviving witness, not necessarily the only witness. The fact that the proxy arrangement of *ekmartyria* (§18), under which a witness deposed to another who then appeared in court, was used in his case may indicate that he too was feeble, since this procedure was available for witnesses who were ill or abroad. The speaker also leans heavily (§§28–9) on the apparent admission of Nikodemos and others that his sister was given to Pyrrhos without a dowry. Although there was no general legal requirement that the bride must bring a dowry, the practice was normal (among people of property at least). The insistence on this point suggests that there was in fact no dowry; this however may mean only that Pyrrhos married a female socially far inferior to him. Marriage was further formalized by the treatment of the children, beginning immediately after birth with the admission of the newborn baby to the father's *oikos* and the bestowal of a name. Here the speaker is on weaker ground, since Phile's uncles have deposed that she was admitted to the *oikos* as a legitimate daughter (§30). Isaios' response is to seize on a superficial inconsistency, that the uncles attest that the name Kleitarete was given in infancy while the estate is claimed under the name Phile. The argument, though pressed with vigour, is not very strong. In the absence of birth registers, names were to a large extent a matter of usage and no special procedure was necessary for changing a name. Perhaps the most telling argument however is the insistence on the incompatibility of the behaviour of the speaker's opponents with the claim that Phile was legitimate (§§40–3, 45).

They allowed Endios to inherit when there was allegedly a legitimate daughter in existence. They also allowed Phile to be married to Xenokles. As Pyrrhos' sole surviving daughter she would be classed as an *epikleros* ('heiress') and her position with reference to Pyrrhos' estate would be protected by law; in order to inherit the estate, the adopted son Endios should by law have married her. All these arguments are repeated, expanded and elaborated during the rest of the speech.

It is very difficult to determine who if anyone is telling the truth in all of this. The readiness of other close relatives to support Phile (though relatives can presumably be bought) suggests that there is some substance to the claim made on her behalf. Without access to independent information concerning the participants any reconstruction must be entirely conjectural. It has been suggested that Phile was the victim of a family plot to deprive her of her inheritance; if so, presumably those who are now supporting her claim have either changed sides or have plucked up the courage belatedly to intervene. Alternatively, it may have been convenient for all concerned for Endios to inherit without marrying Pyrrhos' daughter Phile, as required by law. For instance, there may have been a pronounced antipathy between Pyrrhos' daughter and his adopted son. Or the age of the parties may be an issue. According to §1 Pyrrhos has been dead over twenty years, and §31 tells us that Phile has been married for over eight years. Since Greek girls were normally married at the age of 14–16, it would seem that Phile was a small child when Pyrrhos died. Since Athenian adoption was intended to produce an heir for an *oikos* without an existing male heir, adoptees were usually adults. There may therefore have been a very great difference in age between Endios and Phile. Although Athenians were not normally bothered by large age-gaps between husband and wife, by the time Phile reached puberty, Endios may have doubted his sexual powers; it may therefore have suited everyone to allow the adopted son to inherit in the short term and to place Phile with a husband who could provide an heir, on the understanding that Phile's claim to her father's estate would be made on his death. But the reader will already be aware of the impossibility of demonstrating any of this.

One final feature of the speech is worth signalling. The speaker describes a situation in which Phile, the (allegedly) illegitimate daughter of an Athenian citizen by a female of Athenian descent, was allowed to marry an Athenian citizen. This account is occasionally cited as evidence for the citizen rights of bastards of two Athenian parents, a contentious issue. It is, however, difficult to take the evidence too seriously. Apart from the fact that the speaker's presentation of Phile's case may be complete fabrication, since he is describing the alleged behaviour of opponents it is of no concern to him if that behaviour is illegal. We cannot be sure that the marriage of Phile to Xenokles would have been valid if she were illegitimate and we cannot therefore conclude that we have evidence for the legal rights of bastards.

CASE X: ISAIOS 4 – ON THE ESTATE OF NIKOSTRATOS

The present speech concerns the estate of an Athenian, Nikostratos, who had evidently served abroad as a mercenary and had been away from Athens for eleven years (§8). On his death a sum of two talents arrived in Athens, and according to our speaker a scramble for the estate began. The speech was delivered by a supporting speaker (*synegoros*) on behalf of two brothers, Hagnon and Hagnotheos, who are claimants. They are young men (§26), and this is presumably the main reason for their recourse to a supporting speaker; from the opening it would seem that the factual case has been presented by one of the brothers. They are contesting the claim of a certain Chariades. Chariades, who had served with Nikostratos, adduces a will which makes him Nikostratos' adopted son and heir. The death of Nikostratos is probably to be fixed in 374 BC by the reference to Ake (Akko on the coast of modern Israel) in §7; in that year the Persian satrap Pharnabazos assembled an army at Ake for an expedition to recapture Egypt.

[1] Hagnon here and Hagnotheos are as it happens friends of mine, gentlemen, as was their father before them. I therefore think it proper to speak in their support, as far as I am able.

As far as events abroad are concerned, it is perhaps impossible to discover witnesses; nor is it easy to expose any lies from the opposing party, since neither of my friends has been to the place in question. But what has taken place here would in my opinion be sufficient indication that all the people who lay claim to Nikostratos' property by testament are trying to deceive you. [2] To begin with, gentlemen, it is worth while to examine the issue of the names entered, and to consider which side submitted their plea in a simpler and more natural way. Hagnon and Hagnotheos entered Nikostratos' name as 'son of Thrasymachos'; they declare that they are his first cousins and provide witnesses to these facts. [3] Chariades however and his supporters say that Nikostratos was the son of Smikros, though they are claiming the estate of the son of Thrasymachos. My friends make no claim to knowing the other name or to having anything to do with it; they say that Nikostratos was the son of Thrasymachos, and they claim his property in the same terms. [4] If they were in agreement about Nikostratos' patronymic and disagreed only about the right to the estate, you would have no need to consider anything but whether the Nikostratos on whom both parties agreed had made any will. As it is, how can two fathers be assigned to the same man? For this is what Chariades has done. He himself has claimed the estate of Nikostratos, son of Smikros, but in response to my friends' claim to the estate of Thrasymachos' son he paid his court deposit as though it was the same man. [5] All this is an insult and a plot. They think that if the matter is left simple and there is no confusion introduced, my friends will easily establish that Nikostratos left no will. But if they deny that the father is the same, while nonetheless claiming the estate, they know full well that my friends will have to devote more of their speech to proving that Nikostratos was Thrasymachos' son than that he left no will. [6] Furthermore, if they were to admit that Nikostratos was Thrasymachos' son they could not prove that my friends are not his cousins; but by fabricating another father for the dead man they have introduced a debate about the question of kinship as well as about the will.

[7] You can see that the people who set these devices in motion against my friends are outside the family, not just from this conduct but also from what happened at the outset. Who was there who did not cut his hair in mourning when the two talents came here from Ake? Who was there who did not put on black clothing, with the aim of using mourning to make a claim to the property? How many relatives and sons by testament laid claim to Nikostratos' possessions? [8] Demosthenes claimed to be his nephew, but withdrew when exposed by my friends here. Telephos claimed that Nikostratos bequeathed him all he owned; though he too gave up not long afterwards. Ameiniades brought a son of his, not yet three, to the Archon, despite the fact that Nikostratos had not been in Athens within the last eleven years. [9] Pyrrhos of Lamptrai claimed

that the money had been dedicated to Athene by Nikostratos and had been beqeathed by him to himself. Ktesias of Besa and Kranaos began by claiming that they had secured a judgment against Nikostratos in a suit for one talent, and when they couldn't prove it they pretended that he was their freedman. But they still couldn't prove their claim. [10] These were the ones who immediately rushed for Nikostratos' property at the outset. At that point Chariades made no claim. But later he came along trying to introduce not only himself but also his mistress's son into the family. His aim was either to inherit himself or to make the boy a citizen. But when he too realized that he would be exposed on the question of the boy's birth, he let go the child's claim and paid the deposit for a claim that the estate was his own by testament.

[11] It ought to be the rule, gentlemen, that anyone unsuccessfully claiming an inheritance on ground of testament would not only be fined at the established rate but would have to pay the city a sum equal to what he set out to gain. In this way the laws would not be treated with contempt and families would not be subjected to insult, and above all nobody would tell lies even against the dead. But since everyone is free to lay claim to the property of any other as he pleases, it is your duty to examine the issues as closely as possible and leave out nothing, as far as is in your power. [12] It seems to me that it is only in cases relating to inheritance that one should put more trust in circumstantial evidence than in witnesses. In the case of other agreements it is not very difficult to expose false testimony; for the individual who made the agreement, against whom they testify, is alive and present. But in the case of wills how is one to detect liars, unless the inconsistencies are considerable, when the object of their testimony is dead and the relatives are ignorant of what took place and there is no accurate means of refutation? [13] Furthermore, gentlemen, many men who make wills do not even inform those present of the content of the will, but have them there as witnesses to the simple fact that they are leaving a will. And it is a matter of chance whether a document is substituted and rewritten in a way opposite to the deceased's will; for the witnesses will be equally ignorant if the will which is produced is the one which they were invited to witness. [14] Where it is possible to trick even those who were undeniably present, surely a man would be all the more ready to attempt to mislead you who know nothing of the issue?

And indeed, gentlemen, the law enjoins that wills should be valid not merely if someone makes one but if he is sane when he does so.

So you must ask first of all if a man made a will and then if he was in his right mind when he did so. [15] Since we deny outright that the will was made, how on earth could you decide whether someone was out of his mind when making the will before you are convinced that a will was actually made? You see how hard a task it is to determine whether people who claim an estate by testament are telling the truth. However, in the case of those who claim by right of birth there is no need to provide witnesses to show that the estate belongs to them (for it is universally agreed that the property of the deceased goes to the nearest relatives); [16] furthermore, the relatives are favoured not only by the laws dealing with kinship but also by those which deal with bequests. For the law does not allow anyone to dispose of his property, if his judgement is affected by age or illness or the other factors which are familiar to you also. But as far as claim by birth is concerned, no matter what the state of mind of the deceased the nearest relative receives the property without contention. [17] Besides, to be convinced by wills you must rely on witnesses, and it is possible to be deceived by witnesses (otherwise there would be no prosecutions for false witness), but when it comes to kinship you rely on yourselves; for relatives make their claims according to the laws, which you laid down. [18] Moreover, gentlemen, if the people who are claiming on ground of testament were in fact incontrovertibly friends of Nikostratos, though you would still not know for certain, it is more likely nevertheless that the will would be considered genuine. For it has happened that people who were not well disposed toward their relatives have thought more of friends outside the family than of those who were closely related. As it is, ⟨there is no evidence that our opponents⟩ were his messmates or friends or even in the same company. And we have provided you with witnesses to all of these facts. [19] Now observe this, the most important point, which is the firmest evidence against Chariades' impudence. When a man has neither picked up the body of the individual who adopted him nor burned it nor collected the bones but has left all this to be done by complete strangers, is that man not utterly irreligious, a man who having carried out none of the customary rites sees fit to inherit the deceased's money? [20] But perhaps, since he did none of these things, he administered Nikostratos' property? But on this too you have heard testimony, and most of it is not denied by Chariades himself. I think he will have invented makeshift excuses for each of his actions; what else is left for a man who openly admits the facts?

[21] So you can now see clearly, gentlemen, that these people have no right to Nikostratos' estate, but are trying to deceive you and deprive my friends, who are Nikostratos' kin, of property which the law has granted them. Chariades is not the only one who has done this; many others before now have claimed the property of men who have died abroad, in some cases without even knowing them. [22] They reckon that if they win they will possess someone else's property, while if they fail there is little at stake. There are people willing to give false testimony, and any refutation must be based on facts which are unknown. Briefly, there is a great difference between a claim based on birth and one based on testament. What you must do, gentlemen, is firstly consider whether in your view the will was made. This is both what the laws instruct and the most just course of action. [23] When you yourselves do not know the truth for certain, and when the witnesses were not friends of the deceased but of Chariades, who wants to get hold of someone else's property, what could be more just than to vote to allow the kin their kinsman's property? Indeed, if anything had befallen my friends here, their property would have gone to none but Nikostratos; he would have claimed on the same relationship, as their cousin born of the father's brother. [24] But of course neither Hagnon nor Hagnotheos is related to Nikostratos, according to our opponents; his relatives are different people. And then these relatives give evidence for a man who claims the estate on testamentary grounds rather than claim the estate themselves on grounds of kinship? No, they are not so lost in folly as to trust the will and concede so much money so lightly. In fact, from our opponents' own words it is more to the advantage of these relatives that my friends be awarded the estate of Nikostratos rather than Chariades. [25] For in future, if my friends gain possession of the estate on the basis of a claim by kinship, it will be open to these relatives to enter a claim on ground of kinship whenever they choose, and to demonstrate to you that they were more closely related to Nikostratos, and that he was Smikros' son, not Thrasymachos'. But if Chariades inherits, no relative will be in a position to come forward for Nikostratos' property. For when the successful claimant possesses it by testament, what can claimants by kinship actually say?

[26] So then, please confirm for these young men the rights which each of you would expect. They provided you with witnesses firstly to show that they are cousins of Nikostratos by his father's brother, secondly that they never quarrelled with him, and in addition that

they buried Nikostratos; furthermore that Chariades neither here nor in the camp enjoyed any degree of familiarity with Nikostratos, and finally that the partnership, on which he places especial emphasis, is a fiction.

[27] Even without these proofs, gentlemen, you should rightly examine the characters of the two sides. Thrasippos, the father of Hagnon and Hagnotheos, has already performed public services for you and paid levies, and in general was a decent citizen. These boys themselves have never left Athens except on your orders, and while here they have been useful citizens; they serve in the army and pay their levies, they do their duty and behave, as everyone knows, in an orderly manner. [28] So they could much more properly claim Nikostratos' money as a gift than Chariades. For he, when he was living here, was first of all arrested in the act as a thief and taken to prison. Then after being released by the Eleven along with some others, all of whom you publicly condemned to death, he was later denounced to the Council as a felon; he slipped away and failed to appear, [29] and from that time he did not return to Athens for seventeen years, until the death of Nikostratos. He has never in your service served in the army or paid any levy, except perhaps since he laid claim to Nikostratos' property, nor performed any other public service. Then with a career like this he is not content to evade punishment for his offences but actually lays claim to the property of others. [30] Now if my friends were quarrelsome or like some other citizens, perhaps he might not be disputing possession of Nikostratos' property but be on trial for his life. As it stands, gentlemen, someone else will punish him, if anyone is interested. [31] But as for my friends, you must help them; do not attach more importance to people who seek unjustly to acquire the property of others than to those who are related by birth to the deceased and apart from this have before now been of service to him. Remember the laws and the oaths you have sworn, and in addition the depositions we have provided, and cast your vote for the just cause.

We have a neat antithesis in this speech. Chariades claims the inheritance on the basis of an alleged will, while the brothers Hagnon and Hagnotheos claim it on grounds of birth, as Nikostratos' cousins. The two parties also differ on the identity of the dead man; Hagnon and Hagnotheos identify him as Nikostratos, son of Thrasymachos, while the rival claimant identifies him as Nikostratos, son of Smikros. Since we do not possess a detailed statement of the case for the brothers' claim, it is difficult to assess its strength. On the basis of the present speech however, it does not seem very strong. The speaker relies essentially on bluster. The brothers contest the authenticity of the will. They therefore need to prove that the will is a forgery and to demonstrate both that the dead man was the son of Thrasymachos and that they are his closest surviving kin. The kinship issue was dealt with by the brother who gave the main speech, and witnesses were adduced to demonstrate their relationship to Nikostratos (§26). The speech also sought to prove that Chariades was unconnected with the dead man. One would like to know, however, how effectively the question of the dead man's identity was addressed. Chariades has a clear advantage here, in that he was abroad on military service with the dead man. In the present speech the issue is dealt with only in a cursory way, with no attempt being made to prove that the brothers' version is correct; without that proof, the question of proximity of kinship is left hanging in the air. The attempt to undermine the will consists in part of a series of generalizations about wills in general, the effect of which is to undermine the validity of such documents, and of the superiority of claims based on birth. The only direct attack on Chariades' case consists of an assertion that the witnesses to the will are unreliable as friends of Chariades. The speaker closes with an attempt to sway the judges on the ground of the different characters of the two sides, the brothers loyal to Athens, ready always to do their duty to the state, and Chariades, criminal and disloyal to the city.

Perhaps the most interesting aspect of the speech is the vivid impression it gives of competition for money left by individuals who died abroad.

CASE XI: DEMOSTHENES 55 – REPLY TO KALLIKLES ON DAMAGE TO A FARM

Laws as old as Solon set limits on the activities (such as building, planting and digging) close to boundaries between properties in order to prevent damage to neighbouring land or structures. The present dispute may reflect similar legislation dealing with flowing water. The present speech was made by the defendant in an action for damages (*dike blabes*) arising out of a wall constructed on his family farm to prevent water flowing on to the property. The plaintiff Kallikles alleges that the wall has diverted the water on to his land causing flooding. The date of the case cannot be determined.

[1] So after all, men of Athens, there really is nothing worse than to have a dishonest and greedy neighbour, which is what has now befallen me. In his desire for my properties Kallikles has reduced me to a sorry state with his persecution. First of all he arranged for his cousin to claim my properties; [2] when he was refuted outright and I had got the better of his scheming he secured two arbitration judgments against me by default, one in his own person for a thousand drachmas, the other by his brother Kallikrates here on his instigation. Now I beg all of you to listen to me attentively, not because I shall prove an able speaker but so that you may discover from the actual facts that I am the victim of blatant persecution.

[3] I have a single just response, men of Athens, to all my opponents' claims. This plot was walled by my father almost before my birth, when their father Kallipides was still alive and was his neighbour; and he, I'm sure, had more accurate knowledge than they, since Kallikles was a man by that time and was living in Athens. [4] And though my father lived on for over fifteen years, as many years as their father Kallipides, during all this time nobody ever came forward with a charge or complaint (though obviously it often rained then as now), nor did anyone at the outset prevent my father, if he *was* harming anyone in putting a wall round our property; no, nobody even ordered him to stop or protested at his action in front of witnesses. [5] And yet, Kallikles, it was assuredly open to you at that time, when you could see the watercourse being blocked, to go and complain and say to my father: 'Teisias, what is this you're doing? Are you blocking the watercourse? Why, the water will pour into our farm.' In that case, if he was willing to stop, there would have been no ill-will between us, while if he ignored you and something of the sort happened, you could have used the people who were present as witnesses. [6] And indeed you should have proved the existence of the watercourse to the whole world, so that you could have proved my father's guilt with facts, not just with words as now. Now nobody ever saw fit to do any of this. No, for you wouldn't then have won arbitration hearings by default, as you have against me now, and there would have been no profit for you from pestering me; [7] but if you had produced a witness at that time and appealed to his testimony, my father could have demonstrated an accurate knowledge of all of these details and refuted these people who are so ready to testify. But, I think, you have all dismissed me as a young man and inexperienced in the world. But in response to all these people, men of Athens, I offer their own behaviour as the

most convincing testimony. *Why* did no-one either protest in front of witnesses or make any charge; why, so far from anybody ever even complaining, were they content to tolerate these wrongs?

[8] In my view this is a satisfactory response to their impudence. But so that you may also know the truth about the other aspects of the case, men of Athens, I shall try to show you more clearly still that my father did no wrong in putting a wall round the farm and that all they have said against us is a lie. It is agreed even by our opponents themselves that the farm is our own private property. [9] This being established, men of Athens, the best way for you to realize that I am being prosecuted maliciously would be by seeing the property. For this reason I for my part wanted to entrust the case to the arbitration of people who know, people who are impartial. This was not the wish of my opponents, as they are now trying to claim. This too will be made clear to all of you. Now please, men of Athens, by all that's sacred pay close attention.

[10] There is a road between my farm and theirs. Since the farms are surrounded by mountainous terrain, the rain water which flows down runs, as it happens, partly into the road and partly on to the farms. Now the water which flows into the road, runs down the road where the way is clear, but wherever there is an obstacle, inevitably it overflows into the properties. [11] And indeed it happened, men of Athens, that when a storm occurred the water poured over this farm of ours. The matter was neglected at a time when the property was not yet owned by my father but by a man who disliked the region strongly and was more fond of the town, and so the water overflowed two or three times, ruining the farms and made increasing inroads. Accordingly my father, seeing this happen, so I am told by those who know the facts, and also because the neighbours were encroaching with their livestock and trespassing on the property, built this wall around it.

[12] To prove the truth of my statements, I shall present to you as witnesses the people who know the facts, and presumptive arguments much more compelling than the witnesses, men of Athens. For, though Kallikles claims that I have caused him damage by blocking off the watercourse, I shall prove that this is farmland, not a watercourse. [13] Now if it were not agreed that this is our private land, perhaps we might be harming him, if we were walling off any public property. As it is they do not dispute this fact; and there are cultivated trees on the plot, vines and figs. But who would choose to plant these in a watercourse? Nobody at all. And who again would

choose to bury his ancestors in a watercourse? Again nobody, I think. [14] Now both of these are actually the case, judges. For the trees which are planted were there before my father walled the boundary, and the ancient tombs have been there since before we acquired the property. With these facts established, what stronger argument could there be, men of Athens? For the facts prove the case clearly. Now please take all these depositions and read them.

Depositions

[15] You hear what the witnesses say, men of Athens. Don't you think they attest explicitly that it is a plot full of trees and it has some tombs and the rest of the things which apply to most properties, and furthermore that the plot was surrounded with a wall while my opponents' father was still alive, when neither they nor any other neighbour protested?

[16] You should also hear a response to the rest of Kallikles' claims, judges. Reflect first of all whether any of you has ever seen or heard of the existence of a watercourse beside a road. I don't think there is a single one in the whole country. For why, when water was sure to flow on its way through public land, would anyone have made a course for it through his own private property? [17] Then again, which of you, whether living in the town or in the country, would allow water which was flowing along the road into his own farm or house? Quite the opposite, don't we all as a rule, whenever water forces its way, block it and wall it off? This man expects me to allow the water from the road into my plot and, when it's passed his farm, lead it back into the road. Then in turn the next neighbour with a farm beyond his will complain. For any justification which Kallikles has will obviously apply to all of them too. [18] But if I am to shrink from directing the water into the road, I'm sure I should be rash enough to release it on to my neighbour's property! When I'm subjected to non-assessed suits because the water flowing from the road poured into his farm, what treatment in heaven's name shall I expect from those who receive damage from the water pouring from my property? But when I cannot release the water I have received either into the road or into the farmland, in heaven's name what course is left, judges? Surely Kallikles will not make me drink it!

[19] If there were a watercourse to receive it again, judges, perhaps it would be wrong of me not to allow the water on my land. There are recognized watercourses on some of the farms. And the first owners in line receive the water by means of these, just like the drains from houses, and then others receive it from them in the same way. But at this point nobody passes the water to me or receives it in turn from me. [20] How then can it be a watercourse? Water pouring in has often in the past, I think, caused damage to many because they took no precaution, just as it has now caused Kallikles damage. What is most monstrous is that when the water flows on to his land Kallikles hauls in massive boulders and walls it off, but he has brought an action for damages against me on the grounds that my father was in the wrong in building a wall when this happened to our farm. Yet if all the people who have suffered from the water flowing on that side sue me, even if my possessions were many times their present size they would still be inadequate. [21] The plaintiffs are quite unlike everyone else, in that though they have suffered no loss, as I shall prove to you clearly in a moment, while many others have received much serious damage, they are the only ones who have had the nerve to bring an action against me. Yet everyone had more reason to do this. The plaintiffs, if they really have suffered any loss, are themselves the cause of the damage for which they are harassing me; the other neighbours, if nothing else, at least cannot be accused of this. But to ensure that I don't get everything confused, please take the depositions of my neighbours.

Depositions

[22] Isn't it preposterous, judges? My neighbours make no complaint against me after damage on this scale, nor does any other of those who have been unlucky; no, they accept their misfortune, while this man persecutes me. But he, as you will shortly hear more clearly from the depositions, has himself behaved badly, firstly in making the road narrower by extending his boundary wall to take in the roadside trees, secondly in throwing out his rubbish into the road, with the result that it has become both higher and narrower. [23] What I shall try to show you right now is that he has brought such a serious action against me without having suffered any loss or damage of any significance.

My mother was friendly with my opponents' mother before they tried to harass me. They used to visit each other, as one would expect both because the two of them lived in the country and were neighbours and because their husbands were also friends while alive. [24] My mother called on their mother, who lamented the incident and showed her the damage, and this was how we discovered everything, judges. And I am telling you what I heard from my mother, so heaven help me; and if I'm lying, let the opposite be my fate. I swear that she said she saw, and heard their mother say, that some barley grains were soaked, which she herself saw being dried, but not even three medimnoi, and about half a medimnos of wheat meal. She said that a jar of olive oil had been knocked over but had not been damaged. [25] This, judges, was all that befell them, and for this I am sued in a non-assessed action for a thousand drachmas. For I need not count some ancient wall he built, if it neither fell down nor suffered any other harm. And so if I agreed with them that I am to blame for all that happened, this is what was soaked. [26] But since my father did nothing wrong at the outset in putting a wall round our land, and the other side never made any complaint during all the time which elapsed, while the rest despite their terrible losses make no complaint against me, and every one of you is in the habit of directing the water from your houses and farms into the road, and not (for heaven's sake) allowing it in from the road, what more is there to say? It's obvious from this that I am clearly being persecuted, when I have done nothing wrong, nor have they suffered the damage they claim.

[27] To prove to you that they have thrown rubbish into the road and made the road narrower by extending their boundary wall, and furthermore that I offered an oath to their mother and challenged my own mother to swear the same oath, I ask the clerk to take both the depositions and the challenge.

Depositions, challenge

[28] Could any mortals be more impudent or more blatantly malicious in their prosecution than these men? When they themselves extended their boundary wall and have raised the level of the road, they are suing other people for damages, in a non-assessed action for one thousand drachmas at that, though the sum total of their losses is not even fifty drachmas? But consider, judges, how many people have had the misfortune to have their fields damaged by

water, both in Eleusis and elsewhere. But assuredly each of these men will not (heavens above!) expect to recover the damages from his neighbours. [29] Personally, though I could reasonably resent the narrowing and raising of the road, I let the matter lie. But these people actually go so far, it seems, as to harass the victims of their misconduct as well. However, Kallikles, if you have the right to wall in your own farm, presumably we too had that right. If my father did you any harm by building the wall, now you are harming me by building a wall as you do. [30] For obviously with its course blocked with large stones the water will flow back on to my land, and at some point it will unexpectedly knock down the dry-stone dike. But even so I make no complaint against them on this account; I accept what luck brings and will try to take care of my own property. For I think that Kallikles too is being sensible in protecting his property, though in suing me I consider him thoroughly dishonest and afflicted with some mental illness.

[31] Don't be surprised at his eagerness, judges, nor by the fact that he has now had the nerve to bring a spurious charge. Previously, after he persuaded his cousin to dispute possession of my farm, he brought forward a non-existent contract, and this time too he has secured an arbitration judgment against me by default on another suit similar to this, having entered the name of one of my slaves, Kallaros, on the charge. For in addition to their other misdeeds they have discovered this device too: they are bringing the same suit against Kallaros. [32] Yet what slave would put a wall round his master's land without his master's order? With no other charge to bring against Kallaros, they are suing him for a barrier built by my father more than fifteen years before he died. And if I give up my farm, and either sell it to them or exchange it for other land, Kallaros is guilty of no wrong; if I refuse to abandon my own property to my opponents, they are victims of all the most appalling treatment by Kallaros and they search for an arbitrator who will adjudge the farm to them, or compromises which will give them possession of the property.

[33] Now, judges, if it is right that plotters and persecutors should profit, there would be no point in what I have said. If however you hate people like this and cast your vote justly, since Kallikles has made no loss and suffered no wrong either from Kallaros or from my father, I see no need to say more. [34] But to show you that before now he used his cousin in a plot to gain my land, and that on this occasion he has personally secured a judgment

in a similar action against Kallaros, in an attempt to harass me because I am fond of the slave, and that he has brought another action against Kallaros, the clerk will read out the depositions on all these points.

Depositions

[35] This and much other appalling treatment I have received at their hands; but so far from obtaining redress, I should be content merely to avoid losing the case to them as well. So in heaven's name, judges, do not abandon me to these people when I am innocent. I am worried less about the financial loss, difficult as that is for those with small means; no, they are driving me right out of the deme with their harassment and malicious prosecutions. To show we are innocent, we were ready to entrust the issue to people who knew the facts, unprejudiced and impartial arbitrators, and equally ready to swear the customary oath. We thought that this was the most reliable indication we could provide to you who have yourselves taken an oath. Please take the challenge and the remaining depositions.

Challenge, depositions

The present case appears to fall into a series of disputes between the speaker and Kallikles, not all of which were necessarily connected with the damage caused by the flood. In response to Kallikles' allegations the speaker counters that the wall was built by his father, with no complaint lodged by the plaintiffs before the present. He also denies that the wall interrupted or diverted any watercourse, insisting instead that the water flowed down the roadway adjacent to the farms (evidently a common occurrence) and that the flooding simply resulted from water pouring off the road. He denies that the damage caused by the flash-flood was as great as Kallikles asserts. He also complains of the inconsistency of Kallikles in bringing a charge for alleged damage caused by a construction on the speaker's land when Kallikles himself has narrowed the road with building and rubbish thrown out. The speaker also claims that Kallikles' suit

---

In the manuscripts this sentence occurs in §19. It was transposed to this location by Blass.

is part of a strategy designed to give him ownership of the speaker's farm.

It is possible that Kallikles has (as we are told) manufactured the suit out of a desire to get the speaker's farm, or alternatively to obtain damages for loss which was not the responsibility of the speaker. It is also possible that the wall in question does have the effect of diverting water, and that the damage to Kallikles' farm comes either from an unusually heavy flood or from decay in his own perimeter wall causing the water to pour in. Or the speaker may have made alterations to a structure which was (as he says) built years ago by his father. Almost the only thing which does emerge with any security is the long-standing hostility between the neighbours.

The speech raises interesting legal questions. Normally, it would seem, in cases of damage the compensation paid was set at the actual loss caused (which would be subject to assessment by the two litigants, with the judges choosing between the alternatives offered) in case of accidental damage, or twice the damage caused where the act was deliberate. Here however we have a fixed penalty of 1,000 drachmas (§28). It may be however that the law under which the action was brought was not a general statute dealing with damage but a law which dealt specifically with the kind of damage alleged and which imposed a fixed penalty. A further puzzle is the allegation that Kallikles is trying to get control of the speaker's farm. It has been suggested that the action was brought under a law which compelled a convicted defendant either to pay 1,000 drachmas or to forfeit to the plaintiff either the whole property on which the structure impeding the watercourse was erected or the relevant part of the property. It is perhaps easier to suppose that Kallikles envisages not the adjudication to him of the speaker's land (or part of it) but a situation in which the speaker in order to pay compensation has to sell his farm, which Kallikles will then be in a position to buy.

4

CASES CONCERNING COMMERCE

CASE XII: HYPEREIDES 3 – AGAINST ATHENOGENES

The fragmentary state of this speech reflects the circumstances of its survival. It was preserved in a papyrus rescued from the sands of Egypt, not in medieval manuscripts. Even so, its remarkable vigour is unmistakable. It concerns a purchase made by the speaker. As he tells it, he had fallen in love with a slave boy owned by Athenogenes. He had originally intended to secure the freedom of the boy, his father, Midas, and brother but was induced by Athenogenes, partly under the influence of a prostitute turned pimp named Antigona, to buy the slaves and the perfumery business in which they worked. After he made the purchase he discovered a number of undisclosed debts which Midas had contracted amounting to a total of five talents, an enormous sum. He is now suing Athenogenes, probably by the action for damages (*dike blabes*). The speech cannot have been delivered before 330, for in §31 we are told that the battle of Salamis occurred one hundred and fifty years earlier. Nor can it be later than 324, for the presence of Troizenian exiles in Athens (§33) indicates that Alexander's decree of that year allowing the return of exiles to their cities had not yet been enacted. The speaker is a young man from a farming background.

[1] . . . her. When I had told her the story and said that Athenogenes was being unpleasant to me and refusing to reach any reasonable compromise, she said that he was always like this but urged me to be confident; she would personally collaborate with me in everything. [2] As she said this she had the most sincere manner imaginable and she swore the most solemn oaths that she was speaking with concern for me and complete honesty; and so, judges – I shall

tell you the truth – I was persuaded. So much does desire subvert our natural sense, when a woman's complicity is added. Anyway, by tricking me with these empty claims she got herself for her goodwill three hundred drachmas supposedly to buy a slave girl. [3] I suppose, judges, that it's not so surprising that I was led like a child by Antigona in this way; this woman was the shrewdest of courtesans in her youth and has continued pimping . . . she has ruined the house of . . . of Cholleidai, a property as great as any. Yet if she had such an effect on her own, what do you imagine she will achieve now, when she has acquired Athenogenes as her partner, a speechwriter, a common sort, and most significantly an Egyptian?

[4] Finally, to cut my story short, she sent for me again later and said that after using many arguments on Athenogenes she had at last persuaded him to set free Midas and both his sons for me for forty mnai; and she urged me to provide the money as soon as possible before Athenogenes had a change of mind. [5] I collected money on all sides and pestered my friends and paid the forty mnai into the bank; then I went to see Antigona. She brought the two of us, me and Athenogenes, together and reconciled us and urged us to treat each other kindly in future. I said I would do so, and Athenogenes here in answer said I should be grateful to Antigona for the outcome. 'And now', he said, 'I'll show you right away what a good turn I shall do you for her sake. You', he said, 'are about to pay out the money for the freedom of Midas and his children; I for my part will sell them to you as an outright purchase, first of all so that nobody will obstruct you or seduce the boy, secondly so they themselves will be kept by fear from misbehaving. [6] Most importantly, as matters stand it would appear that they owed their freedom to me; but if you buy them as an outright purchase, and then later set them free at a time of your choosing, they will be doubly grateful to you. However, you will become liable', he said, 'for all the money they owe, the price of perfume due to Pankalos and Prokles, and any other sum paid to the perfumery by any of its customers in the usual way. It is a very small amount, and the goods in the perfumery are worth far more, perfume, scent boxes and myrrh', and he mentioned several other terms, 'from which these debts will easily be settled.' [7] Here, judges, was his trick, his principal deception. If I were to pay the money for their freedom, I stood to lose only what I gave him and would come to no great harm. If I were to buy them as an outright purchase and agree to accept the debts from him thinking them insignificant, since I didn't know in advance, his

intention was to lead the creditors and loan contributors to me, having ensnared me in the agreement. And this is what he did.

[8] The moment I agreed to this suggestion of his, he took from his lap a document and read out the contents, which were an agreement with me. Now I heard them being read out, but I was eager to complete the business for which I had come, and he sealed the agreement immediately right there in the house so that nobody concerned for my interests would hear the contents; he entered the name of Nikon of Kephisia with mine. [9] We went to the perfumery and lodged the document with Lysikles of Leukonoe, and I paid the forty mnai and made the purchase. When this had happened the creditors to whom Midas owed money and the loan contributors came and spoke to me; and within three months all the debts became visible, with the result that including the friendly loans I owed, as I have just said, about five talents. [10] When I realized my appalling situation, I finally called my friends and relatives together and we read my copy of the agreement. In it the names of Pankalos and Prokles were explicitly entered, and the fact that the price of perfumes was owed (these were small amounts and my opponents could claim that the value of the perfume in the shop was sufficient to cover them), but the majority, and the largest, of the debts were not entered by name but as an afterthought as though of no importance, with 'and any other debt which Midas owes'. [11] And only one of the friendly loans was entered, on which there were three instalments outstanding. This was registered under the name of Dikaiokrates; but the others, which accounted for the whole of Midas' borrowing, were new, and my opponent did not enter them in the agreement but concealed them. [12] We deliberated and decided to approach Athenogenes and talk to him. We found him near the perfume stalls, and we asked him if he wasn't ashamed to lie and use the agreement to trap me by not disclosing the debts. He replied that he did not know the debts of which we spoke and was not interested in us, and that he had in his possession a written agreement with me dealing with this. A large crowd gathered and listened to the affair, since the discussion was taking place in the agora; though they shouted him down and encouraged us to arrest him as an enslaver, we were unwilling to do this but summoned him to your court as the law requires. First of all the clerk will read out to you the agreement; from the text itself you will recognize the trickery, which is Athenogenes' own work.

Agreement

[13] So then, you have heard what happened in detail. Athenogenes will shortly tell you that the law instructs that all agreements made by one man with another are to be binding. Yes, just agreements, mister. Unjust agreements, on the contrary, it does not allow to be binding. I shall use the actual laws to clarify this for you. For you've actually reduced me to such a state of abject fear that you and your cleverness may be the ruin of me as to make me examine the laws and study them day and night and treat everything else as irrelevant.

[14] There is one law which bids one speak the truth in the agora, the most decent of all instructions; but you have lied in the middle of the agora and made an agreement with the intention of harming me. For if you demonstrate that you warned me about the friendly loans and the debts or that you included in the agreement all that I later found them to be, I offer no opposition but admit that I owe the money. [15] Then there's another law dealing with agreements which people make with each other, that when someone is selling a slave they must state in advance any physical disability the slave has, or else there is a right to bring the slave back. Yet when there is a right, should anyone when selling a servant fail to disclose chance infirmities, to bring it back, why shouldn't you accept responsibility for misdeeds contrived by you? Yet a slave prone to fits does not ruin his purchaser's fortune besides, but Midas, whom you sold to me, has ruined not just mine but my friends'.

[16] But Athenogenes, observe the way the law deals not only with slaves but also with free persons. You know, I'm sure, both you and everyone else, that it is the children of women who are formally married who are legitimate. Yet the lawgiver was not satisfied that the woman should have been formally betrothed by her father or brother, but he added explicitly in the law: 'the children of any woman a man justly betroths as bride are to be legitimate', not 'if someone betroths some other woman misrepresenting her as his daughter'. No, he makes just betrothals valid and unjust ones void.

[17] Furthermore, the law on wills is similar to these. It grants the right for a man to bequeath his property as he wishes except when affected by age or illness or insanity or under the influence of a woman or subject to imprisonment or compulsion. Now if unjustly made wills are not valid even for one's own property, how when Athenogenes has made an agreement to the detriment of my

property can this be valid? [18] And it seems that if someone writes a will under his own wife's influence, this is to be invalid; yet when I was influenced by Athenogenes' mistress, must I be ruined, despite having the most cogent support in the text of the law, since I was compelled by these people to make this agreement? And do you actually emphasize the agreement with which you ambushed me so that you and your mistress could seal them, for which . . . conspiracy . . . on these grounds . . . And it wasn't enough for you that you had got the forty mnai for the perfume shop; you actually extracted another five talents from me, as though I were caught . . .

[19] ⟨Perhaps Athenogenes will claim that⟩ he did not know . . . Midas . . . ⟨It is incredible that I, who have no experience⟩ in market business discovered all the debts and friendly loans in three months without any effort, while this man, a third generation perfume seller, sitting in the agora every day, the owner of three perfume shops from which he received accounts every month, did not know the debts. In other matters he is no layman, but in dealing with his slave he was so naive that apparently he knew some of the debts, but he claims that he did not know others, as it suits him. [20] An argument of this sort from him is not a defence but an admission that I should not pay the debts. For when he claims that he did not know all the sums owed, he surely cannot maintain that he informed me in advance of the debts; and it's not right that I should pay any debts of which I was not told by the vendor. Now, Athenogenes, there are many things which make it, in my opinion, obvious to everyone that you did know that Midas owed this money, including the fact that you asked for Nikon as guarantor for me . . . able ⟨to meet⟩ the debts [21] . . . I ⟨could⟩ not . . . this argument of yours . . . in this way. If you failed to inform me of all the debts because you did not know, and I made the agreement in the belief that the extent of the debts was what I heard from you, which of us should more rightly pay them, the subsequent purchaser or the long-standing owner at the time the money was borrowed? You, in my opinion. But if we dispute this point, let our arbitrator be the law, which was passed not by people in love or plotting to get the property of others but the most democratic of men, Solon. [22] Aware that many purchases take place in the city, he passed a law whose justice is admitted by everyone, that damage or wrongdoing committed by slaves is to the responsibility of the master at the time. And this is right. For if a slave achieves some success or makes a profit, this becomes the property of his owner. But you ignore the

law and talk about breach of agreement. And though Solon does not hold that even a justly drafted decree should have greater authority than the law, you expect your unjust agreement to prevail over all the laws.

[23] On top of this, judges, he told ⟨my father and the rest of those close to me that⟩ . . . willing . . . gift . . . he told me to leave Midas to him and not buy him, but that I refused and wanted to buy all of them. And they say that this is what he will say to you too, to appear reasonable, as though he would be talking to idiots who would not recognize his cheek. [24] I must tell you what happened; it will be clear that it is consistent with the rest of their trickery. He sent the boy I mentioned just before to me to say that he would not go with me if I did not secure the freedom of his father and brother. When I had already agreed that I would pay the money for all three of them, Athenogenes approached some of my friends and said: 'Why does Epikrates want all this trouble, when he can take the boy and use him . . . [25] . . . chicanery he was up to . . . wrongdoing . . . I trust that . . . the boy . . . I refused . . . forty mnai . . . five talents . . . [26] I am not a perfume seller nor do I have any other trade; I farm the land my father left me, and I was bounced into the purchase by these people. Which is more likely, Athenogenes, that I yearned for your trade, of which I was ignorant, or that you and your mistress conspired against me? I think the latter. And so, judges, I deserve your understanding for being tricked . . . and coming to grief from falling in with a man such as this, while Athenogenes . . .

[27] . . . all be mine but the profits of deception his. And that I got Midas, his bold accomplice, whom he says he let go reluctantly, while for the boy, whom he claims he offered me for free at that time, he should now receive a sum of money far above his value, not for me to own him but for him to be set free by your vote. [28] Personally however I have no intention of being disfranchised by Athenogenes on top of my other calamities. For it would be a harsh fate, judges, if . . . I made a mistake . . . has wronged . . . guilty . . . penalty assessment . . . citizen . . . on occasion . . .

. . . the most . . . of the metics to go unguarded. [29] And in the war against Philip, shortly before the battle he fled the city; he did not join you for the campaign at Chaironeia but went to live in Troizen, in contravention of the law which allows impeachment and summary arrest against anyone who moves abroad during war, if he returns. In doing this he anticipated, it seems, that their city would survive but he had sentenced ours to death. He brought up his daughters amid your prosperity, . . . he gave them in marriage . . . intending to carry on his business on his return, now that peace has come. [30] For this is what . . . these loyal people . . . the peace . . . in times of danger . . . at Plataia . . . they bound . . . Athenogenes . . . though he broke the agreement we all have with the city, he insists on his private agreement with me, as though anybody could be convinced that the man who despised his duty to you would have paid attention to his duty to me; [31] this man who is such a criminal through and through that after the people of Troizen had made him a citizen on his arrival there he fell under the influence of Mnesias of Argos and having been put in authority by him drove the citizens from the city, as they will testify themselves, since they are in exile here. When they were exiled you received them, judges, and made them citizens, granting them a share of all your privileges; you remembered their service against the barbarians over one hundred and fifty years previously and felt that men who had proved loyal in times of danger should be saved by you when in distress. [32] But this wretch, the man who abandoned you and enrolled himself there, behaved in a way quite unworthy either of his citizenship or the city's kindness; he treated the people who had welcomed him so brutally that after . . . in the Assembly . . . in this respect . . . in fear of their revenge he fled back.

[33] And to prove the truth of my statements, he will read out to you first of all the law which forbids metics to move abroad in wartime, then the deposition of the Troizenians, and in addition to these the decree which the Troizenians passed in honour of your city for receiving them and making them citizens. Read it.

Law, deposition, decree

[34] Now please take the deposition of his in-law . . . property . . . bequeathed . . . in order . . . Antigona . . . deposition . . .

[35] . . . events, and the way Athenogenes has plotted against me, and how he has behaved toward you. When a man is wicked in his private life, gave up hope of the city's survival, abandoned you and overthrew the city to which he moved, now you have caught him will you fail to punish him? For myself, judges, I beg and implore you to pity me, bearing in mind that in this case you should . . . feel pity not for the defendant, who if he loses the case, stands to suffer nothing, . . . if he is acquitted . . . I shall be ruined. For I should be

unable [to pay] . . . even the smallest fraction . . . judges . . . themselves . . .

The speaker is evidently in a difficult position. He may well have been misled by Athenogenes. But he appears to have agreed to an open-ended contract (§10) which committed him to honouring any debts incurred by Midas. It is doubtful that the law gave him much protection. Under Athenian law agreements freely entered into were binding. To counter this obvious rejoinder from Athenogenes the speaker responds that the law says that *fair* agreements freely entered into were binding (§13). The problem here of course is that Athenogenes had actually declared the existence of debts, even if he had withheld the number and scale. The plaintiff then strives to find a number of laws which can be used to support his suit. He cites the law forbidding the telling of lies in the agora (§14); but the contract was not made in the agora. He also cites the law which instructs that anyone selling a slave must declare any physical defects for the sale to be valid (§15). The fact that this is the closest law he can find to his own circumstances suggests that there was no law specifically covering undisclosed debts incurred by a slave. Likewise, his appeal to the law which made the master liable for the offences committed by a slave is beside the point, since although the debts were incurred under Athenogenes' ownership the speaker had voluntarily accepted those debts (§21). He draws on the law of betrothals, which validates only honest compacts (§16), and the law of wills (§17), which limits the power of an individual to dispose even of his own property by invalidating wills in which there is duress or pressure; specifically he notes that wills made under the influence of a woman (as his agreement to buy was made under the influence of Antigona) were invalid under the law. But what this amounts to is an argument from analogy, not direct legal support. For the rest, all he can do is insist that Athenogenes as a member of a family of perfumiers, cannot have been ignorant of the debts, while he as a man from a farming background with no commercial experience was a complete innocent, and indulge in character assassination.

The speech casts an interesting light on the activities of slaves. There is no doubt that Midas was a slave. As such he had no legal personality and could not make binding legal agreements. Yet evidently Midas had no difficulty in persuading Athenians to advance substantial sums of money. Presumably they would expect to recoup any debts from the master in the event of default by the slave. But clearly the practical situation of slaves engaged in commercial activity was different from the strict legal position.

CASE XIII: DEMOSTHENES 35 – REPLY TO LAKRITOS' SPECIAL PLEA

This case arose out of a maritime loan. In Athens loans on sea trade were usually secured on the ship or the cargo. In the event of the loss of the security, the loan was cancelled. In view of the high risk attached to such loans, it is not surprising that the interest rates were much higher than those secured on realty. Thus in the contract preserved in §10 the interest rate is set at 22.5 per cent or 30 per cent depending on the date when the ship enters the Black Sea (which of course has implications for weather and therefore for risk). The Athenian laws recognized the importance of the grain trade by allowing for accelerated procedures to deal with mercantile suits (*dikai emporikai*). The conditions for the use of these processes were: (a) that one of the parties must be a ship's captain or merchant; (b) that the case must concern an agreement to sail to or from Athens; (c) that there must be a written contract. The importance of contracts in maritime trade reflects the greater degree of uncertainty involved, since the lender loses control of the security once it sets sail, unless he also travels on board.

The speaker, Androkles, an Athenian, together with Nausikrates of Karystos, had loaned money to two brothers, Artemon and Apollodoros, merchants from Phaselis, for a voyage to the Black Sea; the loan was secured on cargo to be shipped by the two brothers (the ship was independently security for another loan). Androkles is alleging breach of contract. Artemon is now dead, and Androkles is suing his brother Lakritos for the money. Lakritos has entered a special plea in bar of action (*paragraphe*). The *paragraphe* was a later development than the other formal means of barring action, the *diamartyria* (for which see the introduction to Case IX, Isai. 3 on p. 109). It came into existence at the end of the fifth century in connection with the amnesty which followed the restoration of democracy after the fall of the oligarchic regime of the Thirty. In the *paragraphe* the defendant in a suit countersues the plaintiff alleging that the action is inadmissible on technical grounds. The roles of the two parties were therefore reversed for the *paragraphe* hearing. The main suit was suspended while a panel of judges heard the *paragraphe* case. If the *paragraphe* succeeded the main action was either terminated outright (if the plea was that the action could not be pursued because it had been adjudicated already or otherwise formally resolved) or (if the wrong procedure or court had been used) must be initiated afresh in the correct way. If it failed the main action could proceed. To prevent casual recourse to the procedure there was a penalty (*epobelia*) of one-sixth of the sum at issue which fell on the losing party in the *paragraphe* hearing. The *paragraphe* steadily advanced in use at the expense of the *diamartyria*, except in inheritance cases where, because there were only rival claimants (possibly more than two) rather than plaintiff and defendant, there was nobody to countersue, and where the dispute could be checked by a simple statement of fact (the existence of legitimate issue). Since the speech presupposes the existence of the special rapid procedures for settling maritime disputes, it should be dated after 355. Section 40, which suggests that the rhetorician Isokrates is still alive (he died in 338), offers a lower terminus. A date some time in the 340s would suit.

For loans in Athens the reader should consult P. Millett, *Lending and Borrowing in Ancient Athens* (Cambridge 1991) and E.E. Cohen, *Athenian Economy and Society: A Banking Perspective* (Princeton 1992).

[1] The Phaselites are not up to anything new, judges, but their usual practice. These people are exceedingly clever at borrowing money in the trading zone and then, when they've received it and made a maritime contract, straight away they've forgotten the contract and the laws and their duty to repay what they received. [2] They think that if they pay it back they've virtually lost their own property, and instead of repayment they invent sophistries and special pleas and excuses; they are the most villainous and dishonest people in the world. Here is proof of this: though many people, both Greek and barbarian, come to your trading zone, there are regularly more lawsuits involving Phaselites alone than the rest put together.

[3] This is the way they are. Now, judges, I loaned money to this man's brother Artemon under the trading laws for a voyage to the Pontos and back to Athens. Since Artemon died before he could repay the money to me, I have brought this suit against Lakritos here under the same laws under which I made the contract, [4] on the grounds that my opponent is Artemon's brother and possesses all his property, both what he left behind here and what he owned

in Phaselis, and is the heir to his whole estate. He could not demonstrate any law which allows him to own his brother's property and to have dealt with it as he saw fit but not to pay back money belonging to others while claiming that he is not his heir but has disowned the estate. [5] Such is Lakritos' unscrupulousness. But I urge you, judges, to give me a kindly hearing on this issue; and if I prove that he has done wrong to us, the lenders, and to you no less, help as is right.

[6] For myself, judges, I had no personal knowledge at all of these people. But Thrasymedes son of Diophantes, the one from Sphettos, and his brother Melanippos are friends of mine, and we are as close as it is possible to be. They approached me in the company of Lakritos here, whom they had got to know somehow (I don't know how), [7] and they asked me to lend money for a voyage to the Black Sea to Artemon, his brother, and Apollodoros, so that they could engage in trade. Even Thrasymedes, judges, was ignorant of this man's unscrupulousness; he thought they were decent men and exactly the sort of people they pretended and claimed to be, and he believed they would do all that Lakritos here promised and undertook. [8] He was, it transpires, completely deceived; he had no idea what sort of beasts he was dealing with in these people. I in turn was persuaded by Thrasymedes and his brother, and by this man Lakritos who undertook that I would receive all that was my due from his brothers, and I loaned thirty silver mnai together with a guest-friend of ours from Karystos. [9] Now I want you first of all to hear the contract under which we loaned the money and the witnesses who were present when the loan was made; then I shall prove the rest and show how these people burgled us on the loan. Read out the contract, then the depositions.

Contract

[10] *Androkles of Sphettos and Nausikrates of Karystos loaned three hundred silver drachmas to the Phaselites Artemon and Apollodoros for a voyage from Athens to Mende or Skione, and from there to Bosporos, if they choose, keeping to the lefthand coast as far as Borysthenes, and then back to Athens, at a rate of two hundred and twenty five drachmas per thousand, or three hundred drachmas to the thousand if they sail out of the Black Sea to Hieron after Arktouros, on the security of three thousand jars of Mendaian wine which is to be transported from Mende or Skione*

in the twenty-oared ship whose master was Hyblesios. [11] *They offer these goods as security owing no money to anyone else at all on them and will take out no additional loan. They will bring back the replacement cargo from the Black Sea to Athens in its entirety in the same boat. If the goods reach Athens safely, the borrowers will repay the lenders within twenty days of their return to Athens the money which due under the contract completely except for jettison which is made on a collective vote of those on board or any payments made to enemy forces. And they will deliver the goods offered as security intact into the lenders' control until they repay the money due under the contract.* [12] *If they do not pay within the agreed period, the lenders are to have the right to borrow on the goods or sell them at the price obtaining. If there is any shortfall in the sum due to the lenders under the contract, the lenders both individually and collectively are to have the right to recover it from Artemon and Apollodoros, and from all their possessions everywhere, on land and sea, wherever they may be, as if they had lost a suit at law and were in default on payment.* [13] *If they do not enter the Black Sea, they are to wait in the Hellespont for ten days after the dogstar, unload the goods wherever there is no right of seizure against the Athenians and after sailing from there to Athens pay back the interest written in the contract for last year. If the ship in which the goods are travelling suffers irreparable damage but the goods offered as security are saved, what survives is to be the shared property of the lenders. On this issue nothing else is to have greater authority than the contract.*

The witnesses are Phormion of the Peiraieus, Kephisodotos the Boiotian, Hierodoros of Pithos.

[14] Read the depositions as well.

Archenomides son of Archedamas of Anagyros testifies that Androkles of Sphettos, Nausikrates of Karystos, and Artemon and Apollodoros of Phaselis lodged an agreement with him, and that the agreement is still lodged with him.

Read out also the deposition of those who were there.

Theodotos metic with privileged status, Charinos son of Epichares of Leukonoe, Phormion son of Ktesiphon of Peiraieus, Kephisodotos of Boiotia, Heliodoros of Pithos testify that they were present when Androkles loaned three thousand silver drachmas to Apollodoros and Artemon, and that they know that they lodged the contract with Archenomides of Anagyros.

[15] This, judges, was the contract under which I loaned the money to my opponent's brother Artemon. Lakritos here encouraged me and undertook that I would have all that was my due under the contract on which I made the loan; he drafted it himself and joined in sealing it when it was written. For his brothers were rather young still, virtually boys, while this man, Lakritos of Phaselis, was something big, a pupil of Isokrates. [16] He was the organizer of the whole thing, and he told me to deal exclusively with him. He said that he would do all that was right by me and would remain in Athens while his brother Artemon would sail with the goods. At that point, judges, when he wanted to receive the money from us, he said he was both brother and partner of Artemon, and he spoke with remarkable persuasiveness. [17] But as soon as they got hold of the money, they divided it up and used it as they chose, but as for the contract under which they had received the money, they obeyed none of its conditions, great or small, as the result showed. And this Lakritos was the leading figure in the whole business. With each clause written in the contract I shall demonstrate in detail that they have done nothing that was right.

[18] To begin with, the contract states that they borrowed the thirty mnai from us on security of three thousand jars of wine, maintaining that they had security for another thirty mnai so that the total value of the wine was about a talent, including the payments they had to make for the shipment of the wine; these three thousand jars were to be shipped to the Black Sea on the twenty-oared vessel captained by Hyblesios. [19] This is what is written in the contract which you have heard, judges. But instead of three thousand jars these men loaded not even five hundred jars on the boat, and instead of having bought the amount of wine they should they used the money as they chose with no intention or inclination to load the three thousand jars on the boat as in the contract. To prove the truth of this statement, take the deposition of the passengers who sailed on the same boat with them.

Deposition

[20] *Erasikles testifies that he was steersman on the ship captained by Hyblesios, and that he knows that Apollodoros carried on the*

boat four hundred and fifty jars of Mendaian wine, no more, and that Apollodoros carried no other freight on the boat to the Black Sea.

Hippias son of Anthippos of Halikarnassos testifies that he sailed on Hyblesios' boat as overseer and that he knows that Apollodoros the Phaselite carried four hundred and fifty jars of wine from Mende to the Black Sea but no other freight.

They gave their absentee testimony to the following people: Archiades son of Mnesonides of Archarnai, Sostratos son of Philip of Histiaia, Eumarichos son of Euboios of Histiaia, Philtades son of Ktesias of Xypete, Dionysios son of Demokratides of Cholleidai.

[21] So in the matter of the quantity of wine they were obliged to load on the boat this was their conduct; they began with the first clause to default and fail to carry out the written agreements.

Next in the contract is a statement that they offer these goods as security unencumbered, owing nothing to anyone, and that they will take out no additional loan on them from anyone. This is explicitly stated in writing, judges. [22] But what did these men do? Ignoring what was written in the contract they borrowed money from some stripling, whom they tricked by claiming that they owed no debt to anyone. They both cheated us and secretly borrowed on our property and they tricked that young man who loaned the money by pretending that the goods on which they were borrowing were unencumbered. That's the sort of villainy they practise. And all this is the clever ruse of this Lakritos. To prove that I am speaking the truth and that they borrowed additional money in breach of the contract, he will read out to you the deposition of the very man who made the loan. [23] Read the deposition.

Deposition

Aratos of Halikarnassos testifies that he loaned eleven silver mnai to Apollodoros on the security of the merchandise which he was carrying to the Black Sea on the ship of Hyblesios and the replacement goods purchased there for the return, and that he did not know that Apollodoros had borrowed money from Androkles; otherwise he would not have loaned the money to Apollodoros.

[24] Such are the devious tricks of these people.

The next thing written in the contract, judges, is that when they have sold the cargo in the Black Sea they are to purchase replacement goods in turn, load them as return cargo and export the return cargo to Athens, and that on their return to Athens they are to 'repay the money' to us within twenty days in good coin. And until they pay, we are to control the goods and they are to provide them intact until we receive the money. [25] This is written in these precise terms in the contract. But it is precisely here that these people especially showed their arrogance and lack of shame and the fact that they had not the slightest regard for the written terms of the contract but thought that the contract was mere rubbish and nonsense. For they neither bought any replacement goods in the Black Sea nor loaded a return cargo and brought it to Athens. And we, the ones who lent the money, had nothing to seize and nothing to control while waiting to get back our own money. For these men brought nothing into your harbour. [26] Instead we have been treated in a manner without precedent, judges. In our own city, though we have done no wrong nor lost any lawsuit to these men, we have had our own property seized by these people who are Phaselites, as though Phaselites had been granted legal right of seizure against Athenians. For when they refuse to pay back what they received, what other term could one use of such conduct than that they are taking other people's property by force? Personally I have never yet heard of a more vile action than what they have done to us, and all this while admitting that they received the money from us. [27] All matters relating to an agreement which are subject to dispute require a judgment, judges; but matters which are admitted by both contracting parties and which are dealt with in maritime contracts are regarded by everyone as final and it is proper to carry out what is written. That they have in no way whatsoever acted according to the contract, but immediately – right from the very start – they connived and plotted to act quite dishonestly is unambiguously proved both by the depositions and by themselves.

[28] You must now hear the most wicked action of Lakritos here – for he was the manager of all this. When they arrived here, they did not sail into your trading zone but moored in the Thieves' Harbour which lies outside the markers of your trading zone. Mooring in the Thieves' Harbour is the same as if someone were to moor at Aigina or Megara, for it's possible to set sail from this harbour anywhere one wishes whenever one chooses. [29] And the boat was at anchor there for over twenty-five days, while they wandered

around your display-market, and we approached and spoke to them, demanding that they take steps to ensure we received our money as soon as possible. They agreed and said that this was just what they were trying to manage. And at the same time as we approached them we kept watch to see if they were unloading anything from any part of the boat or paying the 2 per cent duty.

[30] When they had been in town for many days and we could not discover that anything had been unloaded or any duty paid in their name, at that point we began to demand payment more urgently. As we made ourselves a nuisance to them, Lakritos here, the brother of Artemon, replied that they were unable to pay and all their goods had been lost. Lakritos stated that he could make a good case on this issue. [31] As for ourselves, judges, we expressed our anger at what he said, but our anger achieved nothing; these people were not bothered at all. Nonetheless, we asked them in what way the goods had been lost. Lakritos here said that the boat had been wrecked sailing along the coast from Pantikapaion to Theodosia and that with the boat wrecked his brothers had lost their goods, which happened to be on the boat. On board were salt fish, wine from Kos and various other things, and all these they said were replacement cargo which they were meaning to transport to Athens, if they had not been lost on the boat. [32] This is what he said. But it is important to hear the vileness and duplicity of these people. They had no contract in relation to the boat which was lost. It was someone else who had loaned money on the cargo from Athens to the Black Sea and the boat itself (the lender's name was Antipatros and he was a native of Kition). The Koan wine (eighty jars of soured wine) and the salt fish were being carried along the coast on the boat from Pantikapaion to Theodosia for some farmer for the use of his farm labourers. Why do they make these excuses? It is not right.

[33] Please take the deposition, firstly that of Apollonides, to show that it was Antipatros who lent the money on the boat and that the shipwreck has no relevance to my opponents, and then that of Erasikles and that of Hippias to show that only eighty jars of wine were being carried on the boat.

Depositions

Apollonides of Halikarnassos testifies that he knows that Antipatros, a native of Kition, loaned money to Hyblesios for a voyage to the Black Sea on the boat captained by Hyblesios and the cargo going to the Black Sea; that he himself was joint owner of the boat with Hyblesios and that his own slaves were sailing on the ship and when the ship was wrecked his slaves came to him and informed him that the ship was sailing empty from Pantikapaion to Theodosia when it was wrecked.

[34] *Erasikles testifies that he was sailing with Hyblesios to the Black Sea as steersman of the ship, and that when the ship was sailing along the coast to Theodosia from Pantikapaion he knows that it was sailing empty, and that there was no wine on the boat belonging to Apollodoros, the defendant in the present suit himself, but about eighty jars of Koan wine were being transported for one of the people of Theodosia.*

Hippias son of Anthippos of Halikarnassos testifies that he was sailing with Hyblesios supervising the ship's cargo, and when the ship was sailing along the coast to Theodosia from Pantikapaion Apollodoros had a container or two of wool loaded on the ship and eleven or twelve jars of wine and some goat skins, two or three bundles, and nothing else.

They gave their absentee testimony to the following people: Euphiletos son of Damotimos of Aphidnai, Hippias son of Timoxenos of Thymaitidai, Sostratos son of Philippos of Histiaia, Archenomides son of Straton of Thria, and Philtades son of Ktesias of Xypete.

[35] Such is the effrontery of these people. As for you, judges, consider in your own minds if you have ever known or heard of people bringing wine to Athens from the Black Sea as merchandise, especially Koan. Quite the opposite, wine is imported to the Black Sea from our area, from Peparethos, Kos, Thasos and Mende and all sorts of other places. The goods imported here from the Black Sea are different.

[36] When they were pressed by us and questioned whether any of the goods had been saved in the Black Sea, Lakritos here replied that a hundred Kyzikene staters remained, and his brother had loaned this gold in the Black Sea to a certain sailor from Phaselis, a fellow-citizen and acquaintance of his own, and was unable to recover it but had more or less lost this as well. [37] This is what this Lakritos said. But the contract does not say this, judges; it instructs them to load a replacement in the Black Sea without our agreement but to provide it intact in Athens for us until we receive back in full the money we lent. Please read out the contract again.

Contract

[38] Does the contract instruct them, judges, to lend our property, and furthermore to a person we do not know and have never seen before, or to load a replacement cargo, transport it to Athens and display it to us intact? [39] For the contract allows nothing to have greater authority than what is written therein nor to bring to bear either law or decree or anything else at all against the contract. But these people right from the start were not concerned about this contract; no, they used our money as though it were their own private property. That's the kind of wicked sophists and unjust sort they are. [40] Personally, by the lord Zeus and all the gods, I have never had a grudge against any man or criticized him, judges, if someone chooses to be a sophist and pay money to Isokrates – I should be mad if I concerned myself in any way with these things. Still, I don't think – by Zeus! – that persons who despise the laws and think they're clever should covet the property of others or try to take it away from them, relying on their skill in speaking. That's the practice of a devious and detestable sophist. [41] Lakritos here, judges, in coming to court in this suit is not relying on the justice of his case, but in full knowledge of their conduct in relation to this loan, and because he thinks he is smart and will easily furnish arguments for an unjust cause, he expects to lead you astray in any direction he chooses. This is what he claims to be clever at, and he demands payment and collects pupils, professing to teach just these skills. [42] To begin with he gave his brothers this training, which you are aware is wicked and dishonest, judges, how to borrow money on maritime loans in the trading zone and rob people of it and avoid payment. Could any human beings be more wicked than the man who teaches such skills and the people taught by him? But anyway, since he is smart and is confident of his speaking skill and the thousand drachmas he paid to his teacher, [43] tell him to demonstrate to you either that they did not receive the money from us or that after receiving it they paid it back, or that maritime contracts should not be binding, or that the money should be used for some purpose other than on the terms on which they received it under the contract. Let him convince you of any of these things he wishes; and I too for my own part admit that he is supremely clever, if he can convince you, the people who judge cases for mercantile contracts. But I am fully aware that he could not demonstrate or convince you of any of this.

[44] Apart from all this, in heaven's name, judges, if the opposite had happened, and instead of his dead brother owing money to me I owed his brother a talent or eighty mnai, or thereabouts, surely you don't think, judges, that Lakritos here would be using the same arguments which he has now used to excess or would be claiming that he is not the heir or is relinquishing his brother's estate? Don't you think he would be demanding payment from me in a very nasty way, just as he has exacted payment from everyone else who owed the dead man either in the territory of Phaselis or anywhere else? [45] And if any of us when sued by him had dared to enter a plea barring suit alleging that the case was not admissible, I know full well that he himself would be indignant and would complain against us, claiming that he was being monstrously abused in defiance of the law if anyone were to vote that the case was not admissible, when it is a mercantile suit.

So, Lakritos, if you think this right for you, why should it not be right for me? Aren't the same laws written down for all of us? Don't we all have the same rights in mercantile cases? [46] But he's such a vile sort, surpassing all mankind in wickedness of character, that he is trying to persuade you to vote that this mercantile suit is not admissible, when you are now judging the mercantile cases. What is it you're demanding, Lakritos? That it shouldn't suffice that we're robbed of the money we lent you but in addition we must be handed over to the prison for owing the penalty fee, if we should fail to pay it? [47] Wouldn't it be outrageous and monstrous and a disgrace to you, judges, if people who have made maritime loans in your trading zone and are cheated should be hauled off to prison by the ones who borrowed the money and are cheating them?

This, Lakritos, is what you are trying to persuade these people to approve. But where should one get satisfaction, judges, in relation to mercantile agreements? Before which official, at what period? [48] Before the Eleven? But they admit prosecutions of burglars, thieves and other felons facing death. Before the Archon? The Archon is charged with taking care of heiresses, orphans and parents. Oh, but the King-archon. But we're not gymnasiarchs and we're not indicting anyone for impiety. Well, the Polemarchos will preside. Oh yes, for abandoning a patron or not having a patron. So all that remains is the generals. But they appoint the trierarchs; they never admit a mercantile case into court. [49] *I* am a merchant, and you are brother and heir to a merchant, the one who received a mercantile loan from me. Where then should this suit come to court?

Instruct me, Lakritos, but just say something that's fair and accords with the laws. But there is no man so clever that he could say something fair in support of a case such as this.

[50] This is not my only outrageous treatment from this fellow Lakritos, judges; apart from being deprived of my money I might have found myself in the most extreme danger as far as he was concerned, had not the contract protected me against them and testified that I gave the money for a voyage to the Black Sea and back to Athens. For you know, judges, how severe the law is, if any Athenian transports grain to any place but Athens or lends money for a shipment to any trading centre but Athens, and how grave and severe the penalties are for these acts. [51] Better still, read the law to them so that they may have a clearer understanding.

Law

No Athenian or metic residing in Athens, nor anybody under their authority, is to be allowed to grant money for a ship which does not intend to transport grain to Athens (and so on and so forth). If anyone grants money in contravention of this law, denunciation and a written schedule of the money may be made before the overseers of the port in the same manner as has been described for the ship and the grain. And the owner is to have no right of suit for such money as he lends for a voyage anywhere but Athens, and no official is to admit a suit on the matter to court.

[52] This is how severe the law is, judges. But these people, the vilest men in the world, though it is written explicitly in the contract that the goods must return to Athens, allowed what they borrowed from us in Athens to be shipped to Chios. For when the Phaselite captain was borrowing a further sum from some Chian and the Chian said he would not lend unless he received as security all the goods which were with the captain and the existing lenders agreed, they allowed these goods, our property, to become security for the Chian and the Chian to gain control of everything, [53] and so they sailed out of the Black Sea with the Phaselite captain and the Chian lender and anchored in the Thieves' Harbour, not in your trading zone. And now, judges, money loaned from Athens for a voyage to the Black Sea and back from the Black Sea to Athens has been taken to Chios by these men. [54] This is what I supposed at the beginning of my speech, that you too are the victims no less

than we who gave the money. Think about it, judges: surely you're the victims, when someone tries to set himself above your laws and invalidates maritime contracts and destroys them and has diverted the money from us to Chios – surely a man like this wrongs you as well?

[55] My argument, judges, is now with these men (these are the ones I gave the money to); their argument will be with that Phaselite captain, their fellow-countryman, to whom they say they lent the money without our agreement in breach of the contract. Not even we know their dealings with their countryman, though they themselves do. [56] But this is what we think is right, judges, and this is our request, that you aid us, the victims of wrong, and punish those who connive and play sophistic tricks as these people do. And if you do this, you will both have cast a vote in your own interest and you will strip unscrupulous people of the cunning tricks which some people contrive in relation to maritime agreements.

Androkles alleges that the borrowers breached the contract in several respects. They loaded less wine than contracted on the outward voyage and obtained additional loans on property already secured to Androkles and Nausikrates. They failed to load a return cargo of the right quantity. And on their return they refused to pay the sum owed on the ground that the ship had been wrecked. They claimed that money or goods to the value of one hundred Kyzikene staters had survived the wreck, but this had been given as security for a loan raised by the Phaselite captain of a second ship which brought them to Athens. These allegations are supported by some (if limited) witness testimony, though how far the borrowers were culpable is not clear, since we are given no clear idea of the response the borrowers might have made on these points. For much of the speech Androkles sets the actions of the borrowers against their contractual obligations rather than seeking to demonstrate their guilt in detail. He also tries to excite hostility on the basis of slurs against Phaselites and uses the stereotype of the sophist, the professional rhetorician, against Lakritos, who was evidently a pupil of Isokrates.

It is difficult to reconstruct the case for Lakritos' *paragraphe* from this speech. Presumably one argument he will have used is that he was unconnected with the loan. Androkles presents him as the arch-mover in the whole business, but no serious attempt is made to prove (as distinct from asserting) this point, and the contract and depositions make clear that it was his brothers who were involved in the transaction, not Lakritos himself. Androkles has a written contract, as the law for maritime suits requires, but it is difficult to connect it to Lakritos. The issue is however affected by the question of Lakritos' relationship to his dead brother. The speaker insists that Lakritos is his dead brother's sole heir. As such he would be entitled to the whole estate and would be liable to his brother's debts. For his part Lakritos insists that he has declined the inheritance. The speaker provides no evidence to support his position on this crucial point. It may be discomfort on this point that makes him try to tie Lakritos directly to the transaction rather than indirectly through the inheritance.

The reader is puzzled by the silence about the third brother, Apollodoros. Androkles says very little about him, and indeed does not always make clear that he is in fact brother to Lakritos and Artemon. There is no reason to doubt that Apollodoros was also Artemon's heir, and unlike Lakritos was party to the contract and its breach (if Androkles is telling the truth). It has been suggested that Androkles has already sued Apollodoros unsuccessfully and is now seeking to obtain from Lakritos the money he feels is due. Equally, it could be that Apollodoros has returned to Phaselis or is otherwise beyond reach; the speaker may be suing Lakritos because he is an available target.

There is a good study of the speech in Italian: U. Albini and S. Aprosio, *Il porto dei ladri* (Venice 1987).

CASE XIV: DEMOSTHENES 37 – AGAINST PANTAINETOS

The veins of silver in Attica were owned by the state, which leased the right to extract the ore according to a system of competitive bidding. The present case is concerned not directly with mining operations but with a plant for the processing of the ore. Pantainetos had borrowed money from the speaker Nikoboulos and his partner Euergos on the security of the factory. The loan was for 105 mnai (1 talent and 45 mnai). The total value of the property was 206 mnai (3 talents and 26 mnai), and it is to be presumed that the difference between loan and total value represented Pantainetos' own stake in the factory (although this is never made clear, since it suits the speaker to present Pantainetos as a man who exploits other people's money rather than risking his own). What makes the speech confusing at first sight is the nature of the loan, which took the form of *prasis epi lysei*, 'sale with the right of/on condition of redemption'. Under this procedure a property is 'sold' to a 'purchaser' but the 'vendor' retains the right to own the property outright on payment of the sum advanced by the 'purchaser'. Until this point the 'vendor' pays interest at an agreed rate (in the present case 12 per cent per annum, §5, a common rate in loans secured by realty) on the capital sum advanced. The property stands as security and is liable to seizure and sale if the conditions of the agreement, including interest payments, are not met. What we have is in fact a loan, but the constant use of language of sale (which is used in this speech both of the loans and of outright sale and purchase) makes the case at first sight impenetrable to the modern reader. The case is further complicated by the fact that there was a series of such transactions; Pantainetos had originally bought the plant with the help of a loan of 105 mnai from three earlier creditors (§§4–5), and Nikoboulos and Euergos had taken over this debt on payment to this group of the sum owed to them by Pantainetos.

According to Nikoboulos, during his absence on a trading voyage his partner Euergos had trouble with Pantainetos, resulting in the seizure of the plant by Euergos. Pantainetos successfully sued Euergos and obtained damages of two talents. He has now after an interval brought an action against Nikoboulos using the streamlined procedures allowed for mining suits (*dikai metallikai*). This speech however was not delivered in the main action brought by Pantainetos but, like Dem. 35, in a *paragraphe* hearing. Nikoboulos has brought a *paragraphe* alleging that the suit could not be admitted to court. The hearing may be dated to the mid-340s, since the original loan had been made in the Athenian month of Elaphebolion (March–April) of the archon year of Theophilos (§6); that is, 348/7.

There is a commentary on this speech based on the Greek text in C. Carey and R.A. Reid, *Demosthenes: Selected Private Speeches* (repr. Cambridge 1992).

[1] The laws, judges, have granted the right to enter a plea barring suit in cases where a man brings an action after giving release and discharge. Since both of these obtain between myself and Pantainetos here, I have entered a barring plea, as you have just heard, to the effect that the suit is not admissible. I felt I should not be released from my right to this, nor, once I prove on top of everything else that he has granted release and I have been discharged, that he

should be able to argue that I am not telling the truth and offer as evidence the claim that if anything of the sort had occurred I would have brought a plea in bar of action against him, but that I should come to court with this plea and demonstrate to you both that I have done this man no wrong and that his prosecution of me is illegal. [2] If Pantainetos had suffered any of the wrongs of which he is now complaining, he would clearly have brought a suit at once during the period when our business dealings took place, since these suits are monthly and we were both in town, and when all mankind are in the habit of showing their indignation right at the moment of their wrongs rather than after a delay. Since he has suffered no wrong – as you too will (I'm sure) affirm when you hear what happened – but is plaguing me from the confidence aroused by his success in the suit against Euergos, the only course left for me is to prove in your court, judges, that I am not in any way guilty and provide witness for my statements in an attempt to save myself.

[3] My request to all of you will be modest and fair: to hear me with goodwill on the issue of my barring plea and to pay attention to the whole of my case. For though many suits have taken place in the city, I think it will be found that no-one has brought a suit more shameless or more unscrupulous than the one he has dared to lodge and bring to court. I shall give you as brief an account as I am able of all our dealings from the beginning.

[4] Euergos and I loaned one hundred and five mnai to Pantainetos here, judges, on the security of a processing plant among the mine workings at Maroneia and thirty slaves. Forty-five mnai of the loan were mine, while one talent belonged to Euergos. As it happened, Pantainetos owed a talent to Mnesikles of Kollytos and forty-five mnai to Phileas of Eleusis and Pleistor. [5] The individual who sold the processing plant and the slaves to us was Mnesikles (he was the one who had bought the property for Pantainetos from Telemachos, its former owner), and Pantainetos leased it from us for the interest accruing on the money, one hundred and five drachmas per month. We made a contract in which were written the terms of the lease and a right for Pantainetos to redeem the property from us within a stated time.

[6] Once this had been completed in the month of Elaphebolion in the archonship of Theophilos, I sailed off to the Black Sea, while this man and Euergos were here. As to their dealings with each other while I was away, I could not say. For their versions do not agree with each other, nor does Pantainetos' version always agree

with itself. Sometimes he says he was evicted by Euergos by force in breach of the lease agreement, at other times that Euergos is responsible for his being listed as a debtor to the Treasury, at others anything else he chooses. [7] Euergos says simply that as he was not receiving the interest payments nor was Pantainetos carrying out any of the other conditions in the agreement he went and took over his own property from Pantainetos with his consent and retained possession of it; Pantainetos then went off and returned bringing with him people to lay claim to the property, and Euergos did not give way to them but did not prevent Pantainetos from possessing the property he had leased, provided that he carried out the agreement. Such are the accounts I hear from them. [8] But this I do know, that if this man is speaking the truth and has been badly treated by Euergos, he has received satisfaction at a level assessed by himself; for he came to your court and secured judgment against Euergos, and it's not fair to get recompense for the same acts both from the perpetrator and from me, when I was not even in town. But if Euergos is telling the truth, then he has been made the victim of malicious prosecution, while I for my part still could not reasonably be sued for the same events. To prove first of all that I am telling the truth in this, I shall provide you with witnesses to these facts.

Witnesses

[9] You hear from the witnesses, judges, that the vendor to us of the property was the man who had bought them originally, that Pantainetos leased the processing plant which was ours and the slaves, that I was not even present at the subsequent dealings between him and Euergos nor in town at all, and that he brought an action against Euergos and never once made complaint against me. [10] So then, when I arrived, having lost virtually everything I had when I sailed out, after hearing and actually finding that Pantainetos had relinquished the property and Euergos was in possession and controlling the property we had purchased, I was profoundly distressed. I saw that the affair had come to a strange pass: either I must share the processing operations and oversight with Euergos or I must have Euergos as my debtor instead of Pantainetos and draw up a new lease and make a contract with him, neither of which was preferable. [11] I was feeling vexed by the events I speak of, and on seeing Mnesikles, the man who had acted as vendor of the property

to us, I complained to him, telling him what sort of a person he had introduced to me, and I asked about the claimants and what it meant. On hearing this he laughed at the claimants; he said that they wanted to meet us, and he would personally bring us together, and would urge Pantainetos to do all that was right by us; he said he thought he would convince him.

[12] When we met – why tell all the details? The people who claimed to have loaned money to him on the processing plant and the slaves which we had bought from Mnesikles came along, and there was nothing straightforward or honest about them. As all their statements were exposed as lies, and Mnesikles confirmed our claim, they issued a challenge to us on the assumption that we would not accept, challenging us either to receive from them all the money owed to us and withdraw or to pay them for their claims, and complaining that we were holding property worth far more than the money we had loaned. [13] On hearing this I immediately without even considering the matter agreed to receive our money and persuaded Euergos. But when it was time to get back our money and this was where the affair had got to, the people who had made this offer then said that they would not give it unless we acted as vendors of the property to them; and on this very point they showed their good sense, judges; for they saw the way we were being pestered by this man. To prove that in this too I am telling the truth, please take these depositions also.

Depositions

[14] So when the affair had reached this point and the people he had brought were refusing to surrender the money, while we appeared to be rightfully in possession of what we had bought, he begged, he urged, he pleaded for us to act as vendors. He pressed and urged repeatedly – what didn't he do? So I acceded to this too. [15] But I saw that he was a bad character, men of Athens, and that at the start he made accusations to us about Mnesikles, that he clashed in turn with the man he was on friendliest terms with, Euergos, that initially when I sailed in he claimed he was pleased to see me but when it was time to do what was right he became disagreeable in turn with me, and that he was friendly with everyone until he had secured an advantage and got what he wanted but then became an enemy and quarrelled with them. [16] So I thought it best to be reconciled and act as vendor on his behalf, and reach a

settlement with him on the basis of a release and discharge from his claims. When we had reached this agreement he released me from all claims and I became vendor of the property, as he was urging me, in the same way as I bought it from Mnesikles. Having got back my property, and being innocent of any wrong against him, I never thought, whatever might happen, that he would ever bring a suit against me.

[17] These are the events on which you will cast your vote, judges, and on account of which I have entered a plea that the suit with which I am being pestered is not admissible. I shall provide witnesses who were present when I received release and discharge from Pantainetos, and I shall then prove that the suit is not admissible under the laws. Please read this deposition.

Deposition

Please read out also the deposition from the buyers, to inform you that I sold the property on his instructions to the people he requested.

Deposition

[18] Not only do I have these witnesses that I was released and am now being prosecuted maliciously but also Pantainetos himself. For when, while bringing his action against Euergos, he ignored me he testified that he had no claim outstanding against me. For if the same wrongs existed and he was making the same charge against both, he would surely not have ignored one and sued the other. But I think that you recognize without even a word from me that the laws do not allow someone to bring a fresh action in situations such as this. Still, read out to them this law as well.

Law

[19] You hear the law saying outright, judges, that on matters where a man gives release and discharge no further actions may be brought. And indeed you have heard the depositions to the effect that both have occurred between this man and us. It is not proper to sue in any circumstance forbidden in the laws, but especially these. For when the state has sold something, one could argue that it had unfairly sold what it should not. [20] And in cases where the court

has given judgment, it can be said that it was misled into doing this. And for each and every other circumstance in the law, an argument could reasonably be made. But in a case where the man has himself been convinced and has given a release, it is of course impossible to argue or to accuse himself of having acted unjustly. People who sue in defiance of any of these other clauses are failing to abide by what others have decided is just, but a man who gives release and then brings a fresh action is failing to abide by his own decisions. So they particularly deserve your anger.

[21] So then, I have proved that he released me from all claims when I acted as vendor of the slaves; and you have heard the law read out just now to prove that the laws do not allow legal actions in such cases. But to prevent anyone from thinking, judges, that I have recourse to this plea because I have the worst of it on the justice of my case, I want to prove that he is lying on each detail of his complaint. [22] Read the actual complaint which he is bringing against me.

Complaint

Nikoboulos caused me damage by plotting against me and my property. He ordered Antigenes his slave to take from my slave the silver which he was taking as an instalment to the city on the mine which I had bought for ninety mnai, and he was responsible for my being entered as debtor to the Treasury for double the sum.

[23] Stop there. All these charges which he has now brought against me are actions of which he accused Euergos when he won his suit against him. Testimony has been given at the beginning of my speech to you that I was abroad when the disputes between these two were taking place; indeed, this is clear also from this complaint. For he has nowhere written that I have done any of these things, but he has written vaguely that I plotted against him and his property and says that I instructed my slave to do this, falsely. How could I have given instructions, since when I was setting sail I had of course no knowledge whatsoever of what was to happen here? [24] Then again, what complete folly, when alleging that I plotted to disfranchise him and inflict the worst damage, to have written that I instructed a slave to do things which not even one citizen could do to another. What's the point of this? In my view, since he is unable to attribute any of these acts to me because of my absence abroad

but still wants to persecute me, he has written in the complaint that I gave instructions. For he would have no argument, if he had not done so. [25] Read what follows.

Complaint

And when I became a debtor to the Treasury, he installed his slave Antigenes in my processing plant at Thrasymos in control of my property, though I forbade it.

Stop. In all this again he will be shown by the facts themselves to be lying. He has written that I installed and he forbade. But this could not be done by a man who was not there. For I did not install my slave, being as I was in the Black Sea, nor did he forbid a man who was not there. [26] How could it be? Why did he find it necessary to write this? I think that at that point Euergos, while he was making the errors for which he has been punished, as an associate and acquaintance of mine took the slave from my house and installed him in his own property to guard it. Now if he had written the truth, it would have been ridiculous. For if Euergos installed him there, what wrong do I do you? In trying to evade this problem he has been forced to write something like this, so that his complaint could be against me. Read what comes next.

Complaint

And then he persuaded my slaves to sit down in the grinding shop to cause me damage.

[27] Now this is completely shameless. It's clear that this is a lie not only from the fact that I challenged him to hand them over and he refused but from every other circumstance. What purpose could I have in persuading them? Oh yes, to get possession of them. But when the choice was offered of owning them or getting back my money, I chose to get my money back, and this has been stated by witnesses. Read out the challenge nonetheless.

Challenge

[28] Now after refusing this challenge and evading it, observe the very next complaint he makes. Read what follows.

Complaint

And he worked the silver ore which my slaves had mined and kept the silver from this ore.

Again, how could I have done these things when I wasn't there and you have successfully sued Euergos for them? [29] Read the next bit to them.

Complaint

And he sold my processing plant and slaves in breach of the agreement which he had made with me.

Stop there. This charge surpasses all the rest by far. First of all he says 'in breach of the agreement which he made with me'. What agreement is this? We leased our property, nothing else, to him for the interest accruing. Mnesikles had acted as vendor to us in his presence and at his urging. [30] Subsequently, in the same way, we sold it to others on the same terms on which we had bought it, with this man not only urging but actually begging us. For nobody was willing to accept him as vendor. So what has the lease agreement to do with it? Why did you include this count, you most vile individual? To show that we sold the property in turn at your urging and on the terms on which we had bought it, read out the deposition.

Deposition

[31] You too attest this. Property which we had sold for one hundred and five mnai you later sold for three talents two thousand six hundred drachmas. Yet who at all would have given a single drachma with you as vendor? And indeed to prove that I am telling the truth in this, please call the witnesses to these facts.

Witnesses

[32] Though he has the price he was persuaded to accept for his property, and though he begged me to act as vendor for the amount I had contributed, this very man is suing for an extra two talents. And the rest of his charges are even worse. Please read out the rest of the complaint.

Complaint

[33] At this point he lumps together many awful charges against me: battery and outrage and violence and wrongs against heiresses. The suits for each of these are distinct and do not go before the same official or involve the same penalties. Battery and violence go before the Forty, actions for outrage before the Thesmothetai, offences against heiresses before the Archon. And the laws also allow one to lodge pleas in bar of action in matters for which there are no magistrates to introduce. Read this law to them.

Law

[34] Though I had entered in addition to the rest of my barring plea the following count, 'and although the Thesmothetai are not the introducing magistrates for the charges laid by Pantainetos', it has been erased and does not form part of my plea. How this came about is for you to consider. For myself, as long as I can display the actual law, it makes no difference at all; for he won't succeed in erasing your power to recognize and understand what is right.

[35] Take the mining law too. With this too I think I shall prove that the suit is not admissible and that I deserve gratitude rather than being prosecuted maliciously. Read it.

Law

This law states clearly the actions for which mining suits should be brought. Now if someone ejects another from his workings, the law makes him subject to legal action. But so far from ejecting him, I gave him control over and restored to him property which someone else was trying to take from him, and I acted as vendor at his earnest entreaty. [36] Yes, he says, but if anyone commits any other wrongful act in relation to the mines, legal actions are available for these too. Quite right, Pantainetos; but what acts are these? If someone causes smoke, if he makes an armed attack, if he extends his digging within another's limits. These are the other acts, and none of them assuredly has been committed by me against you, unless you count as making an armed attack those who took back what they had loaned to you. And if you think this, you may bring mining suits against everyone who lends out their money to you. But that's not fair. [37] Come now, is anyone who buys a mining concession from the state to ignore the common laws, under which all ought both to give and obtain satisfaction, and take action under mining suits if he borrows money from someone? What if he is slandered? If he is struck? If he brings a charge of theft? If he fails to recover his advance payment of the property levy? If he has any other complaint? [38] Personally I don't think so. I think that the mining suits are for people who are partners in a mine and people who bore into their neighbours' workings and in general people who are working in the mines and commit one of the acts in the law, but that the man who lends to Pantainetos and has got it back from him with difficulty and by persistence should not have to face a mining suit on top. No, not a bit of it.

[39] So the fact that I have done Pantainetos no wrong and that the suit is not admissible under the laws can easily be recognized if one considers these points. So since he had no fair argument to make on any single one of his complaints but had written false charges into the complaint and was bringing suit on issues where he had given release, last month, judges, when I was about to bring the suit to court and the courts had already been allotted, he came to me surrounded by his associates, his company of conspirators, and did something outrageous. [40] He read out to me a long challenge in which he demanded that a slave who he claims knows the facts in question should be put to the test, and if his claim is true I should pay his damages without judicial assessment, while if it proved false the torturer Mnesikles would assess the value of the slave. Once he had got guarantors to this agreement from me and I had sealed the challenge – not because I thought it right [41] (for how is it right that it should depend on a slave's body and life whether I stand condemned to pay two talents or the man who brings malicious suits should face no loss), but I agreed because I wanted to win through the greater justice of my conduct. After this he brought the suit against me afresh as soon as he had recovered his court-deposit (so instantaneously did it become clear that he would not abide by conditions established by himself). [42] And when we came before the torturer, instead of opening the challenge, showing the text and acting as seemed right according to its provisions (because of the confusion at the time and the fact that the case was about to be called it was something like this: 'I issue this challenge to you.' 'I accept.' 'Let's have your ring.' 'Take it.' 'Who is the guarantor?' 'This man.' I made no copy or anything else of the sort), instead of acting as I describe he came with another challenge, in which he

demanded that he torture the slave himself, and he seized him and maltreated him – there was no end to his unbridled violence. [43] And I reflected, judges, what a great advantage it is to have a life based on pretence. For I considered that I was being treated in this way because I was despised for living a simple and natural life and in enduring this treatment I was being severely punished.

To prove that I was compelled to issue a counter-challenge, against what I considered proper, and offered to hand over the slave, and that I am telling the truth in this, read out the challenge.

Challenge

[44] Since he evaded this and evaded the challenge which he initially issued, I wonder personally what on earth he will say to you. But so you will know from whom he claims to have experienced this dreadful treatment, take a look. This is the one who ejected Pantainetos, this is the one stronger than Pantainetos' friends and the laws. *I* was not in town, and even Pantainetos does not claim I was.

[45] I want also to tell you how he deceived the judges last time and secured judgment against Euergos, so you will know that this time too he will leave no unscrupulous trick or falsehood untried. Furthermore, you will find that the same lines of defence are available on the charges he is bringing against me; and this is the surest proof that Euergos then was also the victim of malicious prosecution. So he accused Euergos on top of all his other charges of having gone to Pantainetos' house in the country and gone into the presence of the heiresses and his mother, and he brought with him into court the laws concerning heiresses. [46] Even to this day he has never yet had this issue examined before the Archon, who is ordered by the laws to take care of such matters, and in whose court the wrongdoer faces the risk of being punished or fined while the prosecutor can intervene without penalty, nor has he indicted either me or Euergos as guilty of offences; he made the charges at the court hearing and won a suit for two talents. [47] For it would have been easy for Euergos, had he known in advance, according to the laws, the accusation on which he was being tried, to win acquittal by proving what was true and right; but in a mining suit, on charges which he would never have expected to be made against him, it was difficult on the spot to find a way of dispelling the slander. And the anger of the judges tricked by this man found Euergos guilty on the

charge which they were judging. [48] Yet do you think that the man who tricked those judges will shrink from tricking you? Or that he comes to court with confidence based on the facts of his case rather than on arguments and the witnesses who had conspired with him, the unclean and vile Prokles and Stratokles the most plausible and unscrupulous man in the world, and on his intention to weep and wail without reservation or shame. [49] Yet so far are you from deserving any pity that of all mankind you would most properly be hated for the practices in which you have engaged. You owed a hundred and five mnai and were unable to repay your creditors, but as for the individuals who supplied this money and ensured that you did right by the original lenders, apart from the wrongs you did them in relation to the contract, you are trying to disfranchise them as well. And other borrowers can be seen having to give up their property, but in your case it is the lender who has had this happen to him, and for lending a talent he has had to pay out two after being prosecuted on a trumped-up charge. [50] And I, after lending forty mnai, am being sued in this action for two talents. And on property on which you could never raise more than a hundred mnai in loans, and which you have sold outright for three talents two thousand drachmas, you have, it seems, been wronged to the sum of four talents. And by whom? Oh yes, by my slave. What citizen would yield his property to a slave? Or who would admit that my slave should also be held accountable for acts for which he has successfully prosecuted Euergos? [51] Apart from this, Pantainetos has himself released him from all such accusations. For what he should have done was not make these claims now nor write them into the challenge in which he demanded to put him to the test, but to institute proceedings against him and prosecute myself, the owner. In fact, he has instituted proceedings against me and is making accusations against him. But the laws don't allow this. Who has ever initiated proceedings against the master and charged the slave with the acts as though he were the owner?

[52] When anyone asks him: 'And what rightful claim will you be able to make against Nikoboulos?' he says: 'The Athenians hate moneylenders. Nikoboulos is unpopular, and he walks fast, talks loud and carries a stick. All this', he says, 'is on my side.' And he is not ashamed to say this, nor does he think that his hearers realize that this is the reasoning of the shyster, not the victim of injustice. [53] Personally I do not think that any of the people who lend money are doing wrong, though some of them would rightly be

hated by you, those who have made a profession of the practice and are interested neither in pity nor anything else other than gain. Since I have borrowed money on many occasions, not just lent it to Pantainetos, I too recognize these people and do not love them; but I don't try to rob them, by Zeus, or trump up charges against them. [54] When a man has engaged in trade as I have, sailing and facing danger, and having made a small profit has loaned it through a desire both to do a favour and to prevent his money from slipping through his fingers unnoticed, why should one include him among that type? Unless what you mean is that anyone who lends you money deserves public hatred.

Please read out the depositions to show what sort of a man I am to those who do business with me and those who need help.

Depositions

[55] This, Pantainetos, is the sort of man I am, the one who walks fast, and this is the sort of man you are, the one who walks calmly. But on the subject of my walk or my manner of speaking I shall tell you the whole truth, judges, with complete candour. It has not escaped my attention – I am fully aware of the fact – that in this respect I am not one of those who are naturally favoured and who benefit themselves. For if I offend people with behaviour which brings me no advantage, surely I count as unfortunate to this extent. [56] But what's to be done with me? If I lend to so-and-so, should I also lose my case? No indeed. For my opponent will not be able to demonstrate the presence of any baseness or wickedness, nor does any single one of you, numerous as you are, know of any. As to all these other qualities, each of us, I think, is by nature the way he happened to be born. And to resist natural qualities one has is not easy (otherwise we would be no different from each other), but to recognize them on seeing them in another and to criticize is simple.

[57] But what has this got to do with me and you, Pantainetos? 'You have suffered much grievous mistreatment?' So you've received satisfaction. 'But not from me?' No, because you weren't wronged in any way by me either. Or you would never have released me, nor, when you were deciding to sue Euergos would you have let me alone, nor would you have demanded that the man who had subjected you to much grievous mistreatment should undertake the role of vendor. Then again, how could I who was not present or in town have done you wrong? [58] So if one were to grant that he has

suffered the worst wrongs possible and will now be telling the whole truth about these events, this at least I think all of you would agree, that before now many worse wrongs have been experienced by people than those relating to money; unintentional killings, outrages on what is inviolable and many other acts of this nature take place. But nonetheless for all these acts it is established that the fact that they have been induced to grant release is the end and resolution of the dispute for the victims. [59] And so firmly does this principle of justice prevail in all cases that if a man who has convicted another of unintentional homicide and proved convincingly that he is impure subsequently takes pity and grants release, he no longer has the power to have the same man exiled. Nor, if the victim personally before his death releases the perpetrator from guilt for homicide, is it open to any of his remaining kin to prosecute; no, people whom the laws order to be driven out, exiled and executed if they are convicted, if they are given release just once, are freed from all fears by this expression. [60] So then, when the granting of release has such lasting authority where life and the most serious matters are involved, is it to have no significance where money and less important charges are at issue? No indeed! The most dangerous outcome is not if I do not get justice from you but if a practice which has been established from the beginning of time is to be abolished in our age.

Pantainetos has brought several charges, which are carefully itemized and attacked in the speech:

1 Nikoboulos instructed his slave Antigenes to seize ore worked by Pantainetos; this prevented Pantainetos from meeting his obligations to the state on his mining concession and caused him to be listed as a state debtor.
2 He put Antigenes in control of the plant despite Pantainetos' protests.
3 He caused Pantainetos' slaves in the plant to strike (§26).
4 He smelted ore mined by Pantainetos.
5 He 'sold' on the plant (i.e. passed the debt to other creditors) in contravention of the contract.
6 He committed a variety of other offences.

Essentially Pantainetos has charged Nikoboulos with the offences for which he had successfully sued Euergos. He is also suing Nikoboulos for the same sum awarded against Euergos. Although

Nikoboulos claims that Pantainetos in his earlier suit against Euergos had prejudiced the judges with the use of irrelevant charges (on the principle commonly adopted by speakers in Athenian courts that one's opponent's irrelevant accusations are designed to mislead while one's own are intended to alert the judges to the opponent's duplicity and unreliability), the seizure of the plant was obviously a fact. Nikoboulos deals with the events at some length in order to present a response to the main charge as well as stating the case for his *paragraphe*, thus avoiding the impression that he is using the special plea to evade the main issue. His narrative is intended to show that he has adhered to the contract; it was on Pantainetos' insistence that he eventually passed on the debt, and so Pantainetos cannot claim that Nikoboulos has damaged his interests. More importantly, he stresses his alibi plea; he was abroad and therefore cannot have been responsible. Thus although he presents Euergos as having acted properly he is careful to distance himself from a partner who has already been found guilty.

However, formally his case turns on the question of the admissibility of the suit. He offers several grounds for his *paragraphe*. His most important point, stressed at the outset, is that Pantainetos formally relinquished all claims on Nikoboulos when the latter agreed to transfer the debt to other creditors; in such a case the right to sue was forfeited. He also argues that Pantainetos has lumped together charges which belong under different magistrates; *paragraphe* could be entered where the magistrate chosen lacked competence. Thirdly he argues that the procedure for mining suits could not be used, since the offence concerned a processing plant and not a mine. The second of these was evidently struck out of his written plea by the presiding magistrate. Although Nikoboulos gamely suggests some form of collusion, presumably the magistrate took the view that the charges in question were supplementary and did not form the basis of Pantainetos' case.

We can deal briskly with the main issue. There is no reason to doubt that Nikoboulos was absent during the greater part of the quarrel between Euergos and Pantainetos. However, we do not know if the disagreement had already begun before he left and if so how far Euergos was operating with Nikoboulos' agreement. It may be significant that Euergos used Nikoboulos' slave (Euergos may have been anxious to avoid facing the risk of litigation alone and may have wanted at least indirect support from Nikoboulos). The fact that there are witnesses to Pantainetos' formal relinquishment of his claims against Nikoboulos (§17) does however suggest that Nikoboulos is telling the truth when he claims that the transfer of the debt took place with Pantainetos' agreement.

On the *paragraphe* case, it would seem that Nikoboulos was given formal release from further dispute. Here his case seems strong. As to the third ground of his *paragraphe*, from §36 it would seem that the law under which Pantainetos is suing Nikoboulos allowed generally for legal action relating to mining activity. Accordingly, Pantainetos could argue that the seizure of the plant effectively shut down his operation and therefore did impede his mining activities.

It is conceivable that Pantainetos is now suing because he had not realized earlier the extent of Nikoboulos' involvement. Perhaps he feels that he has some prospect of achieving the same success against Nikoboulos as he had against Euergos. Either way, he may still have damaged his chances of suing by granting a general quittance from further action.

5

CASES CONCERNING CITIZENSHIP

CASE XV: [DEMOSTHENES] 59 – AGAINST NEAIRA

The case for which this fascinating speech was written arose out of the political and possibly personal animosity of two minor Athenian politicians of the fourth century BC, and the trial was played out against the backdrop of the rise of Macedon as a major regional power and the rival foreign policies of competing political groups in Athens. The defendant, Neaira, was associated with a man named Stephanos, who probably belonged to the dominant political group, headed by Euboulos, which favoured a cautious approach to Macedon, one based on military preparedness but avoidance of long-distance and expensive operations. There were other politicians with more interventionist agendas, including the prosecutor Apollodoros and his more distinguished younger contemporary Demosthenes. The first collision between Apollodoros and Stephanos, narrated in §§3–8, occurred when Olynthos in the north of Greece was hard pressed by Macedon in 349 and Athens became embroiled in military operations in Euboia in 348. In an effort to fund operations Apollodoros proposed that the *theoric* fund, which had begun as a means of meeting the cost of tickets to the dramatic festivals in the theatre of Dionysos and had grown to cover other festivals and also major public works, should be put to military use (something which Demosthenes had also tried to achieve). He was successfully prosecuted by Stephanos by *graphe paranomon*, the indictment for illegal proposals which played a major part in political struggles in Athens. According to our speech, Stephanos also sought to have Apollodoros convicted of homicide.

Apollodoros is now striking back. He is prosecuting Neaira under the laws governing the marriage of citizens. The Athenians like other Greeks were jealous of the privileges of citizenship. As was noted in the Introduction, from 451/0 Athenian citizenship was confined to those of Athenian parentage on both sides, and by the date of the present trial there was a law in force which prescribed severe penalties (enslavement with confiscation and sale of property) for any non-Athenian who contracted or simulated a marriage with an Athenian. Apollodoros' aim is both to wound Stephanos personally by harming Neaira and also to blacken his public reputation by associating him with abuse of the honours of citizenship and other offences. This association will have been dramatically visible to the judges, since Stephanos appears to have presented the case for the defence. The official prosecutor is actually Apollodoros' kinsman Theomnestos. Apollodoros ostensibly appears as a supporting speaker (*synegoros*), but it is quite clear (as is made explicit toward the end of the speech) that the prime mover is Apollodoros.

The trial can be dated quite closely. The reference in §26 to an individual named Xenokleides, who appears to be in Athens at the time, indicates a date after 343, when Xenokleides left Macedon (Dem. 19.231). On the other hand, the silence of the speech about Demosthenes' successful attempt to divert theoric money to the military fund in 339 suggests that the trial should not be dated later than 340. The dating is significant. At this period there appears to have been widespread dissatisfaction with the peace between Athens and Macedon of 346 (the Peace of Philokrates), and the more bellicose politicians were using this dissatisfaction as a basis for attacks on the group which had dominated politics earlier in the decade. It was at this period that the author of the peace, Philokrates, was indicted (he was wise enough to flee to avoid trial), as was another politician associated with Euboulos' group, Aischines, whose prosecutor was his enemy Demosthenes.

It is generally accepted (and was already suspected by scholars in antiquity) that the ancient attribution of the speech to Demosthenes is erroneous. This belief is flagged in modern editions (as in the present volume) by the enclosure of Demosthenes' name in square brackets. Some, but by no means all, moderns share my belief that the speech was written by Apollodoros himself. There is a modern commentary on the speech (C. Carey, *Apollodoros, Against Neaira: [Demosthenes] 59*, Warminster 1992).

[1] There were many factors which urged me, men of Athens, to bring this indictment against Neaira, and to come before you.

We have been seriously wronged by Stephanos, and we were placed in the most extreme danger by him, my father-in-law, myself, my sister and my wife, so that I shall present this case not as an aggressor but in retaliation; for it was this man who first started the quarrel, though he had never suffered any harm from us either in word or act. I wish first of all to give you an account of what we have suffered from him, so that you will feel more sympathy for me as I seek to defend myself, and to show how we were placed in the most extreme danger of losing both homeland and citizen rights.

[2] When the Athenian people decreed that Pasion and his descendants should be Athenian citizens because of his benefactions to the city, my father concurred with the people's gift, and he gave Pasion's son Apollodoros his daughter, my sister, in marriage; and she is the mother of Apollodoros' children. Since Apollodoros treated my sister and all of us well, and as he felt that true relatives share all they have, I took as wife Apollodoros' daughter, my niece. [3] After a time Apollodoros was drawn as member of the Council. When he had passed the preliminary scrutiny and sworn the customary oath, a war crisis befell the city such that it was possible for you, if you won, to be the most powerful state in Greece and to recover once and for all your possessions beyond dispute and finally put down Philip, or if you were late in sending aid and abandoned your allies, once the army was disbanded for lack of money, to destroy them and be judged untrustworthy by the rest of Greece, and to risk the loss of your remaining possessions, Lemnos, Imbros, Skyros and the Chersonese. [4] When you were about to march out in full force to Euboia and Olynthos, Apollodoros as councillor drafted a decree in the Council and brought a resolution before the Assembly proposing that the people decide by show of hands whether the surplus from the administration should be used for military or festival purposes. For the laws prescribed that in time of war the surplus from the administration should be used for military purposes; he thought that the people should have the authority to do as it wished with its own property, and he had sworn to act as councillor for the best interests of the Athenian people, as you all bore witness on that occasion. [5] For when the vote took place, nobody voted against the use of this money for military purposes; and even now, if ever the issue is discussed, it is agreed by all that he was unjustly treated for offering the best advice. So it is the man who deceived the judges with his arguments who deserves our anger, not the people who were deceived. This man Stephanos

indicted the decree as illegal and came to court; by producing false witnesses to support the slanderous charge that Apollodoros had been a debtor to the Treasury for twenty-five years, and making many accusations irrelevant to the indictment, he secured a verdict against the decree.

[6] On this count, if this is what he chose to do, we have no complaint. But when the judges were voting on the penalty assessment, though we urged him to compromise he refused, and proposed a penalty of fifteen talents with the intention of disfranchising Apollodoros himself and his children and reducing my sister and all of us to absolute poverty and complete destitution. [7] For Apollodoros' property did not amount even to three talents, to enable him to pay so large a fine; and if the debt was not paid by the ninth prytany, the debt would be doubled and Apollodoros would be listed as owing thirty talents to the Treasury; and once he was listed as a debtor to the Treasury, all the property Apollodoros owns would be inventoried as belonging to the state, and once it was sold Apollodoros himself, his children, his wife and all of us would be reduced to absolute poverty. [8] Furthermore, his second daughter would have been unmarriageable. For who would ever have accepted a girl without dowry from a father who was a debtor to the Treasury and a pauper? Such then, was the scale of the calamities he tried to inflict on us, though he had never been wronged by us. To the judges who tried the case on that occasion I am deeply grateful for this at least, that they did not leave Apollodoros to be plundered but imposed a fine of one talent, so that he was just able to pay it; but as for Stephanos, we have, as is just, sought to pay him back in the same coin.

[9] For not only did he try to destroy us like this; he also wanted to exile Apollodoros from his homeland. He brought a false accusation against him that once when he had gone to Aphidna in search of a runaway slave of his he struck a woman and the person died from the blow; he produced some slaves and represented them as Cyrenaeans, and by public proclamation summoned Apollodoros to be tried for murder at the Palladion. [10] And Stephanos here conducted the prosecution, having taken an oath that Apollodoros killed the woman with his own hand, invoking destruction on himself, his race and his household, though it had not happened and he had not seen it or heard it ever from any living man. But it was proved that he was lying on oath and bringing a false accusation, and he was exposed as having been hired by Kephisophon and

Apollophanes to secure Apollodoros' exile or disfranchisement for pay; he received few votes from his five hundred drachmas, and left the court a perjurer and a known scoundrel.

[11] Consider for yourselves, men of Athens, reflecting on the probable consequences in your own minds, what I could have done with myself and my wife and my sister, if Apollodoros had actually suffered any of the injuries which Stephanos plotted against him, either in the first or in the second trial? What disgrace, what disaster would not have befallen me? [12] On all sides people approached me privately and urged me to seek revenge for what was done to us by him; and they reviled me as the most cowardly man in the world, if when I was so closely related to them I failed to exact punishment for my sister, father-in-law, nieces and wife, and by bringing before you the woman who is guilty of such blatant impiety against the gods, outrage against the city and contempt for your laws, and by proving her guilt in my speech, enable you to treat her as you wish – [13] and just as Stephanos tried to deprive me of my relatives, contrary to your laws and decrees, so I too have come before you to prove that this man is living in marriage with an alien woman contrary to the law, that he introduced another's children into his phratry and deme, that he gives the daughters of courtesans in marriage as though they were his own, that he has committed impiety against the gods and is depriving the people of its privilege of granting citizenship to anyone it wishes. For who would seek to obtain this gift from the people, when it would cost much expense and trouble to become a citizen, if he can get it from Stephanos with less expense, if in fact the result for him will be exactly the same?

[14] So then, I have explained to you the wrongs inflicted by Stephanos without provocation which induced me to bring this indictment. You must now be convinced that this woman Neaira is an alien and that she is living in marriage with Stephanos here and has committed many crimes against the city. So I put to you, judges, a request which I think proper for a young man inexperienced in speaking, that you bid me call Apollodoros as my supporter for this trial. [15] For he is older than I am and has more experience in the laws; he has studied all these matters carefully, and he has been wronged by Stephanos, so that there can be no objection if he seeks revenge on the man who started it. It is your duty to listen to the detailed presentation of prosecution and defence and then on the basis of the actual truth to cast your vote on behalf of the gods, the laws, justice and yourselves.

Supporting speech (delivered by Apollodoros)

[16] The wrongs inflicted by Stephanos here, men of Athens, which made me take the stand to accuse this woman Neaira, have been explained to you by Theomnestos; what I wish to prove clearly to you is that Neaira is an alien and is living in marriage with Stephanos contrary to the laws. First of all the clerk will read you the law under which Theomnestos brought this indictment and this trial comes before you.

Law

If an alien lives in marriage with an Athenian woman by any manner or means, any Athenian at will who possesses the right is to indict him before the Thesmothetai. If he is convicted, both he and his property are to be sold, and one-third is to go to the successful prosecutor. The same is to apply if an alien woman lives in marriage with an Athenian man, and the man who lives in marriage with the alien woman so convicted is to be fined one thousand drachmas.

[17] You have heard the law, judges, which forbids an alien woman to live in marriage with an Athenian or an Athenian woman with an alien, or to produce children, by any manner or means. If anyone breaks this law, it allows for an indictment against them, the alien man or woman, before the Thesmothetai, and it instructs that if convicted the person is to be sold. So then, I wish to prove to you in detail, starting at the beginning, that this woman Neaira is an alien.

[18] There were these seven girls bought as small children by Nikarete, a freedwoman of Charisios of Elis and the wife of his cook Hippias, an expert judge of beauty in small children who knew how to bring them up and train them skilfully; for she had made this her trade and she made her living by this means. [19] She called them her daughters, so that she could charge the highest possible fees from men who wished to have relations with them, on the pretext that they were free girls, and when she had exploited the youth of each of them she sold them off together, all seven, Anteia, Stratola, Aristokleia, Metaneira, Phila, Isthmias and Neaira here. [20] Which of them each purchaser acquired and how they obtained their freedom from those who bought them from Nikarete I shall inform you later on in my speech, if you wish to hear and I

have water to spare; but the fact that this woman Neaira belonged to Nikarete and worked as a courtesan on hire to all who wished to have relations with her, this is the point to which I wish to return.

[21] Lysias the sophist, who was a lover of Metaneira, wanted to initiate her, in addition to the other sums he had spent on her; for he thought that, while her owner got the rest of the money he paid, anything he spent on the festival and the Mysteries for her sake would win him the gratitude of the girl herself. He therefore asked Nikarete to come to the Mysteries and bring Metaneira so that she could be initiated, and he promised to initiate her personally. [22] When they arrived Lysias did not bring them into his own house, out of respect for his wife, the daughter of Brachyllos and his own niece, and for his mother, who was rather elderly and who lived with him. He lodged them, Metaneira and Nikarete, at the house of Philostratos of Kolonai, who was still unmarried and a friend of his. Neaira here accompanied them; she was already working as a prostitute, though she was too young as she had not yet reached puberty.

[23] To prove the truth of my statements, that she belonged to Nikarete and accompanied her and was hired out to anyone willing to pay, I shall call Philostratos himself as witness to these facts.

Deposition

Philostratos the son of Dionysios of Kolonai testifies that he knows that Neaira was owned by Nikarete, who also owned Metaneira, and that they stayed with him when they were in town for the Mysteries while they were living in Corinth; that they were lodged at his house by Lysias the son of Kephalos, a close personal friend of his.

[24] Again, men of Athens, afterwards Simos of Thessaly came here for the Great Panathenaia and brought this Neaira. Nikarete came with her too, and they stayed with Ktesippos the son of Glaukonides of Kydantidai; and Neaira here drank and dined with them in the presence of a number of men as though she were a courtesan. And to prove the truth of my statements I shall call witnesses of these facts for you. [25] Please call Euphiletos the son of Simon of Aixone and Aristomachos the son of Kritodemos of Alopeke.

Witnesses

Euphiletos the son of Simon of Aixone and Aristomachos the son of Kritodemos of Alopeke testify that they know that Simos of Thessaly came to Athens for the Great Panathenaia, and with him Nikarete and Neaira the defendant in this trial, that they stayed with Ktesippos the son of Glaukonides, and that Neaira drank with them like a courtesan in the presence of many others who were drinking at Ktesippos' house.

[26] Afterward she carried on her trade openly in Corinth and was a celebrity; among her lovers were Xenokleides the poet and Hipparchos the actor, who hired and had her. To prove the truth of this statement I cannot provide the testimony of Xenokleides; the laws do not allow him to testify. [27] For when under the influence of Kallistratos you were rescuing the Spartans, initially he opposed the sending of aid in the Assembly. As he had bought the right to the 2 per cent tax on grain during the peace and was required to pay his instalments to the Council-chamber each prytany, and was exempted under the law, he did not join in that expedition; but he was indicted for failure to serve by this man Stephanos, slandered by him in his speech in court, convicted and disfranchised. [28] Yet don't you think it intolerable that this man Stephanos has removed the right to speak from citizens by birth who have a legitimate claim to citizenship while he forces in as Athenian citizens people who do not belong, in defiance of all the laws? I shall call Hipparchos in person for you, and force him to give evidence or take the oath of disclaimer as the law prescribes, or I shall subpoena him. Please call Hipparchos.

Deposition

Hipparchos of Athmone testifies that Xenokleides the poet and he hired Neaira, the defendant in this trial, in Corinth as a courtesan who worked for hire, and that Neaira drank with himself and Xenokleides the poet in Corinth.

[29] Later on she had two lovers, Timanoridas of Corinth and Eukrates of Leukas; since Nikarete was extravagant in her demands, expecting them to meet all the daily expenses of her household, they paid Nikarete thirty mnai for Neaira's person and bought her outright from her in accordance with the law of the city to be their

slave. And they kept her and used her for as long as they pleased. [30] But when they were about to marry they declared to her that since she had been their mistress they did not wish to see her working in Corinth or under the control of a brothelkeeper, and that they would be content to receive less money for her than they had paid and see her get some personal advantage. So they offered to remit her one thousand drachmas towards her freedom, five hundred each, and told her to find the other twenty mnai herself and pay them. After listening to what Eukrates and Timanoridas said, she invited to Corinth several of her former lovers, including Phrynion of Paiania, the son of Demon and brother of Demochares, a man with an outrageous and extravagant way of life, as the older among you remember. [31] When Phrynion arrived, she told him what Eukrates and Timanoridas had said to her and gave him the money which she had collected from her other lovers as a friendly loan towards the cost of her freedom and whatever she had saved herself, and begged him to add the rest needed to make up the twenty mnai and pay it for her to Eukrates and Timanorides to free her. [32] He listened readily to these words of hers, and taking the money which had been contributed by her other lovers and adding the rest personally he paid Eukrates and Timanoridas the twenty mnai to secure her freedom on condition that she did not work in Corinth. To prove the truth of these statements I shall call as witness someone who was present. Call Philagros of Melite.

Deposition

Philagros of Melite testifies that he was present in Corinth when Phrynion the brother of Demochares paid twenty mnai for Neaira the defendant in this trial to Timanoridas of Corinth and Eukrates of Leukas, and when he had paid the money he went off to Athens taking Neaira with him.

[33] On coming here with her he treated her in an outrageous and thoughtless manner; he took her to dinner with him everywhere wherever he was drinking; she joined in all his revels, and he had intercourse with her in public anywhere whenever he pleased, making a show of his privilege in front of onlookers. The many people to whose parties he took her included Chabrias of Aixone, when he won the Pythian games in the archonship of Sokratidas with the chariot he bought from the sons of Mitys of Argos, and on

his return from Delphi held a victory feast at Kolias. Many people there had intercourse with her when she was drunk, while Phrynion was asleep, including the servants who had served Chabrias' meal. [34] To prove the truth of these statements, I shall provide as witnesses the people who were there and saw it. Please call Chionides of Xypete and Euthetion of Kydathenaion.

Deposition

Chionides of Xypete and Euthetion of Kydathenaion testify that they were invited to dinner by Chabrias, when he was celebrating his chariot victory, and they were entertained at Kolias; that they know that Phrynion was at this dinner with Neaira the defendant in this trial; that they and Phrynion and Neaira went to sleep and they noticed several people get up in the night and visit Neaira, including some of the servants, who were Chabrias' household slaves.

[35] So then, since she was abused outrageously by Phrynion instead of being cherished as she expected, and he did not grant all her wishes, she gathered together the property in his house and all the clothing and gold jewellery he had bought to adorn her and two maidservants, Thratta and Kokkaline, and ran off to Megara. This was the time when Asteios was archon at Athens, and it was the period in which you were involved in your second war with Sparta. [36] She spent two years in Megara, that of Asteios' archonship and the year of Alkisthenes. But since her trade as a prostitute did not provide enough money to maintain her household she was extravagant, while the Megarians are mean and petty, and there were few foreigners in town at that time because there was a war on, the Megarians took the Spartan side and you had control of the sea; but she could not return to Corinth because the condition on which she was quit of Eukrates and Timanoridas was that she would not work her trade in Corinth. [37] Well, when the peace came in the archonship of Phrasikleides and the battle was fought at Leuktra between the Thebans and the Spartans, at that point this Stephanos came to town and stayed with her as a courtesan and had relations with her. She told him all that happened and Phrynion's insulting treatment; she gave him besides all she had brought from Phrynion's house, and since she was eager to live here but afraid of Phrynion because she had done him wrong and he was angry with her, and she knew

his temper was violent and arrogant, she made Stephanos here her patron. [38] Stephanos spoke encouragingly to her in Megara and inflated her confidence, saying that Phrynion would regret it if he laid hands on her; he would keep her as his wife and introduce the children she had at that time into his phratry as his own and give them citizenship; nobody in the world would harm her. So he brought her here from Megara and three children with her, Proxenos and Ariston and a daughter who is now known as Phano. [39] He established her and her children in the small house he had by the Whispering Hermes, between the houses of Dorotheos of Eleusis and Kleinomachos, the house which Spintharos has since bought from him for seven mnai. So this was the sum total of Stephanos' property. He had two aims in bringing her here, to have a beautiful mistress for free and for her trade to pay for the necessities and maintain the house; for he had no other source of income, apart from what he could obtain as a sykophant.

[40] But Phrynion learned that she was in town and staying with Stephanos, and he went to Stephanos' house with some young men and tried to drag her off. When Stephanos asserted her freedom according to the law, Phrynion compelled her to post bail before the Polemarchos. To prove the truth of this statement, I shall provide the man who was Polemarchos then in person as witness. Please call Aietes of Keiriadai.

Deposition

Aietes of Keiriadai testifies that when he was Polemarchos Neaira the defendant in this trial was compelled to post bail by Phrynion the brother of Demochares, and Stephanos of Eroiadai, Glauketes of Kephisia and Aristokrates of Phaleron went bail for Neaira.

[41] After being bailed by Stephanos, while she was staying with him she continued to work the same trade no less than before, though she charged larger fees from people who wanted to have relations with her, since she enjoyed a degree of respectability and was living with a man in marriage. Stephanos, too, used to help her in blackmail; if he caught any rich and unknown foreigner making love to her, he would lock him up indoors and demand a large sum of money. Not surprisingly, [42] for neither Stephanos nor Neaira had any property to enable them to meet their daily expenses, and the cost of maintenance was high, since she had to keep him and

herself and three children which she brought with her to his house, and two maidservants and a manservant, especially as she had become used to living comfortably before, when other people paid for her needs. [43] Stephanos here had no income worth mentioning from political activity; he was not yet a public speaker but still only a sykophant, the sort who shout by the speaker's platform and hire themselves to bring indictments and denunciations and put their names to other people's proposals, until he fell under the influence of Kallistratos of Aphidna. How and why that happened I shall tell you, when I have told Neaira's tale and demonstrated that she is an alien, and has committed serious offences against you and impiety against the gods; [44] then you will know that this man himself deserves no lighter punishment than Neaira, but much greater, and all the more for the fact that while claiming to be an Athenian citizen he has shown so much contempt for the laws, for you and for the gods that he cannot bring himself to keep quiet from shame at his misdeeds, but by persecuting myself and others he has caused Theomnestos here to subject him and the defendant to such a serious trial, with the result that her origin has been examined and his criminality exposed.

[45] So Phrynion brought a suit against him for asserting the freedom of Neaira and for receiving the property which she took from Phrynion's house, but their acquaintances brought them together and persuaded them to submit the dispute to their arbitration. And Satyros of Alopeke, the brother of Lakedaimonios, sat as arbitrator representing Phrynion, while Saurias of Lamptrai sat for Stephanos here; as impartial arbitrator they chose Diogeiton of Acharnai. [46] They met in the temple and after hearing the facts from both parties and the woman herself they announced their decision, which the parties accepted, that the woman was free and her own mistress, but that Neaira should give back to Phrynion all that she took with her from Phrynion's house, except for clothing and jewellery and maidservants, which had been bought for the woman herself; she was to live with each of them day for day; but any other arrangement arrived at by mutual agreement should be binding; the one who at the time had her in his keeping was to provide for her maintenance; and for the future they were to be friends and bear no grudge.

[47] This, then, was the settlement determined by the arbitrators for Phrynion and Stephanos over this woman Neaira. To prove the truth of my statements, he will read out to you the deposition

concerning these events. Please call Satyros of Alopeke, Saurias of Lamptrai and Diogeiton of Acharnai.

Deposition

Satyros of Alopeke, Saurias of Lamptrai and Diogeiton of Acharnai testify that they brought about a settlement between Stephanos and Phrynion when acting as arbitrators in the matter of Neaira the defendant in this trial; and that the terms on which they effected the settlement were such as Apollodoros produces.

Settlement

They affected a settlement between Phrynion and Stephanos on the following terms, that each is to keep Neaira at his house and have the use of her for an equal number of days each month, unless they reach any other agreement themselves.

[48] Once the settlement was affected, the people who had supported each party in the arbitration and the whole affair, as is often the case, I think, especially when the dispute is about a courtesan, went to dinner at the house of each when he had Neaira with him, and this woman dined and drank with them as if she were a courtesan. To prove the truth of my statements, please call the witnesses who were with them, Euboulos of Probalinthos, Diopeithes of Melite, Kteson of Kerameis.

Witnesses

Euboulos of Probalinthos, Diopeithes of Melite and Kteson of Kerameis testify that when the settlement was made between Phrynion and Stephanos in the matter of Neaira, they often dined with them and drank with Neaira, the defendant in this trial, both when Neaira was at Stephanos' house and when she was at Phrynion's.

[49] So then, I have proved by my account, with the support of witnesses, that she was originally a slave and was sold twice, and that she worked as a courtesan; that she ran away from Phrynion to Megara, and that she was required to post bail before the Polemarchos as an alien. But I wish to prove to you that Stephanos here too has himself testified against her to prove her an alien. [50] Stephanos here gave the daughter of this woman Neaira, whom she

brought to his house as a small child, and who was at that time known as Strybele but now Phano, in marriage to an Athenian, Phrastor of Aigilia, as though she were his own daughter, with a dowry of thirty mnai. When she went to live with Phrastor, a working man who had amassed his resources by careful living, she did not know how to adapt to Phrastor's ways; she pursued her mother's habits and the dissolute way of life in her house, since she had, I suppose, been brought up among licentiousness of this sort. [51] Phrastor saw that she was neither a decent woman nor willing to obey him, and since also he had learned that she was not Stephanos' daughter but Neaira's, and that he was tricked at the outset at the betrothal, when he received her in the belief that she was Stephanos' daughter and not Neaira's, and that she was his daughter by a citizen wife he had before he lived in marriage with Neaira, Phrastor was enraged at all this, and feeling insulted and deceived, he threw the woman out after he had been living with her for about a year, while she was pregnant, and withheld the dowry. [52] Stephanos brought a suit for maintenance against him at the Odeion under the law which prescribes that if anyone sends away his wife he must pay back the dowry, or else pay interest at a rate of nine obols,* and that the guardian may bring a suit for maintenance at the Odeion on behalf of the woman; so Phrastor brought an indictment against Stephanos before the Thesmothetai for betrothing to him, an Athenian citizen, the daughter of an alien, as though she were related to him, under the following law. Please read it out.

Law

If anyone gives an alien woman in marriage to an Athenian man, representing her as related to him, he is to be disfranchised, his property is to be confiscated, and one-third is to go to the successful prosecutor. Those who possess the right may bring an indictment before the Thesmothetai, as for non-citizenship.

[53] He has read you the law under which Stephanos here was indicted by Phrastor before the Thesmothetai. Stephanos realized that if it was proved that he had betrothed the daughter of a foreigner he would be subject to the most severe penalties. He reached a settlement with Phrastor, and gave up his claim to the dowry and withdrew his suit for maintenance, and Phrastor

* i.e., 10 per cent.

withdrew his indictment from the Thesmothetai. To prove the truth of these statements, I shall call Phrastor himself as witness and compel him to give evidence according to the law. [54] Please call Phrastor of Aigilia.

Deposition

Phrastor of Aigilia testifies that when he realized that Stephanos had betrothed Neaira's daughter to him, representing her as his own daughter, he indicted him before the Thesmothetai according to the law, and ejected the woman from his house and stopped living with her; and when Stephanos brought a suit for maintenance against him at the Odeion he came to terms with him with the result that the indictment was withdrawn from the Thesmothetai and the suit for maintenance which Stephanos brought against me.

[55] Now let me produce for you another piece of testimony by Phrastor and the members of his phratry and genos proving that this Neaira is a foreigner. Not long after Phrastor sent away Neaira's daughter, he became ill; he was in a very serious condition and was reduced to complete helplessness. Phrastor had a long-standing quarrel with his relatives, for whom he felt anger and hatred, and he was childless. Beguiled in his illness by the attentions of Neaira and her daughter [56] (they went to call on him, as he was sick and had nobody to treat his illness, bringing all that was needed for his sickness and taking care of him; you know yourselves, I think, how useful a woman is in times of illness as nurse to an invalid), he was persuaded in fact to take back and acknowledge as his son the child which the daughter of this woman Neaira had borne after she was sent away by Phrastor while she was pregnant, because he had discovered that she was not Stephanos' daughter but Neaira's and he was angry at the deception. [57] His reasoning was natural and understandable, that his condition was serious and there was not much hope of recovery; and so to prevent his relatives getting his property and himself from dying childless he acknowledged the child as his and received him into his house. That he would never have done this if he had been in good health, I shall establish for you with a powerful and unambiguous proof. [58] As soon as Phrastor left his bed after that illness and recovered and was reasonably sound in body, he took a wife of citizen birth in accord-

ance with the laws, the legitimate daughter of Satyros of Melite, and sister of Diphilos. So this should be proof for you that he did not take back the boy voluntarily but under compulsion from his illness, his childlessness, their nursing and his quarrel with his relatives, and his desire to prevent them inheriting his property if anything were to happen to him. What followed will provide still further proof. [59] For when Phrastor tried during his illness to introduce his child by Neaira's daughter into his phratry and into the Brytidai, the genos to which Phrastor belongs, the members of that genos, aware I think of the identity of Phrastor's first wife, Neaira's daughter, and of his ejection of her, and that it was on account of his illness that he was induced to take back the boy, rejected the boy and refused to register him among themselves. [60] When Phrastor brought a suit against them for refusing to register his son, the members of his genos challenged him in the presence of the arbitrator to swear by sacrificial victims that he believed the child to be his son by a woman of citizen birth given in marriage to him in accordance with the law. When the genos members issued this challenge to Phrastor in the presence of the arbitrator, Phrastor declined the oath and would not swear.

[61] To prove the truth of these statements, I shall provide as witnesses those of the Brytidai who were present.

Witnesses

Timostratos of Hekale, Xanthippos of Eroiadai, Eualkes of Phaleron, Anytos of Lakiadai, Euphranor of Aigilia and Nikippos of Kephale testify that they and Phrastor belong to the genos called Brytidai, and that when Phrastor claimed the right to introduce his son into the genos, since they knew that it was Phrastor's son by the daughter of Neaira, they prevented him from introducing his son.

[62] Thus I offer you unambiguous proof that even the closest relations of this woman Neaira have themselves testified that she is a foreigner, both Stephanos here who now keeps her and is living in marriage with her and Phrastor who married her daughter: Stephanos by refusing to go to trial on behalf of her daughter when indicted by Phrastor before the Thesmothetai for giving the daughter of a foreign woman in marriage to him, an Athenian citizen, and when he gave up his claim on the dowry rather than recover it; [63]

Phrastor by ejecting the daughter of this Neaira after marrying her, when he discovered that she was not Stephanos' daughter, and by refusing to return the dowry, and later, after he was induced to acknowledge his son because of his illness, his childlessness and his quarrel with his relatives, when he was attempting to introduce it into his genos, by refusing to swear and choosing instead to respect the oath after the clan rejected his son and challenged him to swear, and by subsequently marrying another woman of Athenian birth in accordance with the law. For these actions, which are unambiguous, have provided convincing testimony against them, proving that Neaira here is a foreigner.

[64] Now observe the rapacity and unscrupulousness of this man Stephanos, and this too will make you realize that this woman Neaira is a foreigner. Stephanos here laid a plot against Epainetos of Andros, a long-standing lover of Neaira's who had spent a great deal on her, and who used to stay with them whenever he was in Athens because of his affection for Neaira; [65] he invited Epainetos to the country on the pretext of making sacrifice, then seized him as a seducer caught with the daughter of Neaira here, and by intimidation extorted a ransom of thirty mnai. He accepted as sureties for this sum Aristomachos who had served as Thesmothetes and Nausiphilos the son of Nausinikos who had been Archon and released Epainetos on an understanding that he would pay the money. [66] Once Epainetos got out and was his own master he brought an indictment against this man Stephanos before the Thesmothetai for false imprisonment under the law which prescribes that if anyone falsely imprisons another as a seducer the victim may indict him before the Thesmothetai for false imprisonment, and that if he secures the conviction of the man who imprisoned him and it is decided that he has been the victim of a dishonest plot, he is liable to no penalty and his sureties are quit of their bail; however, if it is decided that he is a seducer, the law prescribes that his sureties are to deliver him to his captor, who may treat him as he chooses in the court, short of using a knife, on the grounds that he is a seducer. [67] It was under this law that Epainetos indicted him. He admitted that he used the woman, but denied being a seducer; he said that she was not Stephanos' daughter but Neaira's, and that her mother knew that she was having relations with him, that he had spent a great deal of money on them, and that whenever he was in town he used to meet the expenses of the whole household; in addition he cited the law which forbids seizing a man as a seducer with any

women who sit in a brothel or parade publicly, and he said that this was what Stephanos' house was, a brothel, that this was their trade, and they made most of their money by this means. [68] In the face of this line of argument and the indictment which Epainetos had brought, Stephanos realized that he would be exposed as a brothel-keeper and a blackmailer and submitted his dispute with Epainetos to the arbitration of the very men who had acted as surety, on the understanding that they were to be quit of their surety and Epainetos was to withdraw his indictment. [69] Epainetos accepted these terms and withdrew the indictment on which he was prosecuting Stephanos; there was a meeting at which the men who had stood surety sat as arbitrators. Stephanos could offer no justification, but asked Epainetos to contribute to the marriage of Neaira's daughter; he spoke of his poverty and the girl's earlier misfortune with Phrastor, and the fact that he had lost her dowry and would not be able to marry her off again. [70] 'You have besides had the use of the woman', he said, 'and it is only right that you should do her a good turn', and other coaxing arguments which a man begging in difficult circumstances might use. The arbitrators, after listening to both sides, arranged a settlement between them; they persuaded Epainetos to contribute a thousand drachmas to the marriage of Neaira's daughter.

To prove all I am saying is true, I shall call as witnesses the very men who acted as sureties and arbitrators.

Witnesses

[71] *Nausiphilos of Kephale and Aristomachos of Kephale testify that they acted as sureties for Epainetos of Andros, when Stephanos claimed to have seized Epainetos as a seducer; that when Epainetos left Stephanos' house and was his own master he indicted Stephanos before the Thesmothetai for falsely imprisoning him; that they served as conciliators and brought about a settlement between Epainetos and Stephanos; and that the terms of settlement are those produced by Apollodoros.*

Settlement

These are the terms on which the conciliators arranged a settlement between Stephanos and Epainetos: that they should bear no grudge for the events relating to the imprisonment, that Epainetos is to give one thousand drachmas for Phano's marriage, since he has had the use of her many times; Stephanos is to offer Phano to Epainetos whenever he is in town and wants to consort with her.

[72] Now although this woman was unambiguously judged to be an alien, and although he had had the audacity to seize as a seducer a man found with her, such was the insolence and shamelessness of this Stephanos and this Neaira that they were not content with claiming she was of citizen birth; observing that Theogenes of the Koironidai, a man of noble birth but poor and inexperienced in public affairs, had been drawn as King-archon, this man Stephanos supported him at his examination and assisted with expenses when he was entering office; he ingratiated himself and bought the post of assessor from him, and gave this woman to him in marriage, Neaira's daughter, betrothing her as though she were his own daughter. Such was his contempt for the laws and for you. [73] And this woman made the secret offerings for you on behalf of the city, and she saw what as an alien she had no right to see; despite her character she entered where nobody else among the vast Athenian population enters, except the wife of the King-archon, and administered the oath to the Venerable Women who assist in the rites; she was given as bride to Dionysos and she carried out on the city's behalf the many ceremonies, holy and secret, handed down by our ancestors. How can it accord with piety for just any woman actually to perform rites which it is not permitted for people even to hear of, especially a woman with a character and career such as hers?

[74] But I want to go back and tell you about the rites in greater detail, so that you will take the issue of punishment more seriously, in the knowledge that you will be casting your vote not only for yourselves and the laws but also for reverence towards the gods, by exacting a penalty for their acts of impiety and punishing the guilty.

In early times, men of Athens, there was a monarchy in the state and the kingship belonged to those who at any time had most prestige because they were indigenous; the king performed all the sacrifices, and the most solemn and secret sacrifices his wife performed, naturally, since she was queen. [75] After Theseus united the people in one city and created a democracy and the population increased, the people nonetheless continued to choose the King by show of hands from men preselected on grounds of excellence; and they passed a law that his wife should be of citizen birth and he should marry a virgin who had never had intercourse with another man, in order that the secret ceremonies should be performed according to ancestral custom, for the city's sake, and the traditional offerings should be made to the gods piously without any excision or innovation. [76] They wrote this law on a stone column and set it up in the temple of Dionysos in the Marshes, by the altar (and this column is standing to this day, displaying its inscription in faint Attic characters); thus the people testified to its piety towards the god and left it as a trust to future generations, showing that we expect the woman who is to be given as bride to a god and who is to perform the sacrifices to be like this. This is why they set it up in the most ancient and holy shrine of Dionysos in the Marshes, so that the inscription would not be known to many; for it is opened up once each year, on the twelfth day of the month of Anthesterion. [77] So then these holy and solemn rites, for which your ancestors showed such noble and impressive concern, you too should treat with gravity, men of Athens, and you should punish those who have shown such outrageous contempt for your laws and committed such shameless impiety against the gods, for two reasons: so that these people will pay the penalty for the crimes they have committed and so that others will take care and feel afraid to commit any offence against the gods and the city.

[78] I wish also to call before you the Sacred Herald, who assists the King-archon's wife when she puts the oath to the Venerable Women at the baskets near the altar, before they touch the victims, so that you may hear the oath and the words which are spoken, as far as it is allowed to hear them, and know how solemn and holy and ancient the traditional rites are.

Oath of the Venerable Women

I live a holy life and am pure and clear from all impurity including intercourse with a man, and I shall perform for Dionysos the Feast of the Wine God and the Rites of Bakchos according to ancestral custom and at the appointed times.

[79] You have now heard the oath and the customary rites of our ancestors, as far as it is allowed to utter them, and you have heard that the woman whom Stephanos gave as wife to Theogenes when he

was serving as King-archon, as though she were his own daughter, carried out these rites and administered the oath to the Venerable Women, and that it is not even permitted for the women who see these rites to divulge them to any other. Let me now offer you a testimony which took place in secret but which I shall prove by the facts themselves to be convincing and true.

[80] When these ceremonies had taken place and the nine Archons had gone up to the Areopagos on the appointed days, the Areopagos, which is generally so valuable to the state in matters of piety, immediately enquired about the identity of the wife of Theogenes, and ascertained the truth. It was concerned for the rites, and was inclined to punish Theogenes to the limit of its power, but in secret and with discretion; for they do not have the power to punish an Athenian citizen as they please. [81] There was a discussion, in which the Areopagos expressed its anger and proposed to punish Theogenes for marrying a woman of this sort and for allowing her to perform the secret rites on behalf of the city. Theogenes implored them, begging and pleading, saying that he had not known that she was Neaira's daughter and that he had been tricked by Stephanos and believed that he was marrying her according to the law as Stephanos' legitimate daughter; that it was because of his ignorance of public affairs and innocence that he made this man his assessor, to manage the business of his office, thinking him a friend, and this was why he had become his son-in-law. [82] 'I shall prove to you I am not lying', he said, 'with strong and unambiguous proof. I shall dismiss the woman from my house, since she is not Stephanos' daughter but Neaira's. And if I do this you should trust my statement that I was tricked; if however I fail to do it, then punish me at once as a criminal guilty of impiety against the gods.' [83] When Theogenes made this promise and pleaded with them, the Areopagos held back, both out of pity for him because of his innocent nature and in the belief that he had really been tricked by Stephanos. When Theogenes left the Areopagos, he immediately ejected the person, the daughter of this woman Neaira, from his house and dismissed Stephanos here, the man who tricked him, from the magistrate's board. And so the members of the Areopagos suspended their trial of Theogenes and abandoned their anger against him, and they forgave him since he had been deceived.

[84] And to prove I am telling the truth, I shall provide Theogenes himself as witness and I shall force him to give evidence. Call Theogenes of Erchia.

Deposition

Theogenes of Erchia testifies that when he was serving as King-archon he married Phano believing her the daughter of Stephanos, but that when he perceived that he had been deceived he ejected the person and ceased to live with her, and dismissed Stephanos from his assessorship and no longer allowed him to serve as assessor.

[85] Take now this law in addition and read it out, so that you may know that not only should she have kept away from these ceremonies, given her character and career, from seeing and sacrificing and carrying out any of the traditional rites of our ancestors on the city's behalf, but from all the other observances in Athens as well. For any woman who is caught with a seducer is not permitted to enter any of the public temples, to which the laws grant the right to enter as spectator or suppliant even to the foreign woman and the slave. [86] These are the only women the laws forbid to enter the public temples, any woman caught with a seducer; and if they enter and defy the law, they may be subjected to any mistreatment at all with impunity by anyone who wishes, short of death, and the law has granted the right to punish them to anyone who comes across them. The reason the law prescribed that she might suffer any outrage but death without any right of redress was to prevent acts of pollution and impiety in the temples; it creates sufficient fear in women to ensure they will be chaste and avoid wrong and do their duty in the house, and teaches her that if she commits an offence of this sort, she will find herself cast out both from her husband's house and from the temples of the city.

[87] You will appreciate the truth of this from hearing the law read out. Please take it.

Law on seduction

And when he has caught the seducer, the person who has so caught him may not live in marriage with his wife; if he continues to live with her, he is to be disfranchised. And the woman who is caught with a seducer may not enter any of the public temples; if she does so enter she is to suffer any mistreatment with impunity, short of death.

[88] I now wish, men of Athens, to provide testimony from the Athenian people, to show how seriously it treats these rites and how much care it has devoted to them. For the Athenian people, though possessing supreme authority over everything in the city and able to do whatever it wishes, believed that the grant of Athenian citizenship was such a noble and solemn gift that it imposed laws on itself defining terms on which it must admit a man as citizen, if they so wish, laws which have now been treated with contempt by this man Stephanos and people who marry as he has. [89] ⟨These laws are familiar to you all.⟩ Still, you will be the better for hearing them, and you will realize that the most noble and solemn awards which are given to benefactors of the city have been defiled.

First of all there is a law binding on the people forbidding it to admit a man as citizen unless on grounds of excellent conduct towards the Athenian people he deserves to be made citizen. Then when the people have been convinced and made the gift, the law does not allow the grant to become valid unless over six thousand Athenians vote for it at the following Assembly in secret ballot. [90] The law bids the Presidents to place the voting urns and submit the vote to the people as they come up, before the foreigners enter and they remove the fences, so that each man on his own authority may consider in his own mind whether the individual he is about to admit as citizen deserves the gift he is about to receive. Next, after this the law has allowed for an indictment for illegality to be brought against him by any Athenian who wishes, who can come into court and prove that he does not deserve the award and has been made an Athenian in contravention of the laws. [91] And before now it has happened that the people have made the award, deceived by the arguments of the people who requested it, an indictment for illegality has been lodged, the case has come to court, and it was proved that the recipient did not deserve it and the court withdrew it. To list the many examples in the distant past would be a long task; but as for events which you all remember, when Peitholas of Thessaly and Apollonides of Olynthos were made citizens by the people the court withdrew it. [92] These events are not so distant for you to be ignorant of them.

Now though the laws governing citizenship, under which a man may become an Athenian, are so fairly and firmly laid down, there is another most binding law laid down on top of all of these; such was the concern the people showed for their own sake and that of the gods to ensure that the sacrifices on behalf of the city should be carried out in accordance with piety. For the law expressly forbids all whom the Athenian people admit as citizens from becoming one of the nine Archons or holding any priesthood; it has admitted their descendants outright to all privileges, and adds: 'if they are born of a wife of citizen status married according to the law'.

[93] And I shall prove I am telling the truth with a convincing and unambiguous testimony. I want to go back in time in my account of the law, to tell how it was passed and for whom its provisions were intended, as men of worth who had shown firm loyalty to the Athenian people. From all this you will understand that the gift of the people which is reserved for benefactors is being degraded and how important are the privileges which Stephanos here and all who marry and have children the same way he has are taking from your control.

[94] The Plataians, men of Athens, were the only Greeks who came to your aid at Marathon, when Datis the Persian King's general, on leaving Eretria after he had gained control over Euboia, disembarked in the area with a large army and began to pillage it. And to this day the picture in the Painted Portico displays a reminder of their courage; for each man is painted rushing to support as fast as he could, the ones wearing the Boiotian caps. [95] Again when Xerxes advanced on Greece, though the Thebans collaborated with the Medes, the Plataians refused to abandon their friendship with you, but alone, unaided by the other Boiotians, half of them faced the advancing barbarian with Leonidas and the Spartans and were killed with them, while the rest embarked on your triremes, since they had no ships of their own, and fought at sea alongside you at Artemision and Salamis. [96] They joined with you and your fellow liberators of Greece in the final battle at Plataia against Mardonios the King's general and made common gift of liberty to the rest of Greece. And when the Spartan king Pausanias tried to insult you and was not satisfied that the Spartans were honoured with the sole command by the Greeks, and that our city though in reality leader in winning liberty for Greece did not compete with Sparta for the honour in order to avoid the jealousy of the allies, [97] the Spartan king, Pausanias, inflated by these honours inscribed on the tripod at Delphi, which the Greeks who had joined in the battle at Plataia and the sea battle at Salamis made jointly and set up in honour of Apollo as a memorial of the victory over the barbarians:

The leader of the Greeks, when he destroyed the Mede host,
Pausanias set up this monument to Phoibos.

as though the achievement and the dedication were his own and not shared by all the allies. [98] The Greeks were enraged, and the Plataians brought an action for a thousand talents against the Spartans before the Amphiktyons on behalf of the allies, and compelled them to erase the distich and inscribe the names of the cities which joined in the task. And for this reason not least the hatred of the Spartans and the royal house pursued them.

At the time the Spartans could do nothing about them, but about fifty years later the Spartan King Archidamos, son of Zeuxidamos, attempted to seize their city in time of peace. [99] He did this from Thebes through the agency of Eurymachos the son of Leontiades, who was a Boiotarchos; Nausikleides and some others opened the gates at night for a bribe. The Plataians, discovering that the Thebans were inside at night and that their city had suddenly been seized while at peace, ran to arms too and confronted them. When day broke and they saw that the Thebans were not many in number, and that only the vanguard had entered (for a heavy rainfall in the night had prevented the whole force from entering; the river Asopos was in spate and it was not easy to cross, especially at night) – [100] when the Plataians saw that the Thebans were in the city and realized that the whole force was not present, they attacked, defeated them in battle and succeeded in destroying them before the others could bring further aid. And they sent a messenger to you immediately to tell you of the incident and of their victory in the battle, and to ask for help if the Thebans should pillage their territory. The Athenians on hearing what had happened quickly sent aid to Plataia; and the Thebans, on seeing that the Athenians had reinforced the Plataians, went home. [101] Now when the Thebans failed in their attempt and the Plataians killed those of them whom they had taken alive in battle, the Spartans were angry; without any pretext now they marched against Plataia, having ordered all the Peloponnesians except the Argives to send two-thirds of the forces from each city and instructed all the rest of the Boiotians, the Lokrians, Phokians, Malians, Oitaians and Ainianians to take the field in full force. [102] They settled down to besiege their walls with a large force and made overtures asking them if they would agree to hand the city over to them, while keeping their territory and enjoying the use of their own possessions, and abandon their alliance with the Athenians. When the Plataians refused and answered that they would do nothing without the agreement of the Athenians, the enemy built a double wall around them and besieged them for ten years, making repeated assaults of all sorts.

[103] When the Plataians were exhausted and in extreme need and were losing hope of being rescued, they drew lots among themselves and one group stayed on to endure the siege while the others, after waiting for a night with much wind and rain, made a sortie from the city, crossed the enemy wall unnoticed by the besieging force, and after massacring the guards reached here safely, against expectation and in a desperate condition. As for those of them who stayed behind, when the city was captured by storm all the grown men were massacred while the women and children were sold into slavery, all of them who had not escaped to Athens when they saw the Spartans approaching.

[104] These were men who visibly proved their loyalty to the people and gave up all possessions, children and wives; see now in what way you gave them a share in citizen rights. For your decrees will make the law clear to all, and you will realize that I am speaking the truth. Please take this decree and read it out to them.

Decree concerning the Plataians

Hippokrates moved that the Plataians be Athenians from this day forward, with rights as the rest of the Athenians, and that they share in all the privileges which Athenians enjoy, both sacred and profane . . . except for any hereditary priesthood or rite, nor the nine Archons, though their descendants may. The Plataians are to be distributed among the demes and tribes. When they have been distributed, it is no longer to be open to any of the Plataians to become an Athenian citizen unless he obtain it as a gift from the Athenian people.

[105] You see, men of Athens, how nobly and justly the public speaker drafted the decree on behalf of the Athenian people. And he required that the Plataians receiving the grant should first of all be examined individually in the lawcourt to determine whether each is a Plataian and one of those loyal to our city, to prevent a large number from obtaining citizenship on this pretext; secondly, that the names of those who had been examined should be inscribed on a stone column, which should be placed on the Akropolis by the

temple of the goddess, so that the grant might be preserved for their descendants and it might be possible for each one to prove to which of them he is related. [106] And he does not allow anyone who is not at this point examined in the lawcourt the right to become an Athenian subsequently, to prevent a large number from procuring citizenship for themselves by claiming to be Plataians. Finally he also in the decree applying to the Plataians defined at once the law in defence of the city and the gods, that none of them should have the right to be appointed one of the nine Archons or to any priesthood, though their descendants should, if they are born of a woman of citizen status married according to the law.

[107] Isn't it monstrous? When, in dealing with men of a neighbouring city who by general agreement had been the greatest benefactors of our city, you defined so properly and precisely each of the terms on which they should receive the grant, will you leave a woman who has blatantly whored throughout the whole of Greece unpunished for insulting the city so shamefully and contemptuously and committing sacrilege against the gods, a woman who was neither bequeathed citizenship by her ancestors nor granted it by the people? [108] For where has she not prostituted herself? Where hasn't she gone to earn her daily wage? Hasn't she been in the whole of the Peloponnese, in Thessaly and Magnesia with Simos of Larissa and Eurydamas the son of Medeios, in Chios and in most of Ionia following Sotadas of Crete, hired out by Nikarete while she still belonged to her? And when a woman is under the control of different men and goes with anyone who pays, what do you expect her to do? Surely to serve her customers in every type of pleasure? So then, will your verdict be that a woman of her character who is known for certain by all to have plied her trade over the breadth of the world is a citizen? [109] And what noble thing will you claim you have achieved when people ask you; from what manner of shame and impiety can you claim innocence? For before she was indicted and brought to trial and everyone learned who she was and what sacrilege she has committed, the crimes were hers, while the city was guilty only of neglect. Some of you were unaware, while others had heard and expressed their anger, but had no practical means of dealing with her, as long as nobody brought her to trial and provided an opportunity to vote on her. But now that you all actually know the facts and have her in your power and you have the authority to punish her, the impiety against the gods becomes yours now, if you fail to punish her.

[110] And what would each of you actually say when he goes home to his own wife or daughter or mother after acquitting this woman, when she asks you: 'Where were you?' and you say 'we were judging'. 'Whom?' she will ask at once. 'Neaira' you will say, of course (what else?) 'because though she is an alien she is living in marriage with a citizen against the law, and because she gave in marriage to Theogenes who served as King-archon her daughter who had been caught in illicit sex, and this woman carried out the secret sacrifices on behalf of the city and was given as wife to Dionysos'; and you will narrate the rest of the charge against her, saying how memorably and carefully each detail was presented. [111] And they on hearing this will ask: 'So what did you do?', and you will say: 'We have acquitted her.' So then the most decent of the womenfolk will be furious with you, because you thought it right that this woman should have the same share as they in public life and religion; while to all the foolish ones you are giving a clear signal to do whatever they please, since you and the laws have given them complete freedom. For it will seem that you too by treating the matter in an indifferent and casual way approve of this woman's way of life. [112] So it would have been far more beneficial if this trial had never taken place than that you should acquit now that it has. For there will then be complete freedom for whores to live in marriage with anyone they please, and to declare anyone at all the father of their children. And your laws will be invalid, while the characters of courtesans will have the power to achieve whatever they wish. So you must also show concern for the women of citizen birth, to prevent the daughters of poor men becoming unmarriageable. [113] For as matters stand, even if a girl is needy, the law contributes an adequate dowry for her, if nature gives her even a remotely moderate appearance. But if the law is brought into contempt by you with this woman's acquittal and becomes invalid, then without a doubt the trade of whores will fall to the daughters of citizens, all those who because of poverty cannot be married, while the status of free women will fall to the courtesans, if they are given the freedom to bear children as they see fit and to share in the civic rituals and ceremonies and rights.

[114] So let each one of you believe that he is casting his vote, one in defence of his wife, another his daughter, another his mother, another the city and its laws and religion, so that those women are not seen to be held in equal esteem with this whore, and that women reared by their kinsmen with great and proper decency and

care and given in marriage according to the laws are not shown to have equal rights with a woman who has been with many men many times each day, in many lascivious ways, as each man wanted. [115] Imagine that the speaker is not I, Apollodoros, nor those citizens who will defend and support her, but that it is the laws and Neaira here who are in dispute with each other over her actions. And when you attend to the prosecution, listen to the laws themselves, by which the city is governed and according to which you have sworn to judge, and ask yourselves what they prescribe and how the defendants have transgressed them; and when you attend to the defence, remember the prosecution made by the laws and the proof offered for their statements, and take a look at her appearance, and consider only this, whether she (Neaira!) has committed these acts.

[116] It is worth while, men of Athens, to bear this in mind too, that you punished Archias who had served as Hierophant, when it was proved in court that he committed impiety by making sacrifice contrary to ancestral custom. Among the charges against him was that during the Haloa he sacrificed for the courtesan Sinope a victim she brought on the hearth in the courtyard at Eleusis, though it is not permitted to sacrifice victims on that day, and the sacrifice was not his concern but the priestess's. [117] Is it not intolerable that a man belonging to the Eumolpidai, born of noble ancestors and a citizen of the state, should be punished, because it was felt that he had offended against an established custom (and neither the entreaty of his kin nor that of his friends helped him, nor the many public services which he himself and his ancestors had performed for the city, nor the fact that he was Hierophant, but you punished him because he was held to be guilty); but this woman Neaira, who committed impiety against the same god and the laws, both herself and her daughter, will you not punish *her*?

[118] For myself, I wonder what on earth they will actually say to you in the defence. That this Neaira is of citizen birth and that she lives in marriage with Stephanos according to the laws? But it has been attested that she is a courtesan and that she was Nikarete's slave. Or that she is not his wife, but he keeps her in his house as his mistress? But the sons who are hers and who have been introduced into the phratry by Stephanos and the daughter who was given in marriage to an Athenian male demonstrate quite clearly that he keeps her as his wife. [119] Now I do not think that either Stephanos himself or anyone else on his behalf will prove that the allegations and the testimony are untrue, and that this Neaira is of

citizen birth; but I hear that he intends to offer a defence of this sort, that he keeps her not as his wife but as his mistress, and that the children are not by her but by another wife of his of citizen birth, a relative of his whom he will say he married previously. [120] In response to the impudence of his claim and the dishonesty of his defence and of the witnesses he has suborned I made him a detailed and fair challenge from which you could have learned the whole truth; I challenged him to hand over the maidservants who remained with Neaira when she came to Stephanos's house from Megara, Thratta and Kokkaline, and those whom she got later when she was living with him, Xennis and Drosis; [121] they know for certain that Proxenos who died and Ariston who is still alive and Antidorides the sprinter and Phano who was called Strybele, who married Theogenes who served as King-archon, are Neaira's children. And if the examination revealed that Stephanos here married a woman of citizen birth and that these children are his by another wife of citizen birth and not Neaira, I was willing to withdraw from the case and to prevent this indictment from coming to court. [122] For this is what living in marriage means: when a man sires children and introduces the sons to phratry and deme and gives the daughters to their husbands as his own. For we have courtesans for pleasure, and concubines for the daily service of our bodies, but wives for the production of legitimate offspring and to have a reliable guardian of our household property. So if he had previously married a woman of citizen birth and his children are by her and not by Neaira, it was open to him to prove it by means of the most accurate testimony, by handing over these servant girls.

[123] To prove that I issued the challenge, he will read out to you the deposition and the challenge. Read the deposition and then the challenge.

Deposition

Hippokrates son of Hippokrates of Probalinthos, Demosthenes son of Demosthenes of Paiania, Diophanes son of Diophanes of Alopeke, Deinomenes son of Archelaos of Kydathenaion, Deinias the son of Phormos of Kydantidai, and Lysimachos the son of Lysippos of Aigilia testify that they were present in the agora when Apollodoros challenged Stephanos, demanding that he hand over the maidservants for examination in the matter of Apollodoros' charges against Stephanos concerning Neaira; that Stephanos refused to hand over the maidservants; and that the challenge was the one which Apollodoros produces.

[124] Read now the actual challenge which I issued to Stephanos here.

Challenge

This challenge was issued by Apollodoros to Stephanos concerning the charge on which he has indicted Neaira, that she is living in marriage with a citizen although she is a foreigner; Apollodoros was ready to take Neaira's maidservants whom she brought with her from Megara, Thratta and Kokkaline, and those whom she acquired later when living with Stephanos, Xennis and Drosis, who possess accurate knowledge about Stephanos' children, that they are by Neaira, Proxenos who is dead and Ariston who is still alive, Antidorides the sprinter and Phano, for examination. And if they should admit that these are the children of Stephanos and Neaira, Neaira was to be sold in accordance with the laws and the children were to be aliens; but if they did not admit that these children were by this woman but by another wife of citizen birth, I was ready to withdraw from the case against Neaira, and, if the slaves had suffered any damage from the examination, to pay for any damage suffered.

[125] When I issued this challenge, judges, to Stephanos here, he refused to accept it. Don't you think then that judgment has already been given by this man Stephanos himself that Neaira is guilty of the indictment I brought against her and that I have told the truth to you and the depositions which I provided are true, while everything this man says will be a lie and he will himself prove that he has no sound case to make since he refused to hand over for examination the maidservants I requested?

[126] And so I for my part, judges, as avenger, both of the gods against whom these people have committed sacrilege and of myself, have brought them to trial and submitted them to your vote. You too must realize that whatever verdict each of you reaches will not go unnoticed by the gods against whom these people have offended, and vote as justice requires and avenge above all the gods and secondly yourselves. And if you do this you will be thought by all men to have given an honourable and just judgment on this indict-

ment which I have brought against Neaira, that she is living in marriage with a citizen although she is an alien.

The speech is fairly typical of the speeches delivered by Apollodoros which have been preserved in the manuscripts of Demosthenes, both in its rather clumsy style and in its heavy reliance on narrative (including a narrative of the siege of Plataia during the Peloponnesian War in the fifth century which draws heavily on Thucydides' account in the third book of his History). Argumentation is brief and is reserved for the closing part of the speech. Much of the narrative is designed to prejudice the judges against Neaira by recounting her earlier career as a prostitute and, through the account of the career of her daughter Phano, associating her with other attempts to abuse the laws dealing with citizenship and with breach of religious law. The latter aspect of the narrative appeals to the strong feelings of fear and caution which underpinned Greek attitudes to religion and to the respect for tradition which the Athenians shared with other Greeks. All this is done with great circumspection. The speaker avoids explicit treatment of sexual matters in order to preserve the appearance of decency while presenting the audience with fascinating sexual gossip.

The case against Neaira, though presented with great vividness and vigour, does not convince the armchair judge, though it will undoubtedly have been a great deal more effective in delivery. Much of the speech concentrates on matters which were probably accepted as beyond dispute by Stephanos, Neaira's slave origin and service initially as a prostitute in a brothel and eventually as a high-class courtesan. When one looks for demonstration of the allegation of illegal marriage, the speech becomes rather perfunctory. Since there is no suggestion of formal betrothal, the case rests on the parentage of the children. Marriage was formally signalled not only by betrothal (*engye*) but also by the acknowledgement granted to the offspring (as Apollodoros notes in §122), and if Stephanos has been treating Neaira's children as his legitimate issue, the relationship is a simulated marriage. In the case of the male offspring, it seems that they have been enjoying citizen rights and have therefore been acknowledged by Stephanos as his sons. However, Stephanos claims (§119) that they are the issue of a lawful marriage to an Athenian wife. Apollodoros' refusal to address this issue at length suggests that Stephanos' claim is true. The amount of space devoted to Phano, however, suggests that here Apollodoros is on firmer ground; that is, that Phano is as he claims Neaira's daughter. And it is possible that Stephanos has been treating Phano as though she were his daughter. If this allegation was accepted by the judges, they might well conclude that Stephanos was treating Neaira as his wife. Again, however, the reader feels uneasy. For most of the allegations concerning Phano the amount of witness testimony is very limited, and it may be that here too Apollodoros is conjuring a case out of thin air. Apollodoros may have felt himself that the case was weak, and this may be one reason for his use of Theomnestos as the official prosecutor. As was noted in the Introduction, there were penalties for failure to obtain one-fifth of the votes cast, and these may have included (in some public actions at least) loss of the right to bring a comparable action again. Given the role of the courts in politics, this was a serious impediment to an active politician, and it would be far better to have someone else face such a penalty.

CASE XVI: DEMOSTHENES 57 – REPLY TO EUBOULIDES

On reaching the age of eighteen, each Athenian was accepted into his deme after a scrutiny (*dokimasia*) to test his age and birth qualifications. His name was then inscribed in the deme register (*lexiarchikon grammateion*) and he was eligible to participate in the meetings of the Athenian Assembly and (in due course) seek office; he was also entitled to participate in the activities of the deme. As well as providing the basis for the exercise of citizen rights, the demes were also responsible for a certain amount of local government, including the organization of local religious activities and the administration of land attached to local cults. The deme functioned in many respects like the Athenian state, with its own Assembly meetings and its own elected officials (most importantly the *demarchos*, demarch). For further information on the demes the reader should consult D. Whitehead, *The Demes of Attica* (Princeton 1986).

In addition to the regular annual scrutinies of new members, we have evidence for two special scrutinies to test the citizen status of existing members during the classical period. The Greek term for these scrutinies, *diapsephisis* (literally 'a voting among/between'), reflects the procedure used, which involved a vote taken collectively by the deme on each member in turn. The first was in 445/4 following a large gift of grain from Egypt for distribution. The second was in 346/5 and was the result of a decree proposed by a certain Demophilos. The present speech relates to the latter. The speaker, Euxitheos, is appealing against ejection by his deme Halimous. Members ejected by their demes had a right of appeal to the law-courts. From the present speech it seems that the hearing which followed took the form of a trial with the appellant as defendant; from §5, where the prosecutor Euboulides is described as 'without liability' (*anypeuthynos*), it seems that the prosecutor or prosecutors acted as representatives of the deme rather than as volunteer prosecutors (as under the procedures for public and private cases); the special scrutinies thus mirrored the appeal mechanisms for the annual *dokimasia* of new citizens (Aristotle, *Ath. Const.*, 42.1). The prosecutor spoke first (§1). The hearing seems to have followed the procedures for public actions, for in §14 (taken literally) Euxitheos introduces what looks like new testimony, and it was only in cases which did not go to public arbitration that this was possible; most private cases went to arbitration, while public cases did not. The nature of the evidence adduced by Euxitheos casts an interesting light on Athenian society, which relied only to a limited extent on documentation. There were no registers of birth or marriage. The deme registers were evidently not trusted as proof of citizenship (hence of course the special scrutinies) and anyone wishing to prove his status would rely on the cumulative testimony of witnesses.

According to the *hypothesis* (summary) of the speech by the writer Libanios preserved in the manuscripts, if the appeal was successful the deme was compelled to reinstate the victim, while the penalty for unsuccessful appeals was enslavement; that is, identical with the punishment for an alien masquerading as a citizen or contracting an illegal marriage with a citizen. Our speech is unclear on this point; it speaks of the magnitude and disgrace of punishment and of ruin (§1). At §65 it appears to envisage exile (his enemies allegedly ransacked his house 'as though I were an exile already'), and the same is implied by §70. If Libanios is correct, it is conceivable his enemies expected him to flee from Athens to evade enslavement, or that enslavement abroad is envisaged, or that the unsuccessful appellant had the option of leaving Attica to avoid enslavement.

An unresolved issue is the relationship between this speech and Isai. 12, which also concerns a case of contested citizenship. It is sometimes supposed that Isai. 12 also belongs to the appeals after

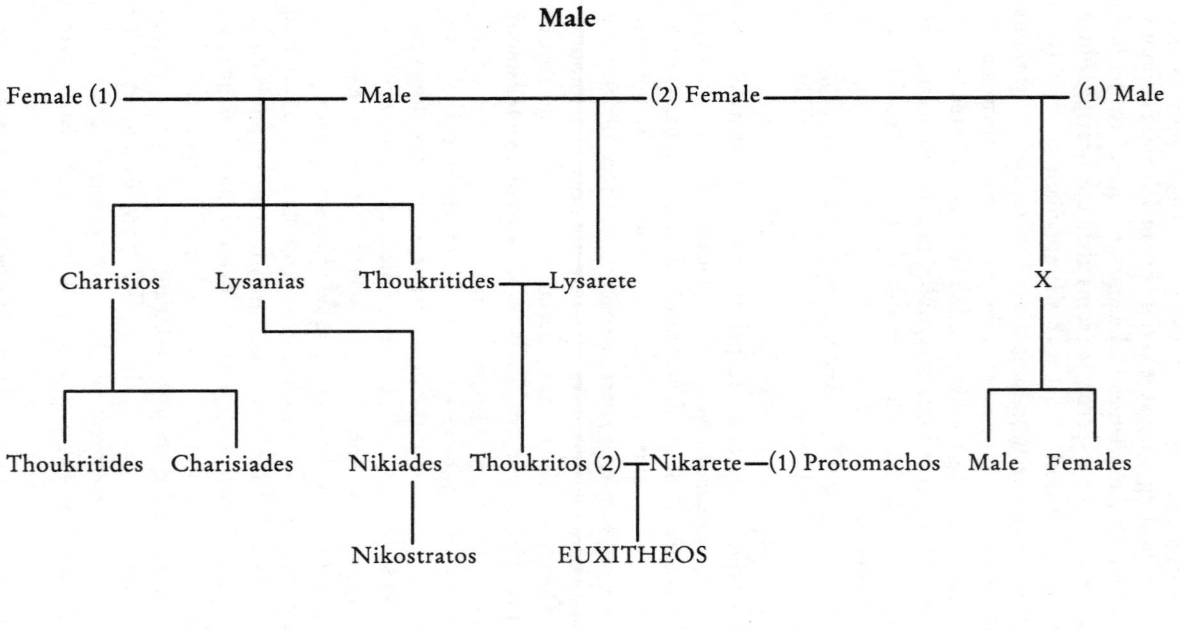
Male
Female (1)
Male
(2) Female
(1) Male
Charisios
Lysanias
Thoukritides
Lysarete
X
Thoukritides
Charisiades
Nikiades
Thoukritos (2)
Nikarete
(1) Protomachos
Male
Females
Nikostratos
EUXITHEOS

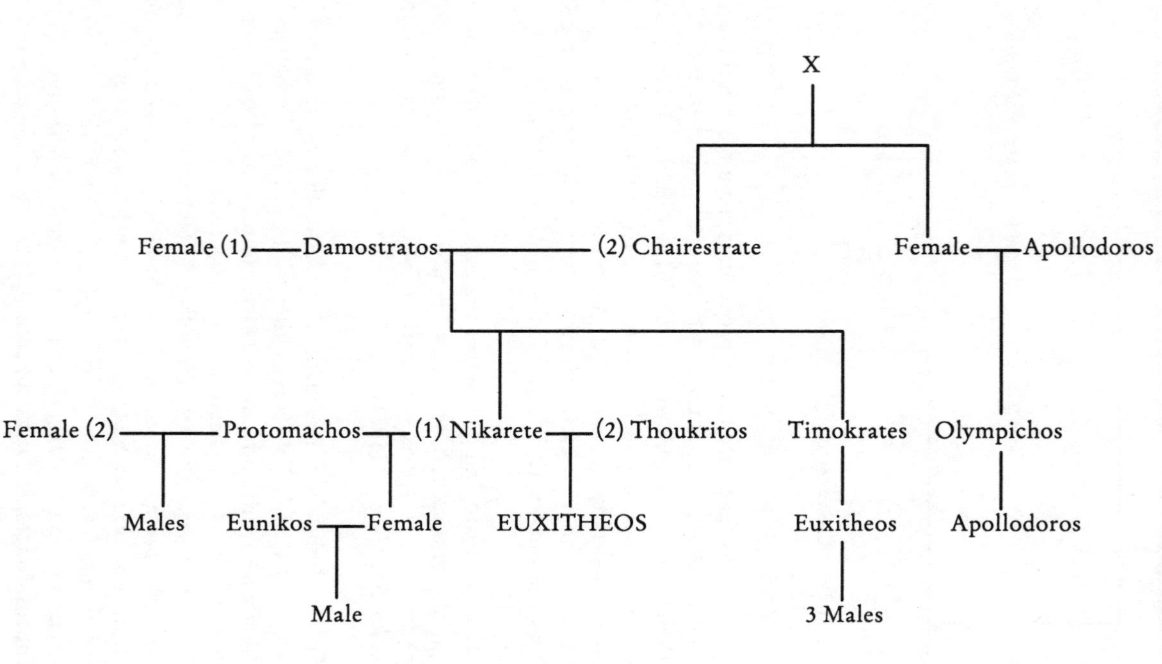
Female
X
Female (1)
Damostratos
(2) Chairestrate
Female
Apollodoros
Female (2)
Protomachos
(1) Nikarete
(2) Thoukritos
Timokrates
Olympichos
Males
Eunikos
Female
EUXITHEOS
Euxitheos
Apollodoros
Male
3 Males

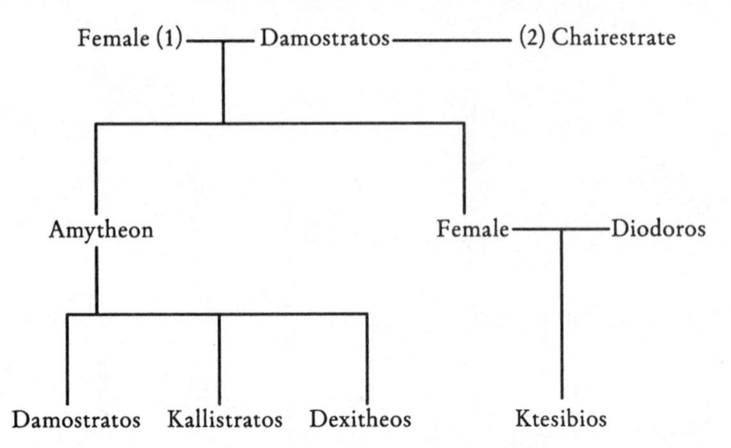

the Demophilos decree. But the procedures there are clearly different. The appellant there is the prosecutor (he spoke first, Isai. 12.8), and there had been public arbitration (§11). It looks as though Isai. 12 is a private suit. As such it is unlikely to be connected with the Demophilos decree. It may be an action for damages, and could have resulted from an extraordinary scrutiny within a single deme (such as the one by the deme Halimous mentioned at §60 of our speech).

In the accompanying family tree the figures 1 and 2 refer to partners in first and second marriages respectively. The reconstruction of the family tree is based in part on W.E. Thompson, *American Journal of Philology* 92 (1971), 89–90.

[1] Though Euboulides has made many false allegations against me and has used abuse which was neither fitting nor just, I shall try by speaking with truth and justice, judges, to prove that we belong to the city and that I have been treated wrongfully by this man. I urge and entreat and implore you all, judges, to take account of the magnitude of the present dispute and the shame which compounds ruin for those who are convicted, and to listen to me too in silence, ideally, if possible, with more goodwill (it's reasonable to be better disposed to people in danger), or if not at least with as much. [2] As it happens, judges, as far as concerns the merits of my case and my right to the city I am confident and have great hopes of contesting the issue successfully, but what I fear is the present situation and the city's passion for pronouncing expulsions. For since many

people have properly been ejected from all the demes, those of us who are victims of intrigue have found ourselves subject to the suspicion attaching to them, and we are tried on the basis of the blame attaching to them, not each on his own case; so inevitably our fear is great.

[3] Nonetheless, despite this situation, I shall tell you what I think is the just way of dealing with these issues at the outset. I think that you should be harsh towards those who are proved to be aliens, if without argument or request to you they shared your sacred and secular rights by deception and against your wishes, but those who are victims of circumstance and prove themselves citizens you should rescue and save. You should reflect that we who have been unjustly treated would suffer the most pitiable fate, if, though by rights we should belong among those who impose punishment with you, we were to find ourselves among those who receive it and suffer injustice because of the anger aroused by the issue. [4] It was my belief, judges, that it was incumbent upon Euboulides and all who are now acting as accuser in the matter of the expulsions to give an accurate account of what they know and bring no hearsay into a hearing of this sort. So unjust has this been judged, and for so long, that the laws do not even allow the giving of hearsay witness evidence, not even in quite trivial suits. And rightly so; for when individuals who have claimed knowledge have been found false, how can it be right to trust what even the speaker does not know? [5] Indeed, where it is not allowed even for someone who incurs liability to harm anyone through things he claims to have heard, how can it be right for you to trust someone who speaks without liability?

Now since this man, knowing the laws (and better than he should), has presented the prosecution in an unjust way with a view to his own advantage, I must speak first of all about the outrageous way I was treated at the deme meeting. [6] And I urge you, men of Athens, not to be predisposed to take the rejection by the deme as evidence that I do not belong to the city. For if you thought that the demesmen would be able to reach a just decision in every case, you would not have allowed the right of appeal to yourselves. In fact you anticipated that something of the sort would arise through rivalry, envy, hostility or other reasons and allowed recourse to you for victims of injustice, and through this to your credit, men of Athens, you have saved all those who have been treated unjustly. [7] To begin with I shall tell you the way in which the vote actually took place in the deme – for I take 'keeping to the issue' to mean proving all the wrongs a man has suffered from intrigue in contravention of the decree.

[8] This Euboulides, men of Athens, as many of you know, indicted the sister of Lakedaimonios for impiety but failed to gain one-fifth of the votes. In that trial I gave evidence which was just but opposed to Euboulides; because of the hostility arising from this he is attacking me. And as a member of the Council, judges, and the man in control of the oath and the list from which the demesmen were called, what did he do? [9] To start with, once the deme members were assembled, he wasted the whole day with speeches and proposals for decrees. This was no accident but a plot against me, to ensure that the vote on me would take place as late as possible; and he succeeded in this. The number of those who had sworn the oath was seventy-three, and we began the voting in the late afternoon; so it came about that it was already dark when my name was called. [10] I was roughly sixtieth, and I was called last of all those who were called on that day, when the older demesmen had gone off to the country; for since our deme, judges, is thirty-five stades from the city and most members live there, the majority had gone off, and those who remained were no more than thirty. These included all my opponent's accomplices. [11] When my name was called, this man leaped up and abused me rapidly and at length and in a loud voice, just like now; he provided no witness, from the deme or the rest of the citizens, but urged the demesmen to vote me out. [12] I demanded an adjournment to the next day because of the late hour, and the fact that I had no supporter present and the suddenness of the crisis, so that he would have an opportunity to make whatever accusations he chose and to provide any witnesses he had and I should have a chance to defend myself among the whole deme and to provide my close associates as witnesses; and I was ready to abide by any decision they made about me. [13] But this man paid no attention to my challenge; he put the vote at once to the demesmen present, without allowing me any defence or providing clear proof. And his accomplices all jumped up and voted. It was dark, and they received two or three votes each from him and put them in the urn. The proof is that while the people voting numbered no more than thirty the votes came to over sixty; so we were all amazed.

[14] To prove that I am telling the truth, that the vote was not submitted to the whole deme and that the votes outnumbered the voters, I shall provide witnesses. As it happens, I have no witness to

support me from among my friends or the Athenians in general because of the hour and the fact that I had not called upon anyone; so I am using the guilty parties themselves as witnesses. So I have written for them such testimony as they will be unable to deny. Speak.

Deposition

[15] Now if, judges, the men of Halimous had put all demesmen to the vote that day, they would probably have been voting until late in order to carry out your decree before going off. If there were more than twenty demesmen left, who had to be put to the vote the following day, and it was in any case necessary for the deme to assemble, what was the difficulty for Euboulides in adjourning to the following day and putting my case first to the vote among the deme? [16] Because, judges, Euboulides was well aware that if I were given a chance to speak and all the demesmen were there for me and the vote was taken honestly, he and his fellow conspirators would be nowhere.

The origin of this conspiracy I shall tell you when I have spoken about my lineage. [17] For now, what do I think right and what am I prepared to do, judges? To show you that I am Athenian both on my father's side and on my mother's and to provide witnesses to this who you will agree are truthful, and to put a stop to the insults and accusations. As for you, having heard them, if you think I am a citizen who has fallen victim to intrigue, you should rightly save me, or if I fail deal with me in any manner you think consistent with your oath. This will be my starting point.

[18] They have maligned my father for having a foreign accent. But the fact that he was captured by the enemy during the Dekeleian War and sold to Leukas, and after meeting Kleandros the actor was restored to his family here after a long interval, this they have omitted; and as though we deserve ruin for those misfortunes, they have accused him of having a foreign accent. [19] Personally, I expect to prove him an Athenian with these very facts. Firstly, I shall provide witnesses to the fact that he was captured and sold, then that on his arrival he was given his share of the property by his uncles, and further that nobody either in the deme or in the phratry or anywhere else accused the man with the foreign accent of being an alien. Please take the depositions.

Depositions

[20] You have heard about his capture and how my father's safe return here came about. To prove that he was your fellow citizen, judges (for this is the reality and the truth), I shall call my surviving relatives on my father's side. Call firstly Thoukritides and Chari-siades. Their father Charisios was the brother of my grandfather Thoukritides and my grandmother Lysarete (my grandfather mar-ried his sister – not by the same mother), and my father's uncle. [21] Then call Nikiades; his father Lysanias was the brother of Thoukri-tides and Lysarete, and my father's uncle. Then Nikostratos; his father Nikiades was the nephew of my grandfather and grand-mother and cousin to my father. Please call all of these. And you, stop the water.

Witnesses

[22] You have heard my father's relatives on the male side, men of Athens, attesting on oath that my father was an Athenian and their kinsman. Surely none of them is swearing falsely on his own destruction with people around him who will know that he is giving false testimony. Now take the depositions of my father's relatives on the female side.

Depositions

[23] So then my father's surviving relatives on both the male and the female side have attested that he was an Athenian on both sides and had a proper right to the city. Now please call the members of the phratry and then the genos.

Witnesses

Now take the depositions of the demesmen, and those of my rela-tives about the members of the phratry, to show that they elected me phratriarch.

Depositions

[24] You have heard the evidence of those who should properly give it, my relatives and members of phratry, deme and genos. From

this you can determine whether the man who had this evidence to offer was citizen or foreigner. For if we had recourse to one or two individuals, we might be suspected of having suborned them. But it is clear that my father during his life and now myself have been scrutinized among all the same groups as each of you – I mean phratry, kin, deme, genos, how is it conceivable or possible that all these have been corrupted and are not truly ours? [25] Now if my father was rich and had clearly paid these people to say that they were his family, it would make sense for him to be suspected of not being a citizen. But if he was a poor man who simultaneously declared the same people as his kin and showed that they gave him a share of their own property, isn't it quite clear that he really was related to these people? For presumably if he was related to none of them these people would not have allowed him into their kinship and given him money in addition. No, he was their relative, as actions proved and as has been attested to you. Moreover, he was elected by lot and held offices after undergoing scrutiny. Please take the deposition.

Deposition

[26] Now does any of you think that the demesmen would ever have allowed that alien, that non-citizen, to hold office among them, instead of charging him? Well, nobody charged him, not a single one, or brought an accusation. Yet emergency votes actually took place in which the demesmen swore by sacrificial victims, when the deme register was lost on them while Antiphilos, Euboulides' father, was demarch; and they ejected some of their number. As to Thoukritos, no one made any such statement or accusation. [27] Yet for all mankind death is the limit of life, and it is right that for matters of which a man is charged while alive his children should have an abiding duty to provide a defence. But in the case of accusations which nobody made during his life, isn't it intolerable if at will anyone can put the children on trial? Now if no account of these issues was put to the test, let us grant that the subject has remained in obscurity. But if an account was given and they took a vote on him and not a single man ever accused him, surely I would rightly be Athenian on his side, since he died without any dispute about his lineage?

To prove I am telling the truth, I shall call witnesses to these facts too.

Witnesses

[28] Moreover, he had four children by the same mother as me; when they died he buried them in the tombs of his ancestors, which are shared by all those who belong to the family. None of these ever forbade him or stopped him or sued him. But who on earth would allow someone to place quite unrelated people in his ancestral tombs?

To prove that in this too I am telling the truth, take the deposition.

Deposition

[29] This is what I have to say about my father to prove he was Athenian, and I have provided as witnesses people who are citizens even on the vote of my opponents here; they attest that he is their cousin. It is clear that he lived so many years here without ever once being exposed as an alien, that he took refuge with these people, his relatives, and they both accepted him and gave him a share of the property as one of themselves. [30] Clearly the timing of his birth is such that even if he was a citizen on one side he was entitled to citizenship; for he was born before Eukleides. I shall speak now about my mother (for they have also used her as a charge against me) and will call witnesses to support my statements. And yet, men of Athens, Euboulides' attack on us with reference to the agora not only contravenes the decree but also the laws, which command that anyone who maligns any citizen, male or female, for work in the agora is guilty of slander. [31] We admit that we sell ribbons and live in a way not of our choosing. And if you think that evidence that we are not Athenians, Euboulides, I shall prove to you the complete opposite, that it is not possible for an alien to work in the agora. Please take and read out first of all the law of Solon.

Law

[32] Now take also the law of Aristophon. For Solon's law, men of Athens, was considered so noble and democratic that you voted to renew it.

Law

Your duty is to support the laws and not think those who work in the agora foreigners, but those who persecute them criminals. For there is another law, Euboulides, on idleness, and though you are liable under it you slander those of us who work. [33] But such is our misfortune that this man is free to indulge in insults irrelevant to the issue and to do as he pleases to prevent me from obtaining justice, while you will perhaps criticize *me*, if I mention the work he goes about performing in the city; and rightly so, for what need is there to say what you know?

Now consider; personally I think that the fact that we work in the agora is the most telling proof that he is casting false accusations against us. [34] As to the woman who he says is a ribbon-seller seen by all, surely what was appropriate was for many individuals who know who she is to give evidence, and not just give hearsay but, if she was a foreigner, examine the market taxes to see if she paid the foreigners' tax, and demonstrate what her nationality was; if she was a slave, ideally her purchaser should have come to court, or failing that the man who sold her, or failing that someone else, and testified either that she had been a slave or that she had been set free. But in fact he proved none of this but has indulged in every possible insult, it seems to me. This is the sykophant, all accusation, no proof. [35] For he has also said this about my mother, that she served as a wetnurse. For our part we don't deny that this happened, when the city was in misfortune and everyone was in a bad way. How and why she served as wetnurse I shall demonstrate clearly to you. And none of you should take it amiss, men of Athens; for even now you will find many women of citizen status wetnursing, and I shall give you their names, if you wish. If we were rich, we should not be selling the ribbons, nor would we be utterly needy. But what has this to do with my birth? In my view, nothing. [36] Under no circumstances despise the poor, judges – for poverty is trouble enough for them – nor those who make the choice to work and to live by honest means. But listen, and if I show you my mother's kin, who are such as befit free citizens, denying on oath the slanderous accusations about her and attesting that she is of citizen status, people whom you will declare reliable, cast your vote for us according to justice.

[37] My grandfather, men of Athens, my mother's father, was Damostratos of Melite. He had four children, by his first wife a daughter and a son named Amytheon, and from his second wife, Chairestrate, my mother and Timokrates. These had children, in Amytheon's case Damostratos, named after his grandfather, Kallistratos and Dexitheos. My mother's brother Amytheon is among

those who served and died in Sicily, and he is buried in the public tombs; this will be attested. [38] His daughter was married to Diodoros of Halai and had a son, Ktesibios. He in turn died in Abydos serving with Thrasyboulos, but of these people Amytheon's son Damostratos, my mother's nephew, is alive. The sister of my grandmother Chairestrate was married to Apollodoros of Plotheia. They had a son Olympichos, and Olympichos had a son Apollodoros, who is alive. Please call them.

Witnesses

[39] So then, you have heard them giving evidence and taking the oath. I shall call an actual relative on both sides, and his sons. Timokrates, my mother's brother by the same father and mother, had a son Euxitheos, and Euxitheos had three sons; and these are all alive. Please call the ones who are in town.

Depositions

[40] Now please take the depositions of the fellow phratry and deme members of my mother's kin, and the people who share the same tombs.

Depositions

This is my proof of my mother's birth, that she is of citizen status on both the male and the female side. My mother, judges, had first of all by Protomachos, to whom her brother by the same father and mother Timokrates gave her in marriage, a daughter, and then me by my father. You need to know how she came to marry my father – as to Euboulides' accusations about Kleinias and my mother's service as wetnurse, all this too I shall tell you about clearly. [41] Protomachos was a poor man. When he inherited a rich heiress, he wanted to give my mother in marriage and he persuaded my father Thoukritos, an acquaintance of his, to take her, and my mother was formally betrothed to my father by her brother Timokrates of Melite in the presence of both his uncles and other witnesses; all of these who survive will give evidence to you. [42] Some time later, when she had already borne two children, because my father was abroad on active service with Thrasyboulos and she herself was in great need she was compelled to wetnurse Kleinias the son of Kleidikos; it turns out that she acted in a manner not favourable – heaven knows – for the dangerous situation which now faces me (for that wetnursing is the source of all the slander about us), but she was doing what was perhaps both necessary and fitting in her existing poverty.

[43] So it can be seen that it was not my father who first married my mother, men of Athens, but Protomachos, and that he had children by her and gave a daughter in marriage; even though he is dead, still he testifies by his actions that she is of native and citizen birth.

To prove I am telling the truth in this, please call first the sons of Protomachos, then the people who were present when she was formally betrothed to my father, and my father's intimates in the phratry, with whom my father celebrated the marriage feast over my mother, then Eunikos of Cholarge who received my sister in marriage from Protomachos, then my sister's son. Call these people.

Witnesses

[44] Surely my plight would be the most pitiful of all, men of Athens, if when these kin who are so numerous testify under oath that they are related to me, though nobody disputes the citizen status of any of them, you were to vote that I am an alien. Please take also the deposition of Kleinias and his relatives, who know, I imagine, who on earth the woman, my mother, was who wetnursed him. For to be true to their oath they must attest not what we claim today but what all along they knew my mother, Kleinias' wetnurse, was reputed to be. [45] If a wetnurse is something lowly, I do not avoid the truth. For we have done wrong not if we are poor but if we are non-citizens. Nor is the present trial about luck or about money but about lineage. Poverty compels free people to perform many slavish and lowly tasks, for which more rightly they would deserve pity, men of Athens, rather than ruin as well. As I am told, many women of citizen status have been wetnurses and wool-workers and grape-pickers because of the city's misfortunes at that period, and many are now not poor but rich. But more of this later. For now call the witnesses.

Witnesses

[46] So then you have all ascertained that I am of citizen status both on my mother's side and on my father's, from the witness testimony you have just heard and from the previous testimony about my father. It remains for me to tell you about myself, most simply and most honestly, I believe, that since I am of citizen birth on both sides and have inherited both property and family I am a citizen. Furthermore, I shall demonstrate all that is required with witnesses, that I was introduced to the phratry, that I was enrolled in the deme, that I was chosen among the most well born by these men themselves to be balloted for the priesthood of Herakles, that I held offices after passing the scrutiny. Please call them.

Witnesses

[47] Isn't it monstrous, judges? If I had been appointed priest as I was initially selected, I should have had to make sacrifice on behalf of these men and Euboulides would have had to join in the sacrifice with me; but now these same people will not even let me join in their sacrifice. It is clear, men of Athens, that throughout the past my citizenship has been admitted by all my current accusers. [48] For Euboulides would presumably not have allowed the foreigner, the metic, as he now claims, either to hold offices or to be selected along with himself and balloted for a priesthood – for he was one of those balloted after preliminary selection. Nor yet, men of Athens, as an old enemy of mine would he have waited for this opportunity, which nobody could predict, if he knew something of the sort. [49] But he did not. And so throughout the past while belonging to the same deme as me and balloting for office he saw none of this, but when the whole city had been stirred to fierce anger against the people who had unscrupulously invaded the demes, then he plotted against me. The earlier period was the opportunity for the man who was sure of the truth of his claim, the present time for the personal enemy and the man intent on persecuting. [50] Personally, judges (and for the sake of Zeus and the gods let nobody heckle or resent what I am about to say), I have assumed myself Athenian just as each of you assumes himself, since I believe my mother from birth to be the woman I declare to you, and am not really the son of another woman pretending to be hers; and my father likewise, men

of Athens. [51] But if it's fair that when people are shown to be concealing their true parents and laying claim to false parents you take it as a sign that they are foreigners, I imagine the opposite should apply to me, that I am a citizen. For I would not have entered the names of an alien man and woman as my parents to participate in the city. If I had any anxiety on this score, I should have looked for people to claim as my parents. But I had none, and so I am keeping to my real parents and expect to participate in the city.

[52] Furthermore, I was left an orphan; and yet they say that I am rich and that some of the witnesses attest they are my relatives for payment. And at one and the same time they both cite against me the disgrace which poverty brings and malign my birth, and say that because of my wealth I can buy everything. [53] So which of their claims should one trust? It was surely open to these people here, if I were bastard or alien, to be heirs to all my property. So then, do these people prefer to receive a small sum, risk prosecution for false testimony and take a false oath rather than have everything, and in safety at that, and not invoke destruction on themselves? This is impossible; no, in my opinion they are relatives doing what is right, helping one of their number. [54] And they are not doing this now for an inducement, but when I was a child they immediately took me to the phratry, to the temple of Ancestral Apollo and the other shrines. Yet I assume that I did not persuade them with money to do this when I was a child. Moreover, my father himself while alive swore the customary oath to the phratry when he introduced me, that he knew I was his son by a formally married wife of citizen status, and this has been attested by witnesses. [55] So am I a foreigner? Where did I pay the metic tax? Who of my family ever did? Where did I go to another deme and fail to persuade them before enrolling myself in this one? Where did I do any of the things which people who are not pure citizens are seen to have done? Nowhere; quite simply, I too clearly participate in the same deme as my father's grandfather, my own, and my father. And now how could someone more convincingly show you that he belongs to the city? [56] Each of you should consider, men of Athens, by what other means he could prove that his relatives have been the same all along from the start than mine, by their bearing witness, taking an oath.

This is why with confidence in my case I took refuge with you. For I perceive, men of Athens, that the lawcourts are more powerful, not only than the deme of Halimous which ejected me but also than the Council and the Assembly, rightly; for in all respects the judgments in your courts are most fair.

[57] Consider this too, those of you who belong to the big demes, that you do not deprive anyone either of the right to accuse or of the right to a defence. And I wish much good fortune to all you who have dealt fairly with this issue, because you have not deprived individuals who requested delay of an opportunity to prepare. By this means you exposed those who sought to persecute or who plotted out of personal enmity. [58] And you deserve praise, men of Athens, while those who have dealt with a noble and just measure in an ignoble way deserve condemnation. In no deme at all will you find worse abuses have occurred than the ones in ours. For this deme has in the case of brothers by the same mother and father rejected some but not others, and they have rejected older men who are needy while leaving their sons as members. And I shall provide witnesses to these facts, if you wish.

[59] The most terrible of all the things the conspirators have done (and let nobody, for the sake of Zeus and the gods, take it amiss if I attempt to prove that the men who have wronged me are wicked; I think that in proving their wickedness I am speaking to the issue of what befell me), is that these people, men of Athens, when some foreigners, Anaximenes and Nikostratos, wished to become citizens, divided the money between themselves, five drachmas apiece, and accepted them. And this is something of which neither Euboulides nor his associates could deny knowledge on oath. And they did not eject these people on this occasion. What individual crime do you think is beyond the men who dared to do this collectively? [60] There are many men, judges, whom Euboulides' fellow conspirators have destroyed or saved for money. For even earlier (I shall speak to the issue, men of Athens), when Euboulides' father Antiphilos was demarch, as I said, he played a trick with a view to obtaining money from people; he said that the general register was lost, and as a result he persuaded the men of Halimous to hold a vote on themselves; he accused ten of the members and ejected them, all of whom but one were readmitted by the lawcourt. This is known to all the older men. [61] They were far from leaving some non-Athenians in the deme, when they connived to eject true citizens, who were readmitted by the lawcourt. And though he was a personal enemy of my father, on that occasion not only did he not accuse him, he did not even vote that he was not Athenian. How is this demonstrable? Because he was judged Athenian by every vote.

Why speak of our fathers? Euboulides here himself, when I was enrolled and the demesmen all voted fairly on me, he neither accused me nor cast his vote against me. And on that occasion again everyone voted me a deme member. And if they claim I am lying, let anyone who wishes attest the opposite in my water allocation. [62] If then, men of Athens, this seems to be their most convincing statement, that the demesmen ejected me this time, I can demonstrate that on four previous occasions, when they voted piously without connivance, they voted both me and my father members of their deme; firstly when my father had his scrutiny, then when I had mine, then in the earlier special vote, when these people did away with the register, and finally when they selected me and voted me one of the most well born to be balloted for the priesthood of Herakles. All this has been attested by witnesses.

[63] If I must speak of my time as demarch, which made some resentful of me, and during which I made myself unpopular by exacting from many of them the rents for the sacred land and other sums which they had filched from the deme, I should like you to hear it, but perhaps you will consider this beside the issue. Since this too I can offer as proof that they have conspired; they erased from the oath the promise to vote according to one's most just opinion and without favour or hostility. [64] This came out into the open, as did the fact that they committed sacrilege on the armour (it must be said) which I dedicated to Athena, and defaced the inscription which the demesmen voted in my honour, these people from whom I extracted the public money, and conspired against me. And their effrontery reached such a scale that they went round claiming that I had done this with a view to my defence. Now which of you would hold me guilty of such lunacy, judges, as to commit acts punishable by death for the sake of evidence of this importance for my case, and to eradicate objects which brought me honour? [65] But the most monstrous thing of all I suppose they would not claim I had contrived. No sooner had my misfortune befallen me than immediately, as though I were an exile already and ruined, some of these people came to my cottage in the country at night and tried to plunder its contents. Such was their contempt for you and for the laws. And I shall call the people who know these facts, if you wish.

[66] There are many other acts committed by these people and lies they have told which I can prove; and I should be happy to tell you, but since you consider it beside the issue, I shall omit it. But

remember and observe this, that I have come to you with many just arguments. I shall interrogate myself in the same way you question the Thesmothetai. 'Sir, who was your father?' Mine? Thoukritos. [67] 'Do any relatives bear witness for him?' Yes indeed; first of all four cousins, then a nephew, then the men who married his female cousins, then members of his phratry, then the members of his genos who share Ancestral Apollo and Zeus of the Fence, then those who share the same tombs, then the demesmen who attest that he has often passed scrutiny and held office, and they themselves have clearly passed the revision. On my father's side, how could I prove my case more fairly and more transparently? I shall call my relatives for you, if you wish. Now hear my mother's side. [68] My mother is Nikarete, daughter of Damostratos of Melite. What relatives of hers bear witness? First of all a nephew, then two sons of her other nephew, then a second cousin, then the sons of Protomachos who was my mother's first husband, then the man who married my sister, Protomachos' daughter, Eunikos of Cholarge, then my sister's son. [69] Furthermore the members of her relatives' phratry and deme have attested this. So what more could you need? For the fact that my father married her according to the laws and celebrated the marriage feast among his phratry has been attested by witnesses. In addition I have shown that I too personally have everything which free citizens should have. So in every respect if you cast your vote in a just and fitting way for us you would be keeping your oath. [70] Furthermore, judges, you ask the nine archons if they treat their parents well. I was orphaned by my father, but as for my mother I beg and implore you to restore my right through this trial to bury her in her ancestral tombs; do not prevent me, and do not render me stateless or deprive me of my relatives who are so numerous or destroy me completely. For rather than abandon them, if I cannot be saved by them, I should kill myself, so as to be buried by them at least in my homeland.

At first sight the case against Euxitheos does not look very strong. Euboulides has attacked the citizenship of his parents. His father apparently spoke with a foreign (i.e. non-Athenian) Greek accent. And his mother had worked in the market-place and served as a wet-nurse, activities which he has presented as base and servile. In a society which placed a premium on the invisibility of women of status and which regarded the farmer, as being financially independent of others, as an ideal, there was a bedrock of prejudice from which to attack such employment. Moreover, although Athenian citizens certainly worked in the market, the fact that aliens could not own land in Attica meant that they would earn their living from commerce rather than farming.

Euxitheos' replies to these points are compelling. His father, he says, had been captured in war and sold into slavery in north-west Greece, where the dialect was Doric, and this explains the accent; on the other hand, his relatives had accepted him without demur on his return and had readily granted him his share of the inheritance. His mother's employment is evidence of poverty, not servile or foreign extraction. Euxitheos also tries to cast doubt on the honesty of the deme's decision, by claiming that Euboulides, whom he represents as a personal enemy, rigged the vote.

Euxitheos may as he claims be the victim of a plot, though he never proves the point. Yet the reader cannot but be struck by the brevity of his treatment of his own case In the case of his parents, Euxitheos proceeds very carefully, painstakingly itemizing all the proofs of citizenship. With his own qualifications he calls *en bloc* witnesses to his introduction to the phratry and enrolment in the deme, to the fact that he was put forward for selection by lot as priest of Herakles and held deme offices after undergoing the *dokimasia*. The slow and detailed demonstration is replaced by one which lumps together and hurries through the individual items. The haste is surprising, since it is important for him to demonstrate that these are his real parents. Among other details which strike the modern reader is the fact that Euxitheos is evidently rich, while his parents were, on his own admission, paupers. One is also struck by the failure of his male relatives on his father's side, members of the same deme, to support him at the scrutiny when he was rejected by the deme. Though he claims to have been taken by surprise, the importance of the occasion should have induced him to ensure a supply of witnesses. It may be that Euxitheos distorts the main thrust of his prosecutor's case. Euboulides may have attacked the parents only in passing and concentrated instead on Euxitheos himself. It is possible, for instance, that he claims Euxitheos is a rich metic who has bought his way into a poor family. Or he may be arguing that Euxitheos joined the family in infancy (as has been suggested). According to Euxitheos his mother lost four children. A childless couple, eager to preserve the family unit and in need of money, might agree to present an alien child as their own; the mother's trade as wetnurse might well introduce her to a rich metic family with ambitions for their son. It is also possible that Euxitheos is a bastard. The status of bastards with two Athenian parents is controversial. If, as some scholars believe, such people were classed as non-citizens, then Euxitheos would properly be classed as a metic (resident alien). But even if (as I believe) bastards were entitled to citizenship, such people would find it difficult to defend their status under an extraordinary scrutiny, since bastards were not full members of the *oikos* (family); they therefore lacked the proofs of paternity (such as admission to the *oikos* at birth, admission to the phratry) bestowed on legitimate issue. Euxitheos would then be lying in claiming to belong to a phratry. Unfortunately it is easier to form than to prove hypotheses in the absence of further information.

6

SLANDER

CASE XVII: LYSIAS 10 – AGAINST THEOMNESTOS

This speech is our only surviving text which deals in detail with the law of slander (*kakegoria*). Under British law, which defines defamation, including slander, as utterances likely to lower the esteem in which the victim is held by right-thinking people, slander is a fairly nebulous concept and accordingly subject to misuse. Athenian law however is more narrow; it is not interested in defamation in general but in certain types of utterance, contexts and categories of victim. We have evidence for a number of laws dealing with *kakegoria*; these laws forbade the utterance of slander in certain places, the slandering of the dead and (according to a cryptic passage in Dem. 57.30) people working in the market-place; they also designated a number of specific allegations as forbidden (*aporrheta*) and therefore subject to action by the individual maligned. We know from this speech that accusations of homicide, throwing away one's shield, and beating one's father or mother were covered. How many other serious allegations were forbidden it is difficult to say. What does seem clear however from the present speech is that the law did not exempt statements before public bodies. The case arises out of an allegation made in a previous trial; there Theomnestos, on trial for addressing the Assembly despite having allegedly thrown away his shield in battle (an act which barred him from the exercise of citizen rights), had stated that the speaker killed his father (§1). The date can be fixed from §4, where the speaker states that the trial took place in the twentieth year (i.e. nineteen years) after the restoration of the democracy (403 BC) following the brief and brutal regime of the oligarchy of the Thirty. The speech was therefore delivered in 384/3.

[1] I don't expect to have any shortage of witnesses, judges; for I see that many of you who are now sitting in judgment were present at the time, when Lysitheos impeached Theomnestos for addressing the Assembly when he had no right, having thrown away his arms. In the course of that trial he said that I had killed my father. [2] Personally, if he had accused me of killing his own father, I would have forgiven him the statement (I considered him wretched and worthless). Nor would I have prosecuted him if I had been called any of the other forbidden terms; for I think it demeaning and over-litigious to sue for slander. [3] But as it stands I think it shameful not to take revenge on the man who said this about my father, who has proved his worth both to you and to the city; and I want to find out from you whether he is to be punished or if he alone of the Athenians has the exclusive right to do and say what he chooses in defiance of the laws.

[4] I am thirty-two years of age, judges, and since you returned from exile it is nineteen years. It can be seen that I was thirteen years old when my father was executed by the Thirty. At that age I neither knew what oligarchy was, nor was able to protect him from the wrong that was done him. [5] And indeed I could not sensibly have plotted against him for his property, for my older brother Pantaleon took over his estate and on becoming guardian defrauded us of our inheritance. So there are many reasons why I should wish he was alive.

Well now, I have to speak of these matters, though there is no need to speak at length, for nearly all of you know I am telling the truth. Even so I shall provide witnesses to the facts.

Witnesses

[6] Perhaps, judges, he will offer no defence on this subject, but will say to you too what he had the nerve to say before the arbitrator, that it is not one of the forbidden terms if someone says that a man has killed his father; the law does not forbid this, but does not permit someone to call a man 'murderer'. [7] But it is my view, judges, that you should take issue not with expressions but with their meaning, and that you all know that all who have killed are murderers and all who are murderers have killed. It would be an enormous task for the lawgiver to write down all the words which have the same meaning; no, in mentioning one term he indicated

them all. [8] Presumably it's not the case, Theomnestos, that if someone called you 'father-beater' or 'mother-beater' you would expect satisfaction from him, while if someone said you struck your female or male parent you would think he should go unpunished since he had not uttered one of the forbidden terms. [9] I should be pleased if you would tell me – for you are an expert in this area and you are well versed both in practice and in speech – if someone said you had cast off your shield (and the law says: 'if someone says that a man has thrown it away, he is liable to action'), would you have refrained from suing him and been content with the term 'cast away the shield', claiming to be unconcerned, on the ground that 'cast away' and 'throw away' are not the same thing? [10] And if you were one of the Eleven, you would refuse to receive a prisoner arrested by someone claiming he had been stripped of his robe or had his tunic removed, and would release him on the same principle, because he is not being called a clothes-stealer?* And if someone was caught abducting a child, you would not state that he was a kidnapper, if you are going to base your argument on names and pay no attention to the facts which cause names to be applied.

[11] Consider this too, judges. I think that from laziness and idleness he has not even been up to the Areopagos. You all know that there, when they are trying cases of homicide, the parties do not use this term in making their oaths but the one which was used to malign me; the accuser swears that the defendant killed, the defendant that he did not kill. [12] Wouldn't it be ridiculous to let off the perpetrator when he admitted he was a murderer, because the accuser stated in his oath that the defendant had killed? How does this differ from Theomnestos' argument? You yourself prosecuted Lysitheos for slander when he said you had cast away your shield. Yet the law says nothing about casting away, but instructs that if anyone says that someone has thrown away his shield he is to pay a penalty of five hundred drachmas. [13] Isn't it intolerable that when you need to take revenge on your enemies who have maligned you, you interpret the laws as I do now, but when you malign someone else against the laws, you don't expect to be punished? Is it that you're so clever that you can use the laws as you choose, or that you're so powerful that you expect that your victims will never get their revenge? [14] And aren't you ashamed to be so stupid that you

---

*The *lopodytes*, literally 'clothes-stealer', was a footpad or mugger, a thief who set upon and stripped his victims.

think your profit should come not from good deeds done to the city but from evading punishment for wrongs you have done? Please read out the law.

Law

[15] I think, judges, that you all know that I am stating the matter correctly, while he is so dull-witted that he can't understand a word that's said. Now I want to enlighten him on this matter using other laws, in the hope that even now on the stand he may be taught and not cause us trouble in the future. Please read out these ancient laws of Solon.

Law

[16] *To have his foot confined in the stocks for five days, if the court make this additional assessment.*

The stocks are the same thing, Theomnestos, as what is now called 'being confined in the wood'. Now if someone so confined were on his release to bring an accusation at the audit of the Eleven that he had not been confined in the stocks but in the wood, wouldn't people think him an idiot? Read out another law.

Law

[17] *He is to vow by Apollo and give surety. If in dread of judgment, let him flee.*

Here the term 'vow' means 'swear', and 'flee' is what now we call 'running away'.

Whoever debars with his door, when the thief is inside.

'Debar' is understood as 'shut out'; don't dispute that.

[18] *Money is to be set at whatever rate the lender chooses.*

'Set' here, my dear Theomnestos, is not to put in the balance but to exact whatever rate of interest he chooses. Again, read out the last part of this law.

[19] *All women who strut overtly,*

and

For damage to a lackey he shall pay double the amount.

Observe carefully. 'Overtly' means 'openly', 'strut' is 'walk', 'lackey' is 'servant'. [20] And there are many other examples of this sort, judges. But I think that if he is not made of wood he will have recognized that the realities are the same now as in olden times, but in some cases we do not use the same terms now as we did formerly. And he'll prove it, because he'll leave the stand without a word. [21] If he doesn't, judges, I ask you to vote as is just, in the realization that it is a far worse insult to have it said that one has killed one's father than that one has thrown away one's shield. For myself I would rather have thrown away all the shields there are than to harbour any such notion about my father.

[22] This man, though he was guilty as charged and was faced with a lesser disaster, not only secured your pity but actually had the witness disfranchised. And I, who saw him do what you too all know he did, who kept my own shield safe, who have been accused of such an unholy and monstrous act, when the disaster which faces me if he is acquitted is the most dire, while he faces no danger of any significance if he is convicted of slander, shall I not get satisfaction from him? [23] What charge do you have to bring against me? That I was justly accused? No, not even you could say this. Well then, that the defendant is a better man and from better stock than I? But not even Theomnestos would claim this. Well then, that I have thrown away my arms and am now suing a man who kept his safe? But this is not the tale that is spread throughout the city.

[24] Remember that you have made him a large and handsome gift in that verdict. And who would not pity Dionysios for meeting such a catastrophe, a man who proved himself extremely brave in times of danger, [25] who left the court saying that the expedition on which we served had been a complete disaster, in which many of us had died, while those who kept their arms safe had been convicted of false testimony by the ones who threw theirs away, that it would have been better for him to have died than to return home to face such a misfortune? [26] Do not then feel any pity for Theomnestos for being insulted as he deserves and sympathize with him for outrageous acts and words in defiance of the laws. For what greater catastrophe could befall me than this, when I have been subjected to such a disgraceful accusation relating to a father such as mine? [27] A man who served as general many times and faced

many other dangers in your company. And his person was never in the hands of the enemy nor was he ever convicted at audit, but at the age of sixty-seven under an oligarchy he was killed for his loyalty to you the people. [28] Isn't it right to be furious with a man who has said such things and to support my father, since he too has been slandered? What could cause him greater pain than to be killed by his enemies and have it said against him that he was killed by his sons? When even to this day, judges, the memorials to his courage hang in your temples, while for my opponent and his father the memorials of their baseness hang in those of the enemy. So deeply is cowardice ingrained in their nature. [29] And indeed, judges, the taller and more impressive and dashing their looks, the more they deserve anger. For it's clear that they have the physical strength but are morally weak.

[30] I am told, judges, that he will resort to the argument that he said this in anger because my evidence supported that of Dionysios. But you must bear in mind, judges, that the lawgiver grants no indulgence for anger but punishes the speaker, if he cannot prove that what was said is true. I have given evidence about this man twice in the past; for at that stage I didn't know that you punish the witnesses and forgive the ones who throw their arms away.

[31] I don't know that I need say more on this matter. I beg you to convict Theomnestos, in the realization that I could face no more serious trial than this. At present I am prosecuting for slander, but on the same vote I am being tried for the murder of my father, though I singlehandedly, once I passed my scrutiny as an adult, prosecuted the Thirty at the Areopagos. [32] Remember this, and give your support to me, my father, the established laws and the oaths you have sworn.

It was a defence under slander law to argue that the accusation was true. According to the speaker, Theomnestos does not base his defence on the accuracy of the allegation, nor does he deny making the statement. He argues that the statement does not count as ***kakegoria*** because he did not use the term forbidden in the law. The law spoke of allegations that an individual was a homicide (*androphonos*), while Theomnestos had not used this term but had merely said that the speaker had killed his father. The plaintiff argues that the law is concerned with meanings, not expressions. It is of course possible that the prosecutor is distorting the defence position; according to §30, Theomnestos may have stated that he spoke in anger (not a technical defence but a bid for understanding from the judges), and it is possible that he argued both that his statement was not only not actionable under the relevant law but also that it was anyway true. But we can be fairly certain that he did contest the interpretation of the law, if only as part of his defence. The case went to public arbitration (§6), and so the speaker was well informed on the lines of argument likely to be used by the defence.

It is not entirely certain who is in the right on the technical issue; modern scholars have sided with both interpretations. Since, as the tenor of prosecution and defence arguments in this case makes clear, the law contained no explicit clause rendering all forms of a given allegation actionable, we cannot be sure whether it was generally understood as forbidding the allegation itself (irrespective of the words used) or specific insulting expressions alleging serious misconduct. On the analogy of the law dealing with work in the market, it is perhaps more likely that the intention of the law when passed was to discourage certain types of insult rather than the use of certain terms. It is also to be borne in mind that Athenian juries (to judge from surviving speeches) were in general more interested in the thrust of a law than in its wording. Ultimately it was for the judges to decide. In his attempt to refute Theomnestos' interpretation of the law, the speaker argues from a number of laws that it is never the letter of the law but its tenor which counts. The result is a lively and witty argument, and (in both prosecution and defence) an attention to the specific phrasing of laws which is unusual in the Athenian courts.

The uniqueness of our speech may be no accident. The speaker appears ill at ease with a prosecution for defamation, and it may be that Athenians were in general reluctant to go to court over words rather than material damage, despite the fact that since this was a private suit the penalty (500 drachmas, a substantial sum) went to the successful plaintiff. There may also have been a fear (well-founded, as many modern litigants have found to their cost) that prosecution merely fans the flames of public gossip.

A detailed commentary on this speech can be found in M. Edwards and S. Usher, *Greek Orators I* (see p. 43, above).

Appendix I

ATHENIAN CURRENCY

The following represents the relative values of Athenian currency:

6 *obols* = 1 *drachma*
100 *drachmas* = 1 *mna* (usually anglicized in the latin form *mina*)
60 *mnai* = 1 *talent*

Given the quite different economic environments, it is not only difficult but quite misleading to translate Athenian currency into any modern currency. An idea of the value of money in Athens can be gained from the fact that at the end of the fifth century a labourer could earn 1 drachma per day, while in the latter part of the fourth century an unskilled labourer might earn $1\frac{1}{2}$ drachmas, a skilled man 2 or even $2\frac{1}{2}$ drachmas. A man with property of three talents was evidently reasonably wealthy, since this was the threshold for liability to perform liturgies (see introduction to Case IV: Antiphon 6 on p. 63) for the deme (though the threshold may have been as high as four talents for state liturgies). For further details the reader should consult A.H.M. Jones, *Athenian Democracy* (Oxford 1957), p. 135, J.K. Davies, *Athenian Propertied Families, 600–300 B.C.* (Oxford 1971), pp. xxiii–xxiv. A comparison of these figures with the various sums reported in the speeches included in this volume will show that the individuals we meet in the selected speeches (and this is true of virtually all speeches surviving from classical Athens) do not form a cross-section of Athenian society but are drawn either from the rich or from the relatively well-to-do.

Appendix II

THE ATHENIAN CALENDAR

The Athenian year was divided like our own into twelve months, though the start and end of individual months do not coincide with ours. The year began in midsummer and the succession of months was as follows:

1 Hekatombaion
2 Metageitnion
3 Boedromion
4 Pyanopsion
5 Maimakterion
6 Poseideon
7 Gamelion
8 Anthesterion
9 Elaphebolion
10 Mounichion
11 Thargelion
12 Skirophorion

SELECTED FURTHER READING

The scholarly literature on Athenian law is substantial. Listed below are a number of general works which will enable the reader to pursue in greater detail the issues raised by the speeches in this volume. The list includes a number of key modern studies of Greek values and Athenian democracy in addition to works devoted to Athenian law and Greek oratory.

Bonner, R.J. (1927) *Lawyers and Litigants in Ancient Athens*, Chicago.

Bonner, R.J. (1905) *Evidence in Athenian Courts*, Chicago.

Bonner, R.J. and G. Smith (1930–8) *The Administration of Justice from Homer to Aristotle* (2 vols), Chicago.

Cartledge, P., P. Millett and S. Todd (eds) (1990) *Nomos: Essays in Athenian Law, Politics and Society*, Cambridge.

Cohen, D. (1991) *Law, Sexuality and Society*, Cambridge.

Cohen, D. (1995) *Law, Violence and Community in Classical Athens*, Cambridge.

Cohen, E.E. (1992) *Athenian Economy and Society: A Banking Perspective*, Princeton, N.J.

Dover, K.J. (1974) *Greek Popular Morality in the Time of Plato and Aristotle*, Oxford.

Dover, K.J. (1978) *Greek Homosexuality*, London.

Edwards, M. (1994) *The Attic Orators*, London.

Fisher, N.R.E. (1976) *Social Values in Classical Athens*, London.

Fisher, N.R.E. (1992) *Hybris: A Study in the Values of Shame and Honour in Classical Greece*, Warminster.

Gagarin, M. (1986) *Early Greek Law*, Berkeley and Los Angeles.

Garner, R. (1987) *Law and Society in Classical Athens*, London and Sydney.

Hansen, M.H. (1991) *Athenian Democracy in the Age of Demosthenes*, Oxford.
Harrison, A.R.W. (1968, 1971) *The Law of Athens* (2 vols), Oxford.
Hunter, V.J. (1994) *Policing Athens: Social Control in the Attic Lawsuits, 420–320 B.C.*, Princeton, N.J.
Isager, S. and M.H. Hansen (1975) *Aspects of Athenian Society in the Fourth Century B.C.*, Odense.
Jones, A.H.M. (1957) *Athenian Democracy*, Oxford.
Just, R. (1989) *Women in Athenian Law and Life*, London.
Kennedy, G. (1963) *The Art of Persuasion in Greece*, Princeton, N.J.
Lacey, W.K. (1968) *The Family in Classical Greece*, London.
MacDowell, D.M. (1963) *Athenian Homicide Law in the Age of the Orators*, Manchester.
MacDowell, D.M. (1978) *The Law in Classical Athens*, London.
Millett, P. (1991) *Lending and Borrowing in Ancient Athens*, Cambridge.
Pomeroy, S.B. (1976) *Goddesses, Whores, Wives and Slaves*, London.
Schaps, D. (1979) *The Economic Rights of Women in Ancient Greece*, Edinburgh.
Sealey, R. (1990) *Women and Law in Classical Greece*, Chapel Hill.
Sealey, R. (1994) *The Justice of the Greeks*, Ann Arbor.
Sinclair, R.K. (1988) *Democracy and Participation in Athens*, Cambridge.
Todd, S. (1993) *The Shape of Athenian Law*, Oxford.

INDEX

For reasons of space it has not been possible to explain all legal and constitutional terms and structures encountered in this selection of speeches. To assist the reader who wishes to pursue these issues in the *Selected Further Reading* (see pp.242–3) I have included in this index the Greek equivalent of English terms used in the translation.

adoption 110, 122, 126, by testament 121, 128
agon atimetos, agon timetos, see penalties, assessed/unassessed
aikeia, see battery
amphidromia 125
Amphiktyons 204
apographe 11
Apollo, Ancestral (*Apollon Patroos*) 227, 230
Apollonides of Olynthos 202
appeal (*ephesis*) to a court 3
arbitration (*diaita*) 90, 103, 134, 135, 139, 140, 191, 192, 195, 197, 234, 239
Archias 208
Archidamos 204
Archon 160, 172, 174, 203, 205–6
Areopagos 4, 27, 75, 90, 91, 200, 235, 238
Aristophon 22 n.12, 222
arrest, summary (*apagoge*) 44, 85, 132, 147, 235
Artemision 203
atimia, *see* citizenship, loss of
audit (*euthyna*) of magistrate on expiry of office 71

banks (*trapezai*) 143
bastard (*nothos*) 117, 123, 124, 126–7, 227, 232, inheritance rights of 124
battery (*aikeia*) 75, 84, 94, 97, 101, 172
betrothal (*engye*) 113, 125, 145, 149, 211, 224
blocking actions 23 n.31, 74; *see also diamartyria, paragraphe*, counter-prosecution
bouleusis of homicide 36, 43
burial 70, 130, 132, 222, 224, 230

calendar, Athenian 241
Chabrias 188
Chaironeia 20, 147
challenge (*proklesis*) 16, 17, 37, 67, 68, 73, 91–2, 93, 140, 167, 170, 173, 174, 195, 209–10, 218
character (*ethos*) 18, 23 n.26, 60, 62, 82, 96, 109, 147f., 149, 176, 223
children, acknowledgement of 115, 125, 194–5, 211
chorus producer (*choregos*) 57, 63; *see also leitourgia*
citizenship 6, 7, 181, 185, 193, 203, 212–3, 219, 226, loss of (*atimia*) 8, 187, grants of 202ff., indictment for non-citizenship, i.e. masqerading as a citizen (*graphe xenias*) 116, 193
clothes-stealer, *see lopodytes*
complaint, formal (*enklema*) 169ff.
concubine (*pallake*) 32, 117, 209

contracts (*syngraphai*) 15, 149, 150, 152–3, 154–6, 159, 163
Council of Five Hundred (*Boule*) 70, 71, 182
counter-prosecution 10, 23 n.31, 70, 74, 150
court fees 97, 118, 128, 173

damage (*blabe*) 133, 141, 142
dekate (tenth day ceremony) 115, 122, 125
Delphinion 27
demarch (*demarchos*) 228, 229
deme (*demos*) 5, 124, 209, 212–3, 218, 221, 226; deme register 212, 228
Demophilos, decree of 213
diamartyria 109, 150–1
diapsephisis 212
dike epitropes, see guardian
Dionysia 65
Dionysos 198, 199
divorce 193, 224
documentation, absence of 15, 125, 213
dokimasia (scrutiny) of officials 5, 182, 221, 230 (Thesmothetai), of candidates for deme membership 212
dowry (*proix*) 104, 115, 116, 118, 125, 183, 193, action for return of 112, 124; *see also* maintenance
drains 136
Drakon 2–3, 26
duty, customs ('the two per cent tax') 157, 187

eisangelia, see impeachment
ekmartyria, see witness, absentee
ejectment/eviction, action for (*dike exoules*) 11, 121
Eleven, the 43, 132, 160, 235, 236
emotional appeal (*pathos*) 18, 82, 94, 109, 148, 174, 206, 207, 210, 211, 230
endeixis 42
ephetai 27
epobelia 24 n.39, 151
Ephialtes 5, 55
epikleros, see heiress
Euboia 180
Euboulos, 84, 180, 192
Eukleides 222
euthyna, see audit
evidence 14, 15
exchange of property (*antidosis*) 78
Executors (*praktores*), the 72

felon (*kakourgos*) 42, 61, 132
Forty, the 172
freedman (i.e. freed slave, *apeleutheros*) 9, 129
friendly loan (*eranos*) 144, 188

Generals, the (*strategoi*) 160
genos 195, 220, 230
grain trade 150, laws 161
graphe paranomon, see indictment for illegal legislation
guardian (*epitropos*) of orphans 102, action against (*dike epitropes*) 102, of woman *see*, *kyrios*

hearing 13ff., duration of 12, 14
heiress (*epikleros*) 117–8, 121, 122, 123, 126, 172, 174, 224, action for maltreatment of (*eisangelia/graphe epiklerou kakoseos*) 118, 121
Hekate 93
Hellenotamiai 55
homicide (*phonos*) 7, 26–7, 41, 71, 73, 90, 177, 183, 235, laws of 45, exile in certain homicide cases 61, 64, 183, proclamations in homicide cases 26, 59, 64, 70, 71, 183, pardon in homicide cases 177, prohibitions on persons accused of homicide 44, 70, 71, 74; *see also bouleusis*
homosexuality 8, 83, 142
hybris, see outrage

idleness (*argia*) 223
impeachment (*eisangelia*) 22 n.10, 70
impiety, indictment for (*graphe asebeias*) 218
indictment for illegal legislation (*graphe paranomon*) 4–5, 22 n.12, 180, 183, 202
inheritance 120, 121, 151–2, 160, 162, 234; *see also* bastard, heiress
interest rates, 105, 150, 164, 193
intimidation 9–10, 13, 18
Ithyphallos 88

judges (*dikastai*) 5–7, 12, number of 7, 22 n.20, voting of 17

kakourgos, see felon
Kallistratos 187, 191
King-Archon (*basileus*) 70, 71, 160, 198, 199
Kleisthenes 4, 22 n.10

kleteusis ('sub poena') 24 n.34, 187
Koroneia 75, 81
kyrios 8

laws, written 2, access to 7f., collection of 10
legal actions: public (*dikai demosiai*) 9–10, 12, 14, 23 n.32, 26, private (*dikai diai*) 9–10, 14, 26
legitimacy (*gnesiotes*) 145; *see also* bastard
leitourgia 57, 63, 75, 82, 84, 108, 132, 208, in deme 132; *see also* chorus producer, tax on wealth, trierarch
Leokorion 84
Leonidas 203
Lesbos, revolt of 43, 56–7, 61, 62
Leuktra 189
levies on property (*eisphorai*) 63, 132, 173
litigiousness 12–13
liturgy, *see leitourgia*
loans 164, maritime 150
logographer (*logographos*), *see* speechwriter
lopodytes ('clothes-stealer', mugger) 43, 85, 90

Macedon 180
maintenance, suit for (*dike sitou*) 112, 124, 193
Marathon 203
marriage (*gamos*) 2, 8, 11, 102, 121, 126, 145, 148, 180, 182, 185, 193, 207, 208, 211, 220, marriage feast (*gamelia*) 124, 225, 230; *see also* divorce
Melite 86
mercantile suits (*dikai emporikai*) 150
metic, see resident alien
metic tax (*metoikion*), *see* tax
military service, 94, 132, military offences 187 (failure to serve), 234 (throwing away one's shield)
mines 114, 163
mining suits (*dikai metallikai*) 164, 172, 174, 178
moichos, *see* seducer
money, value of 240
moneylenders 175
mugger, *see lopodytes*
Mysteries, Eleusinian 186

oath 15, 27, 45, 59, 60, 64, 66, 93–4, 96, 132, 138, 140, 142, 182, 195, 199, 218, 219, 220, 221, 223, 224, 227, 229, 230, 235, 238
Olynthos 180
orphans (*orphanoi*) 102, 106, 107
outrage (*hybris*) 75, 84, 85, 90, 94–5, 101, 172

Palladion 36, 63
Pantikapaion 157, 158
paragraphe 109,150, 164 178; *see also* blocking actions, *diamartyria*
parents, treatment of 230
Pausanias 203
Peisistratos 3
Peitholas of Thessaly 202
Peloponnesian War 108, 211
penalties 7, 17, 18, 24 n.51, 44, 61, 185, 193, assessed/unassessed 7, 22 n.16–17, 44, 136, 138, 141, 147, 183, 236, for prosecutors 8, 12, 13, 24 n.39, 118, 174, 212, in the *paragraphe* 151, in inheritance cases 129; *see also epobelia*
Persephone 86
Pharnabazos 127
Philokrates, Peace of 181
phratriarch (*phratriarchos*) 220
phratry (*phratria*) 123, 124, 195, 208, 219, 220, 224, 225, 226, 230
pimps (*pornoboskoi*) 142, 143, 185, 188, 197
Plataia 203–5
Polemarchos 160, 190, 192
politics in the courts 4–5, 13, 74, 180–1, 212
pollution (*miasma*) 26–7, 57–8, 64
prasis epi lysei, see sale with the right of redemption
Presidents (*prytaneis*) 72, 202
probability (*eikos*), argument from 18
prodikasia 26–7, 71, 73
professionalism 12, 13, 19
property (*ousia*), invisible (*aphanes ousia*) 103, visible (*phanera ousia*) 103
prosecutor, volunteer (*ho boulomenos*) 3, 10, 11, 18, 23 n.28, rewards for 11, 185
prostitutes (*hetairai, pornai*) 142, 185, 186, 187, 189, 196–7, 206, 209, 211
Providers (*Poristai*) 72
public service, *see leitourgia*
purification 64, 70

release from legal action (*aphesis*) 164, 168, 177, 178

relevance/irrelevance 18, 27, 45, 61, 65, 81, 174, 175, 178, 218, 223, 228, 229
resident alien (*metoikos*) 8–9, 153, 231; *see also* tax
roads 135, 137, 138, 140

Sacred Herald (*hierokeryx*) 199
Sacred War 84
Salamis 203
sale 149
sale with the right of redemption (*prasis epi lysei*) 164
seducer (*moichos*) 34–5, 190, 196, 201
self-help 34
Sellers (*Poletai*) 72
Sicilian Expedition 43, 224
Simos of Thessaly 186, 206
slander (*kakegoria*) 89, 98, 222, 233, 238–9
slaves (*doulo*i) 9, 16, 24 n.48–50, 37–8, 68, 139, 142, 145, 149, 173, 175, 188, manumission of 143, 188; *see also* freedman
Solon 3, 133, 146, 222, 236
sophists (*sophistai*) 19, 159, 162
Sparta 92
speeches 17–18, 19
speechwriter (*logographos*) 19
state debtors 8, 169, 178, 183
sub poena, *see kleteusis*
supporting speaker (*synegoros*) 13, 14, 102, 127, 181, 184
sykophant (*sykophantes*) 12, 13, 24 n.40, 57, 191, 223
synegoros, *see* supporting speaker

tax, on aliens working in the market 223, on wealth, *see also* duty, *leitourgia*, levies, metic tax (*metoikion*) 9, 227
tenth day ceremony, *see dekate*
testimony 10, 15, hearsay 15, 217, 223, action for false (*dike pseudomartyrion*) 11, 13, 16, 109, 130, 131
Thargelia 65
theoric fund (*theorikon*) 180–1, 182
Theseus 198
Thesmophoria 30, 124
Thesmothetai 67, 70, 98, 172, 185, 193, 230
Thieves' Harbour 156
Thirty, the 20, 97, 150, 233, 238
Thrasyboulos 224, 225
Thrasyllos 103, 104
time limit for action (*prothesmia*) 41
torture (*basanos*) 15, 16, 37–8, 41, 42, 62, 68, 173, 209–10
trauma ek pronoias, *see* wounding
trierarch (*trierarchos*) 94, 107

Venerable Women (*Gerarai*) 198
wages 6, 240
waterclock (*klepsydra*) 14, 112, 123, 186, 220, 229
wills (*diathekai*) 129, 130, 131, 133, 145, 149
witness (*martys*) 7, 10, 11, 23 n.33, 67, 68f., 114, 129, 218, role of 15–6, evidence of absentee witness (*ekmartyria*) 15, 113, 114, 123, 125, compulsion of witness 10, 187, witness to a summons (*kleter*) 10; *see also kleteusis*, testimony
women 7–8, 23 n.22–24, 23 n.27, 104, 109, 113, 138, 174, 186, 192, 193, 201, 207, 218, 223, 230
wounding (*trauma ek pronoias*) 75, 82–3, 89

Zeus of the Fence (*Zeus Herkeios*) 230